Under the Walnut Trees

A tale of a childhood

MARY WHITE

Watercolour illustrations by Sue Tudge

Copyright © 2020 Mary White

The moral right of the author has been asserted.

Apart from any fair dealing for the purposes of research or private study, or criticism or review, as permitted under the Copyright, Designs and Patents Act 1988, this publication may only be reproduced, stored or transmitted, in any form or by any means, with the prior permission in writing of the publishers, or in the case of reprographic reproduction in accordance with the terms of licences issued by the Copyright Licensing Agency. Enquiries concerning reproduction outside those terms should be sent to the publishers.

Matador
9 Priory Business Park,
Wistow Road, Kibworth Beauchamp,
Leicestershire. LE8 0RX
Tel: 0116 279 2299
Email: books@troubador.co.uk
Web: www.troubador.co.uk/matador
Twitter: @matadorbooks

ISBN 978 1838595 548

British Library Cataloguing in Publication Data.
A catalogue record for this book is available from the British Library.

Printed and bound in the UK by TJ Books, Padstow, Cornwall
Typeset in 12pt Adobe Caslon pro by Troubador Publishing Ltd, Leicester, UK

Matador is an imprint of Troubador Publishing Ltd

*To
Ellie-Mai and Isabel Molly.
With love from
Grandma.*

Contents

The Farmhouse	1
Family	10
Around the Farm	26
School Days	42
Out and About	64
Walnut Trees and Others	81
Domestic Affairs	89
"To Reap and Sow, and Plough and Mow"	113
All the World's a Stage	145
Food: Glorious and Not So Glorious	182
Pastimes	208
Church and Parish	238
Medical Matters	259
Further Afield	279
A History of the Owners of Wansley Barton	325
Acknowledgements	327

When the sun rises, I go to work,
When the sun goes down, I take my rest,
I dig the well from which I drink,
I farm the soil that yields my food,
I share creation, Kings can do no more.

Anon (Chinese, 2500 BC)

The Farmhouse

The ancient farm lay in the far corner of a remote parish. It was situated down one of Devon's long lanes and not visible from any public road. It would only have been known to local people and there was nothing to indicate its existence – certainly in the days of my childhood. There was just a weathered field gate and, beyond, a rutted road with potholes. A casual passer-by may have suspected there was a dwelling further along, and even someone more inquisitive, who bothered to walk for a distance along the track, could easily have given up after deciding there was nothing to be seen except more fields.

These days it is different, as visitors are sought after and encouraged to stay in the holiday homes created from the old farm buildings. Smart pillars and a tasteful sign now proclaim to people that they have at last arrived.

There were few strangers in the 1940s and '50s likely to visit the farm or even the small village. Roborough village and parish lie well off the beaten track and not on a route to anywhere else. Even today most visitors would have a specific reason to be there. The word Roborough means "Rough Hill", and that says it all. The village is perched on the top of a hill with beautiful views, especially south towards Dartmoor and west into Cornwall. It is exposed and vulnerable to winds from all directions, and the houses, mostly detached, straggle along the road by the church. I imagine that it has always been a relatively poor parish. There is one gentleman's house at Ebberly, about a mile from the village, and the rest of the parish consists of outlying farms, cottages and smallholdings.

Wansley Barton lies on the outer boundary of the parish, a good mile and a half from the village itself. If our inquisitive traveller had persisted with his walk along the rutted lane he would have been rewarded, for after following the high ridge for some distance, the lane suddenly turns left and opens out to twice the width, as though to say, "A-ha, there is something special here after all." It then gently slopes down towards the old farmhouse and buildings.

I think that all of us felt the warmth of a homecoming whenever we returned to the farm after a period away, whether it was after a short visit to town or market or an absence of a longer period. As it approached the house, the lane curved between the old stone walls on the left which were covered with Virginia creeper and the walnut trees on the right, then it turned the corner and brought us to the back door.

The stone-built house was large and rambling. It was L-shaped and the south-facing part which formed the foot of the L was older than the rest. These stone walls seemed to grow out of the ground, as this part had been built into the slope. The window ledges inside were at waist height but outside they were at ground level. This meant there was always a problem with damp in those rooms, particularly in the dining room as the fire was not lit there often. These rooms though were the heart of the house and the central hub of everything that went on. All visitors, whether acquaintances or strangers, friends, family, farmhands, travellers or reps, followed the road around the corner and then walked through the small courtyard to the back-kitchen door.

The kitchen was not especially large as farm kitchens go, and a passage led to the dining room, which doubled up as a sitting room when I was young. Another passage led off to some pantries and the dairy and salting house. These passages were quite a feature, and as a child I would race up and down, play ball or do handstands against the walls and even use my skipping rope. The pleasure was not as great in later years when I was old enough to be useful and expected to get down on my hands and knees and scrub the slate and flagstone floors.

The old house needed modernising even when I was young. The fireplace in the kitchen was a huge open one, with smoke-blackened walls and chimney crooks hanging down. There were two bread ovens, one on each side, and these were typical Devonshire clay ovens. The one on the left had not been used for its original purpose for many years. It no longer had a door and it was used as storage for lightings for the fire. The farm cats considered it to be a warm snug hidey-hole and through the years many kittens were born at the back behind the kindling sticks. It was not a wise choice, as the kittens were soon found and disposed of.

The oven on the right side was still in a good condition and had been in use until comparatively modern times. Faggots of wood were put in to heat the clay, then when ready, the ashes would be scraped out and the dough placed on the hot surface by means of an oven peel. This was a wooden implement, rather like a spade with a long handle. This way of making bread was routine in Great-Aunt Leah's day, but I cannot remember seeing the oven in use. My mother had seen bread being made this way or maybe had done it herself, so I think that I only just missed it.

Wansley kitchen must have been the only one in the parish where the cooking was still done in such an antiquated way over an open fire. During my primary school years I visited friends' homes, and whether farm or cottage, large or small, I knew of no one else who cooked with chimney crooks and a brandis (trivet) over the flames and coals. As I became aware of these things I felt rather embarrassed about it, as everyone else had at the very least a cosy black range, and most of the farmhouses boasted an Aga or Rayburn.

However, I do have fond memories of that old fireplace. It was so large that there was room on the bricks at the side of the flames to put a little stool, and many childhood hours were whiled away watching the sparks flying, listening to the logs snacking, and visiting imaginary worlds as I gazed at the changing pictures in the hot coals and flames. There was no better way to round off a cold day than to sit in the chimney corner with a basin of bread and milk broth, watching the glowing embers. A bowl of broth, either savoury or milky, was a normal suppertime repast. Mother would cut a slice of bread into small squares, and put it into a china basin with some sugar. I would watch the milk as it heated on the brandis over the coals, then when it was ready she would pour it over the bread and I would be given the delicious sweet broth. I would stir it and fish out the bread piece by piece with a spoon. Father would usually have finished the day's work by then, and he and Mother often relaxed with a book or they might listen to the wireless. The Tilley lamp gently hissed and one or two favoured cats, who had been allowed to stay in, purred, and it was all very comforting and satisfying. Then it was off to bed.

Bedtime meant leaving the warmth and comfort of the kitchen and making my way with a small candle or night light along the dining room passage, through the door at the end and into the other half of the house. This section ran at right angles to the older part and formed the upright part of the L shape. It was thought in the family that this had originally been a barn which at sometime had been converted into part of the dwelling house. There were some beautiful panelled and curved shelves on either side of the fireplace in one of the rooms, which probably dated the conversion to the seventeenth century. During the war years when I was growing up, this room was not furnished. There were other more pressing matters and no one had the money, time or inclination. I was able to use it as a playroom and no one bothered me. The few toys, dolls and books that I had were scattered around and I played quite happily, unaware that I shared the space with damp, dry rot, mice and probably rats.

The main entrance hall was in this part of the house but inexplicably no one ever used the front door. When I was old enough to think about such things, I realised that in order to reach the front gate and walk down the path to the front door, the visitor would first have to walk across a patch of rough grass. This was only cut occasionally during the summer months, so rather than get their shoes wet, everyone walked or drove around to the back entrance.

The hall was pleasant enough and deserved to have visitors. It was sparsely furnished, just a table and two or three chairs on the old flagstone floor. During the summer months it was a cheerful space, as Mother always stood a large pot of flowers on the table. I particularly remember the lilacs, and the perfume would waft down the passages and up the stairs. There were two oil paintings of rural scenes in large gilt frames, and a huge framed photograph of Great-Great-Great-Uncle Francis hung on the wall over the table. It was a full-length photo taken by a professional photographer, although not in a studio. Some photographers travelled into the countryside and villages, Mr Elliott of Merton being one such person. I imagine it was taken in a country lane somewhere around Ebberly or Roborough, and Great-Great-Great-Uncle Francis (often called Frank) was leaning on his stick, and most surprisingly gazing at the camera with a beaming smile. This was most unusual in a Victorian photograph and we felt that his benign presence was watching over us.

Francis Squire was a sort of father figure in the family, and was obviously one of the movers and shakers in the Squire clan. He had farmed at Wansley during the 1870s until the 1890s and then set up his two great-nephews, Jack and Bob Squire, to take over. He then moved to Landkey to set up another nephew in a farm, before eventually retiring to Rumsam House in Barnstaple. When I was very young his grandfather clock stood by the hall table, and as my bedroom was immediately above the hall, I was lulled to sleep at night by the comforting tick-tock.

I always felt that the contrast between the two sections of the house was startling. If anyone asked my mother whether such an old house had any ghosts, she was adamant that the house was extremely friendly and there were no ghosts or unwanted presences – but I wasn't entirely convinced. I had never actually seen anything but as I walked the passage at night with my candle, I knew that sometimes the old section of the house was bursting with activity. Unseen lives were bustling away with the domestic chores of the past: farmers' wives, housemaids and servants were cleaning, scrubbing, cooking, making butter or cheese and doing all the various tasks connected to farm life. Sometimes the house pulsated with life. She was right about one thing though: the old part of the house, at least, was friendly and I never felt worried or frightened by the presence of these people from the past. I also felt that they were firmly rooted in their time zone and had no idea that a little girl with a night light was walking among them.

It was a different matter in the other part that we thought was a barn conversion. The change was instantaneous as I opened the hall door and stepped from the old house into the newer section. It was like leaving a busy bustling street, and suddenly entering an empty black alley. That part of the house felt empty, distant and remote, and at night, not at all friendly.

The great glory of the house was the main staircase which was situated just off the hall. An antique dealer, one of many who scoured the villages and farms after the war and into the 1950s hoping to snap up bargains from gullible country folk, thought that it was Jacobean hand-carved oak. It was certainly special and a feature we all loved. It may well have begun life somewhere more upmarket than a farm, probably a gentleman's house, and could have been inserted after the barn had been converted into dwelling quarters. A downstairs window had been blocked up to accommodate it.

I loved the staircase, and in the daytime spent many hours playing there with friends or by myself. There were two flights with a landing halfway up. The staircase was wide and the steps very shallow so one could glide up and down in a dignified and elegant manner, although I have to say I usually took them two at a time. The banisters were wide and definitely made for sliding down; they were irresistible. The landing halfway up was a very good place for playing with toys, doing handstands, or playing ball.

There was a second landing and corridor which ran along the top, past the balustrade and my bedroom. This corridor had a door at each end. When these doors were opened they made good goals, and the corridor morphed into a long narrow hockey pitch. On several occasions as a young teenager, I can remember playing hockey with my friend Alice and using balloons as balls. I can also remember filling the balloons with water to make them heavier. It was lucky that the stairs and floors were covered in linoleum then. Even so, Mother was not pleased when she caught us. The staircase seemed to bring out the fun in everyone. Uncle Jack loved to chase us children around the house and, when caught, he would grab us by the ankles and dangle us over the balustrade. I never wriggled in case he dropped me.

There was a back staircase with bare scrubbed wooden steps that ran up from the kitchen but that route to bed was not available during my childhood years. It led straight into a bedroom that was always in use for live-in help. Sometimes it was domestic help, or a young lad to help around the farm. Then there were Land Girls and later German Prisoners of War.

To reach my bedroom, I had to brave the main staircase, and during the dark winters I did not relish it much. At night, rather like Jekyll and Hyde, the stairwell changed character. To me it seemed a vast space and the light from my flickering candle did little to pierce the gloom. All the artefacts around the walls did not help either and there were certainly some unusual objects. Great-Aunt Leah, Great-Aunt Hannah and other ladies of the house had from time to time bought pictures and other items from auctions and sales to try and cover the walls. In my earliest years there was a huge oil canvas which was almost entirely painted in black. In the background a plate and jug were just visible through the gloom, and in the foreground was a piece of cheese with a little mouse. I could never understand why anyone would want such a boring monstrosity on the wall. Apparently, my mother must have thought the same because it was eventually replaced with a shipwreck – not much better because you could tell by the look of horror on their faces that everyone knew they were doomed.

Other items on the walls included an African war shield painted in black, white and red, with strange stylised eyes and mouth, which was quite scary. There were two hand-stitched collages which depicted Egyptian scenes, not frightening but not reassuring either. There was the head of a red deer complete with antlers and shiny glass eyes, and horns from assorted African antelope.

I always had the feeling that something or someone was watching me at night on the staircase, so my strategy was to appear nonchalant. It was no use saying anything to Mother, as she always said:

"Well, it's exactly the same in the dark as it is during the daylight – it's just that you can't see anything."

I never ran up the stairs, as I did not want to appear scared, although I did not linger either. I stepped up quite briskly past the scary war shield and the deer's head, turned the corner by the Egyptians, and then marched up the second flight under the antelope horns. By then I was on the home straight, along the corridor to my bedroom and safety.

The lane curved between the old stone walls on the left, which were covered with Virginia creeper, and the walnut trees on the right, then it turned the corner and brought us to the back door.

Great-Aunt Hannah with the pony and trap. Early twentieth century.

Family

Great-Uncles and Aunties

The Squire family's tenure at Wansley Barton began with Francis Squire, who was born in 1822. He farmed at Wansley from 1870 until the 1890s. In 1871 he married Fanny Symons, a widow. At the time of the marriage Francis would have been forty-nine and Fanny fifty-three. Fanny died in 1880 and Francis must have found married life agreeable, as he married again in 1882 to a Grace Taylor who lived in the village. It was during the 1890s that Francis, who was my Great-Great-Great-Uncle Frank, set up his two great-nephews, John and Robert Squire, to farm at Wansley, while he moved on to pastures new.

Great-Great-Great-Uncle Frank had an entrepreneurial spirit and was considered by other members of the family to be very well off. There was always a rumour when I was young that he had buried his gold somewhere on Wansley, and many a childhood hour was passed with friends, searching for Uncle Frank's gold. Needless to say nothing was ever found, and if he had any gold sovereigns I imagine he put them to better use than burying them. However, he was outwitted by his first wife, Fanny.

She had a son from her previous marriage, Henry Symons. Apparently Henry wanted to buy a horse from Francis and they agreed on a price. Perhaps Francis was wary of banks and this gave rise to the rumour that he buried his money, but Fanny knew that he kept his money in a box under the bed. She stole the sum agreed upon for the horse and gave it to her son to pay Francis. Presumably, Henry knew nothing about this deception and Fanny later confessed on her deathbed. Uncle Frank's smiling face beamed down at us from his photograph in the hall for many years after his death, and it is not difficult to believe that he forgave Fanny her actions. It certainly did not put him off marriage, as he married again within two years, and Henry was still working on the farm as a servant after Fanny's death.

My great-uncles Jack and Bob were born at Ebberly, and the family home was High Downs. Their father, William Squire (my great-grandfather), was a carpenter and wheelwright. I understand that Jack and Bob worked at Wansley with their great-uncle before the tenancy of the farm was transferred to their names, and then Francis moved to Rumsam House in Barnstaple. Jack and Bob farmed for a number of years as bachelor farmers and their sister Hannah became housekeeper.

In 1912 Bob married Hannah Margaret Squire, known as Maggie. She lived at Roborough Mill, which was about half a mile away, and was the daughter of Henry and Emily Squire. Henry was a builder or mason. There are several instances in the family of a Squire marrying a Squire, and in North Devon the name Squire is as commonplace as Smith or Jones in other areas.

Bob and Maggie made the decision to emigrate to Canada, and thought that it would be wonderful to begin their adventure by crossing the Atlantic on a new liner named *Titanic* which was making her maiden voyage. We are not quite sure why they changed their plans and sailed on another ship, but a Canadian relative thinks that it was to do with an illness in the family. Lucky illness for Bob and Maggie, although initially they were disappointed to miss the opportunity.

During the early years of the twentieth century, farming was depressed and times were quite hard. Emigration to Canada or Australia was a regular occurrence in the farming community at the time. Even so it must have been a big decision to make; it was so final and the severance from home, friends and family was total. There were no telephones, no emails, no Skype, only the long-awaited letter. All gossip and news of births, deaths, marriages, dreams, hopes, disappointments and struggles came sporadically via the postman, and certainly in Bob and Maggie's case long after the event.

The wedding of Francis Robert Squire (Uncle Bob) and Hannah Margaret Squire (Aunt Maggie). Back row, L–R: Hannah Squire, Liza Squire, Arty Squire, Tryphena Squire, Elizabeth Prouse, Robert Prouse, Eleanor? Squire, George Squire (Roborough Mill). Front row, L–R: John Squire, Leah Squire (Wansley), Sarah Squire (Sally Davey), Groom, Bride, Ellen Squire? Prouse? Florence Squire? Sitting, L–R: Mrs Squire (Ebberly), Emily Squire, Henry Squire. Boy standing, Harry Prouse (Thelbridge) and Creedy Barton.

Bob and Maggie travelled as far as they could on the American continent, eventually settling on the Pacific coast of British Columbia. They made their home in Victoria on Vancouver Island. This was well before the days of air travel, and the journey was covered by ship, train and boat over a period of many weeks, likewise all the letters which over the years winged their way over and back across ocean and continent. Everyone knew that they would be most unlikely to meet again, although by now photography was more readily available and within the means of ordinary folk. Bob and Maggie had two children, Bill and Grace, and a photo of Grace always stood on Aunt Leah's piano. I was told, "That is Cousin Grace from Canada," and I believe that was when my long-held dream of visiting Canada began.

Jack had married before Bob. A trim and sprightly new headmistress, with an eye for fashion and an extrovert nature, had taken over the helm at Roborough School in 1901. Jack was smitten and so began a long courtship, for she played "hard to get". Eventually

(Left) William Snell, blacksmith, 1836–1916.
(Right) Ann Snell, née Chanter, 1835–1912.
Charcoal and pencil drawings by their daughter, Leah Snell.

they were married in April 1908 and Jack's feelings for her never wavered; he adored her for the rest of his life.

Leah Snell was the thirteenth and youngest child of a blacksmith, William Snell, and his wife, Ann, of Northparks, Burrington. Leah had done very well for herself, and as a self-made career woman in Victorian and Edwardian times she was quite a rare species, especially coming from such a modest rural background. She was born in 1878, and became a pupil-teacher at her local primary school in Burrington.

A pupil-teacher is much what it sounds like. Pupils who were capable and able stayed on after school-leaving age, which at the time was fourteen, and trained to be teachers under the tutelage of the headteacher and other staff. In North Devon this was reinforced by lectures at Barnstaple, and there was also coursework which was sent through the post. There was a system of exams culminating with a certificated exam in Bristol. Leah then worked at Burrington School for several years before applying for the post of headmistress at Roborough School.

A perusal of the Roborough School logbook shows that during the twelve months prior to Leah becoming headmistress, the school was beset with problems. There had been a succession of temporary teachers and the 1901 inspectors' report stated:

> *The condition of the school as regards its control, discipline and instruction is lamentably unsatisfactory. The instructions of inspectors are apparently ignored, little real work has been done and the boys are unruly and troublesome.*

There was obviously pressure on Leah to turn the school around and she was just the person to do it. She was strong willed, sharp tongued, talkative and quick witted. She was also a hard worker and a strict disciplinarian, and apparently, for a small, slight person, surprisingly handy with the cane. I was a little bemused in later years to discover that most of the men in the village, about my parents' age or older, whom I regarded as amiable, inoffensive and blameless old men, had all been caned by Aunty.

It took Jack a long time to persuade Leah to become his wife. There is no doubt that farm life in those days was hard, with long hours of physical labour for women as well as men. In common with all of rural England at the turn of the century there was no electricity, in fact the villages in our particular patch of Devon were not connected to the national grid until the early 1960s. Water was pumped from the well, brought indoors in a bucket, and then heated in a copper or kettle over the fire. The logistics of preparing food, cooking, cleaning, washing and ironing were not for the faint hearted, and Jack mulled over in letters to Leah what could be done to make life easier for her, should she become his wife.

Jack wrote many letters to her and there are several beautiful Victorian or Edwardian Christmas cards. The bundle of letters, tied with string, has lain in Aunt Leah's carved wooden box for over one hundred years. They speak of a long-vanished way of life in pastoral England: of long walks on summer evenings, bicycle rides home in the dark after "courting", the effect of the vagaries of the weather on harvests of long ago, the gossip and latest romances in the village, and he briefly alludes to a whiff of scandal in Leah's own family. In all the letters Jack's integrity, loyalty and faithfulness shine through as he discusses the ups and downs of daily life, and speaks of his feelings as he tries to win Leah's heart. The letters are a precious account of the past, and they even allude to the birth of my father in 1905, and the first appearance of my grandmother downstairs, after "lying-in" for two weeks after the birth.

Jack was born in 1873, one hundred years before my children were born. He would have had very little formal education, just the local village school, and he may well have left school at twelve years old. In fact, the school-leaving age was not raised to twelve until 1889, by which time Jack would have been sixteen, so there is the possibility that he left school at ten years old, although I imagine that he stayed until he was fourteen. Nevertheless, Jack had a very legible style which many people these days would be pleased to own, and his letters are interesting as he chats about life on the farm and gossip around the village, and of course his feelings for Leah.

Leah always considered herself to be "delicate". The fact is, none of us could remember her having a day's illness in her life. She readily admitted that she escaped all the childhood illnesses such as measles, whooping cough and chickenpox, in spite of being in the same room, or bed, as sisters and brothers who were suffering. She also sailed unscathed through epidemics of diphtheria and scarlet fever as a pupil and as a teacher at Burrington School. We can none of us remember her even having a cold or the flu, but somehow or other she managed to make her health a big issue and let us know that she had to take care of herself. Jack pondered this and wrote in a letter:

> *But I don't like the drudge in a farmhouse for you, I wish I could get at something so as it will be easier for you. We will talk it over and see what can be done.*

Leah must have been happy with the arrangements to make life easier. They included breakfast in bed and an afternoon nap. This was to continue for the rest of her life.

"She must be the only farmer's wife in Devon to have breakfast in bed," my mother would mutter darkly as she carried the tray up the wide staircase.

In reality, Leah was as tough as old boots, but perhaps we should all take note: it could be the recipe for longevity, as she lived to be almost 103 years old.

My Parents

Father

My father, William John Squire, always known as Bill, came to work at Wansley when he left school just before his fourteenth birthday.

(Top Left) Leah Snell,
Great-Aunt Leah, 1878–1981.

(Middle Left) John Squire,
Great-Uncle Jack, 1873–1960.

Jinney Bright was married on Tuesday I heard the Bells I thought when I heard them that I wish it was ours

Uncle Jack and Aunt Hannah standing by the house, probably early twentieth century. Not long after this, a wall was built to separate the farmyard from the front of the house.

(Left) Uncle Jack.
(Right) Uncle Jack, Aunt Leah and my father, Bill Squire, on the rough grass outside the front gate.

He always said that he wanted to work with the horses on his uncle's farm, and he probably began to work there in April 1919. His father, William Henry, was a brother to Jack and Bob, and was also involved with farming, but as a bailiff or hind, which was more the role of a farm manager. My father was born at Wansley – I suppose because it was the Squire family home.

William Henry, known as Will, worked for several years as a shepherd for General Buller. General Buller was a veteran of the Boer War and there is a statue of him on his horse in Exeter. He had a big estate at Crediton, and some of my father's earliest memories were of walking the fields around Crediton with his father, presumably on the rounds caring for the sheep. Later the family moved to Sidbury, which is a small village in South East Devon, not far from Sidmouth. My father and his two younger sisters, Doris and Gwendoline, went to school at Sidbury, and that was where the family was living when Father began working at Wansley.

Unfortunately, about eighteen months later tragedy struck. On 5 October 1920 my father's mother, Beatrice, known as Beattie, died in childbirth. It must have been devastating for the family, but sadly it was a calamity that happened all too frequently in those days. My father continued to live with Aunt Leah and Uncle Jack, and the two girls were cared for by maternal family, who lived at Dolton. I think that later my grandfather, William Henry, took up a position on Lundy Island for a while, and Doris and Gwen had holidays there. No such luck for my father though. I think that Uncle Jack and Aunt Leah kept his nose to the grindstone and he had little time off, and was not given much opportunity for socialising or leisure-time activities. I do not believe this was because they were unkind or oppressive in any way; in fact, they were very fond of him, and looked upon him as their own son. It was the way that they had been brought up themselves. Farm life involved hard work and long hours; hobbies or outside interests during daylight hours were considered to be wasteful of time and frivolous.

Mother

Aunt Leah had a brother called Lewis who was a water bailiff. He lived at High Bickington, and as was common in Edwardian times had a large family. His eldest daughter, Mary Jane, was studying to become a teacher like her Aunt Leah. Mary Jane was always called Molly. This does seem to be a feature of the age. A child is given a name at their christening and then always called something else. Molly, like her Aunt Leah, trained to be a teacher via the pupil-teacher route and carried on with her studies at High Bickington School after school-leaving age.

During the school holidays Molly enjoyed visiting her aunt and uncle on the farm at Roborough, and that was how she met Bill. They were both born in 1905, and they were married on 27 April 1937. It was two generations of a Miss Snell, school teacher, marrying a Mr Squire, farmer. When I was born a year later, it meant that Leah and Jack were both blood relations to me, for Leah was my mother's aunt, and Jack was my father's uncle.

Leah and Jack did not have any children of their own, and they always treated me as a grandchild. Indeed, strangers and people who came into the parish in later years always assumed they were my grandparents. They were both fond of me, although I was not aware how much when I was younger. As products of their time they were quite strict and reserved and kept their emotions firmly under control. It is only when I look back now, having grandchildren of my own, that I realise how much I meant to them and how much pleasure they had from my company.

*

They say that opposites attract and this was certainly true of my parents. I always felt that Father was the sunshine and Mother was the rock. My father, like most of the Squires, especially the Ebberly branch of the family, was kindly, gentle, unassuming and easy-going. He certainly did not think highly of himself and was totally unselfish, always putting other people first, at times to his own detriment. He was not a talkative man but he had a quirky sense of humour and could be guaranteed to set everyone chuckling with a few throwaway remarks. He also had an infectious laugh and could light up a room with his smile. The Ebberly Squire family was mostly short, stocky, solid and staid. My father definitely cut more of a dash and had that indefinable ingredient called charm, although I believe he was totally unaware of it. Perhaps it came from his rascally grandfather, the soldier Richard Gartland, whom I have since discovered was of Irish descent. (Incidentally, after twenty years of family history research, and tracing the Squire family back to the late fifteenth century and the Snells back to the early eighteenth century, Richard Gartland seems to be my only ancestor who didn't come from North Devon.)

In addition to all his other characteristics Father was blessed with film-star good looks – well, I certainly thought so – although once again I am not sure that he realised it. He certainly had no airs and graces. Apparently others must have thought the same. Shortly after his death I remember two elderly ladies telling me that when he came to a dance, all the girls wanted to dance with him.

Well, my mother, Molly Snell, was the one who eventually got him, and a very good couple they made. Mother was tiny; she did not quite make four feet eleven even as a young woman and was much shorter than that when she grew old. She was vivacious and talkative, with black hair, dark brown eyes and a skin that looked as though she had been in the sun even in the depths of winter. Like most of the Snell family, she had a quick temper underneath the surface but life had taught her to keep it firmly under control. She loved bright colours, flamboyant clothes and jewellery. As she said, she had to be careful with choice of earrings or she could soon look like a gypsy.

Mother was the perfect antidote to my gentle, quiet, unassuming father but she was not just a brightly coloured bird. She had real strength of character and a toughness hidden underneath the surface. In spite of his easy-going ways and calm and pleasant personality, my father was an inveterate worrier. I think that most people were unaware of this, as he was always so genial and full of fun and made us laugh. However, he worried about everything, whether it was necessary or not, and at times it led to depression. My mother supported and protected, encouraged and cajoled him through thick and thin. She was the rock that we all relied upon when life took a downturn, and she had the ability to batten down the hatches and pull herself and everyone else through, until better times were reached. I certainly learnt from her that no matter how hopeless, painful and worrying the situation, it is possible to plod on a day at a time and eventually reach the other end.

I think that Mother had learnt from an early age that life was not easy. She was the oldest of a family of eleven and there was never very much money. My grandmother struggled to keep them clothed and to put food on the table. It was a shameful thing in those days not to be able to go to school because you had no shoes to wear, and although my grandparents managed to keep their brood shod, I believe it was a close-run thing at times. Apparently potato pie meant just that, potato covered in pastry. My grandfather was for a time a gamekeeper and then a water bailiff. I have heard tales of illicit salmon from time to time, and of course rabbits were part of the staple diet as they were in my childhood, but I think that it was a battle to keep the stomachs full.

Mother was able to stay on after school-leaving age for an extra four years to study and train to be a teacher under the pupil-teacher scheme. My grandparents were unable to do this for any of the other children so she was privileged. They were all bright and intelligent, and these days would have expected to go to university. As the older ones left school they contributed financially to help the family. My mother had to work hard and spent many hours studying. Coursework was sent through the post and there were external exams at Barnstaple. Mother always had a curvature of the spine, even when she was in her twenties. She said that it was the result of spending hours hunched over the table studying, but I suspect that the poor diet during her formative years may have also contributed to it.

There were those in the family who did not believe that Bill and Molly were a good match. We still have a letter written to Aunt Leah by her sister Annie Snell. Annie must have got out of bed the wrong side that morning, as the letter is full of derogatory remarks about members of the family. She wanted to know whether Bill and Molly were still courting, and whether Leah was going to have "her" (Molly) in the house.

Wisely Leah and Jack let events take their own course, and my mother moved into Wansley after the marriage. Dear Uncle Jack was always kindly and always appreciated everything that my mother did for them, but Aunt Leah was quite a difficult person to live with. She considered herself to be "top dog" and Mother was frequently reminded of her place, which was a few notches below. Leah had reason to be grateful to my mother though, as Mum did her duty, and cared for her well into her old age.

(Left) My father, William (Bill) Squire.
(Right) My grandmother, Beatrice (Beattie) Squire, in First World War Land Army uniform.

(Left) Aunty Doris and Aunty Gwen, my father's sisters.
(Right) My grandparents, William Henry and Beatrice Squire. Another example of a Squire marrying a Squire. Beattie was a member of the Squire family of Furse Barton, Ashreigney.

(Left) My parents' wedding on 27 April 1937 at St Mary's Church, High Bickington. (Right) My grandparents, Mary Ann and Lewis Snell.

My parents on honeymoon in Torquay.

Around the Farm

After the farm lane had passed between the old house and the walnut trees, turned the corner and escorted the traveller to the back door, it was evident that its journey was not yet over, for it continued down the gentle slope, beckoning enticingly. It was now no longer confined between two hedges, and the aspect opened out to a big green space full of grass and trees. On the left was the farm courtyard, bounded on three sides with stone buildings; on the right, a swathe of grass ran up to a Devon bank topped with young beech trees. In the middle of this grassy area stood an old oak tree, and next to it, an ash tree, planted in more recent times by some Victorian amateur weather forecaster. We all knew the rhyme.

If the oak before the ash, then we'll only have a splash,
If the ash before the oak, then we'll surely have a soak.

We always watched to see which leaves came out first and the delicate golden-green leaves of the oak were usually the first to unfurl. I honestly cannot remember now whether the summer weather followed as predicted.

The lane ran between the courtyard and the grassy area and continued unhampered as a broad stony track. It passed by the cart linhay and trap house, and skirted a stand of tall fir trees as it led the visitor towards the pond. Beyond the pond more buildings were visible, some thatch and cob, some stone and slate. All this time the visitor's eye was drawn beyond the immediate surroundings, to the patchwork of small fields stretching to the distant Ebberly high ridge. Ebberly House itself, long, low, with white pilasters glinting in the sunlight, gazed across the fields at us.

The farm had at one time been part of the Ebberly estate, and the manor house still seemed to be keeping a friendly eye on proceedings. The only other dwelling that looked directly across at us was Winscott, which was another ancient farmstead in the parish of

Aunt Leah feeding the pigs outside the backdoor.

St Giles in the Wood. It was not our nearest neighbour by any means, but it was comforting to look across to another habitation, even if it was quite distant. The two farms seemed to be companions nestling together in this secluded area of Devon.

The lane still seemed to be in a hurry to entice its traveller on. It passed through the cluster of buildings beyond the pond. Here was the barn and granary and an old thatch and cob linhay to shelter animals. On the left on slightly higher ground was a small plat called the Mowstead, where the ricks were made and Mother kept poultry. The banks of the Mowstead were topped with hazel bushes, and by now a small stream trickled beside the lane. This was the overflow from the pond. Once again, after passing the linhay, the lane became wedged between two high Devon banks. On the right bank towered two wonderful elm trees; they spread their branches, almost touching the hazel bushes on the Mowstead bank, casting a welcome shade in the summer. Here, where the lane narrowed, was a gate so that any animals could be contained in the Lower Court by the barn.

After passing through the gateway, the lane once again managed to shake off its restrictive high hedges, and gradually reverted to a stony track passing through a grassy meadow. It then headed towards a small copse. Here several springs bubbled up amongst the trees, which meant the track was always muddy except in the driest weather. Another gate marked the end of the copse and in some indefinable way the end of that part of Wansley – for the fields now belonged to a part of the farm called Little Wansley.

The track hugged the hedge and wound its way up the side of the field called Lower Stone-Park, then through a gateway into Higher Stone-Park. These fields were south facing and always seemed to bask in the sun. Vetch, toadflax, knapweed and clumps of mallow grew here in the hedges. The lane then passed through another gateway into First Meadow and then into Barn-Park. The old thatch and cob barn was still there when I was young and could have been saved, but it was allowed to deteriorate and now no longer exists. This must have been the only building left of the smallholding called Little Wansley.

The track could now see its goal and headed straight for it. This was a winding public road which scouted the perimeter of the farm before heading towards Ebberly House. By now the track was not quite as obvious as it was overgrown with grass and looked like part of the field. My father recalled that when he was young, an avenue of lime trees stretched from the entrance on the public road to the old barn. This avenue is shown on the old Ordnance Survey maps. All local people knew that it was a direct route to the farm, and anyone from that side of the parish who wished to visit always walked in that way. Maybe even now, sometimes on a summer's evening, shadowy figures – a lady in a long dress, a peddler with wares to sell, a farmer with his horse and cart or children skipping and chattering – pass underneath the shady lime trees to go about their business in the long-vanished farm.

*

Unless the men were working in the fields the daily routine revolved around the two courtyards. The one nearest the house was Higher Court and the one beyond the pond was Lower Court. There was always something of interest going on, and outside the back door, the grassy area leading to the pond was full of life. I loved playing there on the grass amongst the trees, and the animals found it a pleasant place to linger as well. I was wary of the cows; they were big and not always predictable, loitering on their way to and from milking, especially in the summer, relishing noisy slurps from the pond. Most of the time however, the area was left to the poultry and the pigs, for when I was young there was usually a sow or two wandering around. The horses also enjoyed the shade of the oak tree, and Bobby and Flower would crop the grass while the men were having dinner. I came at the very end of the working horse era, and Father was already doing most of the farm work with a tractor when I was born.

The courtyard itself consisted of stone and slate buildings on three sides. There was the stable at the far end, two-storeyed with a tallet above. There were stalls and a loosebox for a colt. Harnesses belonging to faithful workers from the past hung from the walls, and the smells of leather, horse and hay still lingered on. Father stored straw up in the tallet, and this was also home to a pair of barn owls who nested there for many years. There was a loophole slit in the end wall facing Grinding Stone Meadow and the owls made their nest just inside on the ledge. Occasionally I would clamber up over the straw to see the nest and check if there were any eggs, and sometimes I would go with Father to have a look at the little fluffy owlets. I was always aware of the owls, even if I did not see them regularly, as my bedroom was on the front of the house near the stable. I liked their presence and even found their shriek a comforting sound as I snuggled into my feather mattress at night. The young would make a hissing noise, presumably when their parents brought supper, and I would try and imagine what tasty morsels of mice or vole Mr and Mrs Owl had provided.

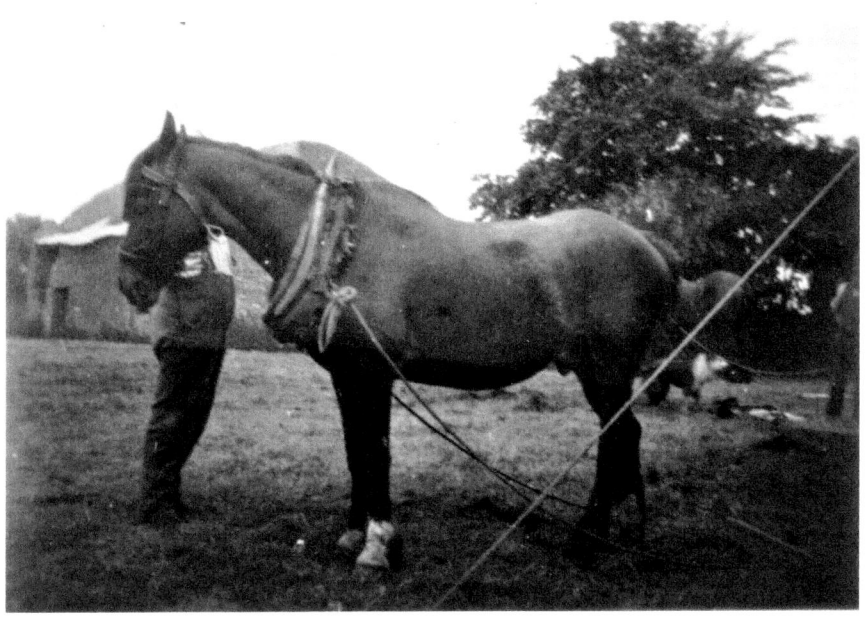

A horse working at Little Wansley. The old barn is in the background.

The stable area always seemed to be a male domain, although by the time I was born, the horses were second to the tractor; nevertheless, the stable still retained an aura of manly businesslike importance. I only visited for a specific reason and rarely just played there. In complete contrast was the turnip house on the adjoining side of the court. The turnip house was a central feeding store, and as well as turnips, depending on the season, there were just as likely to be swedes or mangolds in a heap in the corner. The mangold cutter stood nearby ready to slice them for consumption, and a maund, which was a deep oval-shaped basket made of woven strips of wood, stood underneath the blade ready to catch the slices.

I suppose the turnip house was the farmyard kitchen, for not only were there root crops of one sort or another, but also linseed cattle cake and meal, which Father ground himself, and hay was tossed down from the tallet above, ready to put in the hay racks. There was a walkway leading from the turnip house to the shippens and an open linhay, so that the animals could all be fed without anyone having to go outside and brave bad weather. The turnip house was cosy and had a pleasant sweet aroma of hay and cattle cake. It was south facing and the sun streamed in when the double doors were opened. It was a natural gathering place, and the men would stop and have a chat; the cats would congregate there waiting for their saucers of warm milk straight from the cow. Even Rover and Lassie and other sheep dogs over the years were happy to rest on the hay, on call, waiting for the signal that the cows were unchained and ready to be escorted back to the field.

Of course, all this was well before the days of milking parlours, and each cow knew her place in one of the three shippens and usually retained that place for the rest of her milking life. They were chained up and a scoop of cattle cake, meal or swede put in the troughs. Sometimes that would be my job and the men would pitch some hay into the racks. One of the shippens faced into the turnip house, and those cows were the lucky ladies, for not only were they able to watch proceedings, drooling at the mouth in anticipation, but sometimes by stretching their necks as far as the chain would let them they could grab a little extra. Edna was the luckiest lady, as her stall was near the ladder where the hay was tossed down from the tallet, and she was often able to have a second helping. During the summer months, the cows were let out again after the evening milking and they returned to the field until it was time for the morning session. During the cold winter weather though, they stayed in the shippens all night, and considerable amounts of root crops, hay and cattle cake were required to supplement the grass in the fields. The dung heap which was in the middle of the yard grew all winter, until eventually it was drayed away in the spring to be spread on the fields.

When I was very young the cows were milked by hand and usually two people did the milking, each with their pail and three-legged stool. They washed the udders, then, sitting on their stools, they tucked their heads against the cows' flanks and rhythmically squeezed the milk into the buckets with a satisfying ping, ping, while the cows munched contentedly away.

I think that my father bought the Gascoigne milking machine and petrol two-stroke engine to run it not long after I began school. The petrol engine was put in the corner of the turnip house, and air pipes to create suction were run through to all the shippens and the linhay. I sensed that the adults were very excited about this innovation and it was considered to be very modern. It was certainly much quicker, and the milking could then be done by one person in less time.

Situated above the turnip house, two of the shippens and a calves' house was a large tallet, and this was one of my favourite spots. It was a sweet-smelling place full of hay and straw. The sun shone in the opening, and it was a good place to sit in the sun and read a book or just relax. When friends came over it was a favourite place to play, and we jumped off the beams onto the soft hay, made slides and practised somersaults.

This tallet was also the preferred choice of the farm cats. They had no problem climbing up via the shippen and the ladder, and it made a very cosy maternity ward. Many generations of kittens were born up there. I would take up saucers of milk and then wait quietly until the mother came to feed, and the little ones followed her. Not many kittens grew to adulthood, Father saw to that. He usually managed to find them before their eyes opened and disposed of them. Occasionally though, a cat managed to rear her brood until they turned into fluffy, wide-eyed innocent beauties that no one could resist, and then we would have to find homes for them. We usually had four or five cats around the farm buildings – no more. My mother was not especially fond of cats.

"When I came to Wansley there were fifteen cats," she retorted. "More fuss made of the cats than humans!"

*

The pond was a focal point and always a place of interest. I cannot remember ever being warned not to go there. Like water everywhere it was a magnet for children. There was no problem anyway, as it was quite shallow around the edges where we would wade in to collect toad or frogspawn. It was also muddy, and more than once I left a welly stuck in the mud and had to go back to retrieve it. The mallards usually built their nest on an island of brambles close to the edge, and it was possible to keep an eye on the eggs. Unfortunately, the fox could do the same, and during dry periods when the water level fell after the ducklings had hatched, they began to disappear.

The moorhens however were wiser, and they built their nests where it was just too deep to wade and the water started to pour over the tops of our wellies. The moorhens were fierce little creatures and very protective of their nests and their young. We called them dip-chicks and they frequently chased the poultry. It was not at all unusual to see a hen running for her life up towards the Higher Yard away from the pond, with a little black dip-chick, head outstretched, noisily chasing it.

I was cautioned to be careful on the bank at the back edge of the pond where the water was deeper. A hedge with brambles covered most of this bank, and there was only one place where there was access. Here a tall wooden post stuck out of the water.

The pond with the old linhay, barn and Plantation in the background.

This was the plug which was removed occasionally to drain the pond and clean it.

At sometime, someone had gone to a lot of trouble to make the area around the pond an attractive place. At the side of the deep end and running along the little feeder stream was a small plat that we called The Plantation. There was a lovely beech tree, several larches and some sycamore and hawthorn. It was an interesting place to play and I spent a lot of time there. The feeder stream for the pond came from a spring in a nearby field called Rushy Plat. A deep stone gully had been built to channel the water, and this formed the boundary on one side of The Plantation. Trees grew along the top of the gully, moss covered the stone walls, and in the spring, primroses and violets peeped out.

Mother kept a poultry house in The Plantation and another one on the other side of the hedge in Rushy Plat, so there was always plenty of activity in the area. Some of the hens preferred to nest in the hedges, so after the morning and afternoon feeds when we collected the eggs, we had to search the hedges as well as collect from the hen houses. We knew where most of the nests were, but when I was playing in the area I would keep my eyes open in case I spotted a hen heading towards an undiscovered hiding place. Hens like to build up a clutch of eggs, so we always left one egg in the nest to encourage them to go back to the same place again. We had china eggs to leave in the nests and being unable to count, the poor dears never seemed to realise that we had taken all the rest.

There was a lot of poultry kept down in the Lower Court, for as well as the two houses in Rushy Plat and The Plantation, a building between the granary and the linhay was used for poultry. There was another hen house in the middle of the courtyard and there were always several chicken houses in the Mowstead. The hens wandered everywhere, scratching and pecking, contentedly squawking and clucking, interspersed every so often with a noisy crescendo from someone who had just laid an egg. Occasionally a hen would outwit us and one morning would appear proudly leading a brood of little yellow fluffy, cheeping chicks. Mother then would have to find a coop to put them in, to protect them from the fox. The chicken coops were usually put in the Mowstead, and Father had made several runs out of wire netting with wooden frames. The coops had wooden bars in the front so that the hen could put her head between the bars to eat and drink. During the daytime the bars could be lifted, so that hen and chicks could roam safely in the wire netting run

The barn was the largest and most important building in the Lower Court and was a busy place. The front entrance consisted of a large double door, and immediately opposite there was another set of double doors, so that it was possible to drive right through. There was a thresher along the back wall, and although during my childhood most of the threshing on the farm was done by contractors, Father found it useful to be able to do small quantities now and again. The corn which was produced sometimes needed to be put through the winnowing machine to clean it and remove the douse; I think that it depended on what my father wanted it for. When I was older I was expected to turn the handle. I seem to remember that it had to be turned quite fast and it made my arm ache. The winnowing machine struck me as an unusual piece of machinery because as far as I could tell it seemed to be made entirely of wood. Perhaps there were some internal metal moving parts that I was unaware of.

The mill was the implement used most frequently, as Father regularly ground corn into meal for feeding the cattle. There was also a chaff cutter and a room called the chaff house where the short dusty straw and other items were stored. This room was sturdily built of wood in a corner of the barn, and had a wooden ceiling and its own door. The chaff cutter stood on the ceiling of the chaff house, and the chaff fell through and was contained in the small room.

All the barn machinery was powered by a Lister Blackstone engine, which to me seemed a gleaming monster. It was kept in the engine house which adjoined the back wall of the barn, and as far as I was aware it was the only door on the farm which was always locked. I was terrified of, and fascinated by, this monster in equal parts. The room smelt strongly of oil and grease and was dominated by this black, green and gold beast. To a young child it seemed huge. I think it ran on TVO (tractor vaporising oil) which was similar to paraffin, and Father had to heat something first, possibly the plugs. Then he had to turn the huge flywheel to bring the monster to life. My mother was frightened of it as well, I could tell. She always worried that Father's arm would become trapped in the wheel, and she insisted on someone being there when he started it up. If there were no men around she would go and stand guard, and when I was little I went with her.

A shaft ran through the wall from the engine house to the barn, and a system of pulleys and belts enabled the engine to power all the machinery in the barn. Father could switch them to work the thresher or the mill or chaff cutter as was needed. In later years when modern tractors had power drives, the engine became redundant and Father powered the mill from the tractor. I believe that the old Lister Blackstone engine has survived and is in an agricultural museum somewhere, possibly Winkleigh or Holsworthy.

Next to the engine house was the carpenter's shop, and I sensed that my father would have liked to spend much more time there. This room also had its own unique smell of sawdust and wood. Long benches lined two of the walls, and the planes and chisels and other woodworking tools were neatly lined up. This room had a most unusual beam supporting the roof. It was a complete tree trunk, bark removed, and even starting to fork into two against the wall where it adjoined the engine house. It was definitely out of the ordinary and people always commented.

Father's grandfather had been a carpenter (Master Carpenter had been written on his death certificate) and possibly some of the tools had belonged to him. There was no fancy carpentry carried out in our carpenters' shop, it was mostly enterprises connected to the farm, but Father always seemed happy when he was working on some project there, and he had endless patience which enabled him to get things exactly right.

The granary was built against the front of the barn and the entrance was next to the barn's big double doors. It was boarded out into five hatches, and this is where the sacks of grain were tipped after threshing days. Planks of wood were slotted into the front of the sections, and we leant over the top and scooped up buckets of corn to feed the poultry. As the level of the grain went down, these planks could be removed to enable us still to reach the corn.

Needless to say, this was the home of many rats and when we entered they could be heard scurrying in all directions. A round hole had been cut into the door so that the farm cats could enter whenever they wished. When the rats became really troublesome Father would call the rat catcher, Mr Jack Rogers, who lived in Beaford. Mr Rogers could turn his hand to many things. He was our pig killer, rabbit and mole trapper, and I think that he did some thatching for us from time to time. He always seemed pleased to come to Wansley, possibly because we made some very good scrumpy cider. He walked over from Beaford, which was nearly three miles, and would arrive with rosy red cheeks. He was a little, talkative man, active and wiry. By the time he had drunk two of three glasses of our cider he was laughing and talking even more, and his cheeks were rosier than ever. We always assumed that he made it back home safely afterwards.

The oldest building in the Lower Court was the linhay. This ancient building was typical Devon cob and thatch, and Father overwintered yearlings or steers there. There was a tallet above where hay was kept and in a slee to the side there was a mangold cutter. The building provided good shelter and there were two openings on the front so that the animals had access to a small enclosed yard. The yard was created by a stone wall and there was a gate at either end. As well as hay racks and mangers inside the building, wooden troughs ran alongside the stone wall in the little yard, and meal, cattle cake or other food could be placed over the wall into the troughs, making it unnecessary to enter the yard.

As well as being the oldest building, the linhay was also the last building in the Lower Court and nestled against the high bank under one of the tall elm trees. Together they must have watched over many generations of farmers as they went about their business, the tasks changing little over the years. None of us could have foreseen that by the end of the century the elm trees, the linhay and much of that Lower Court would be obliterated, and there would be no trace left of their existence.

William Squire, 1846–1927. Carpenter and wheelwright of High Downs Ebberly. My Great Grandfather.

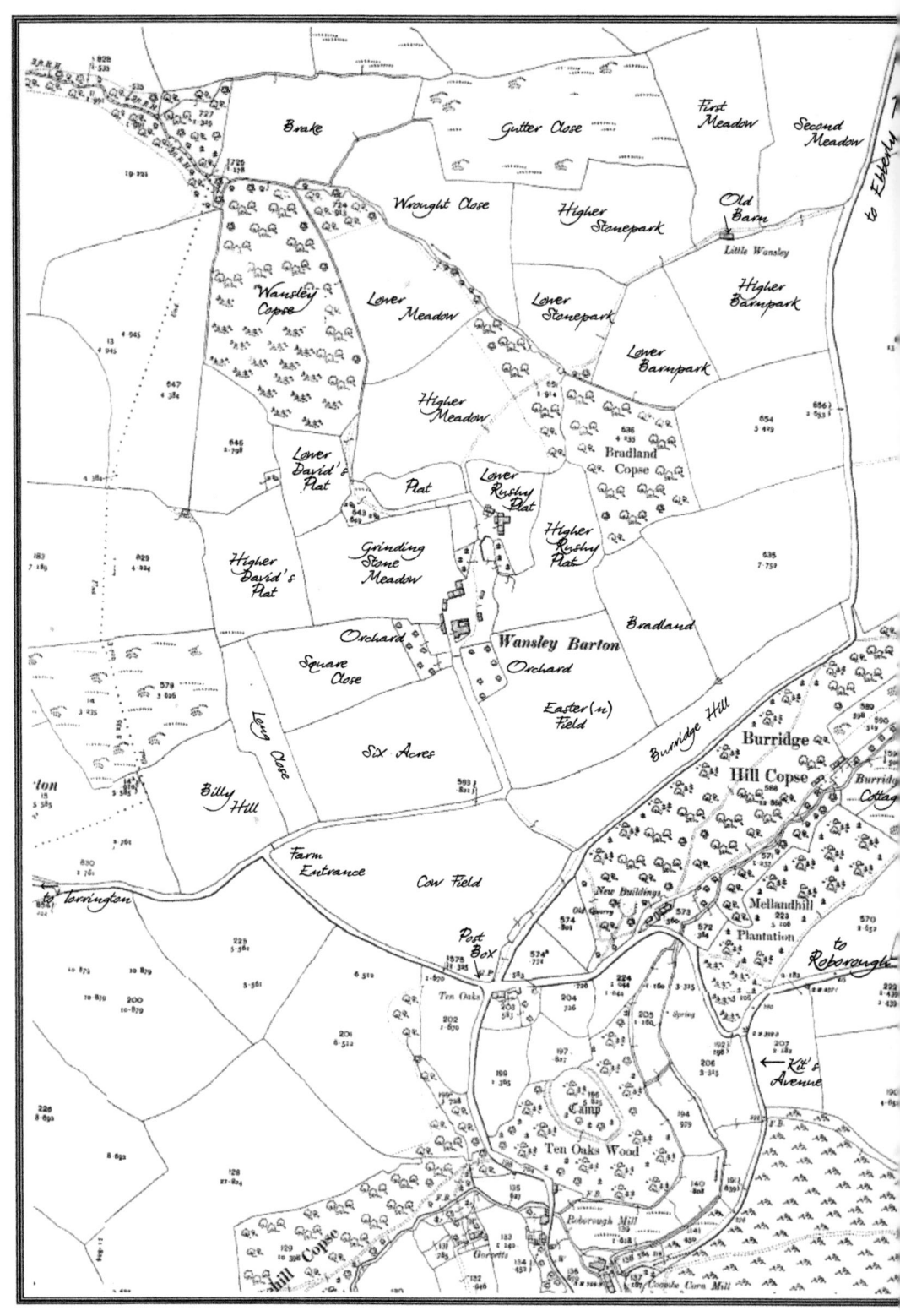

School Days

It was surprising that Mother seemed to be unaware that I had very little idea about the meaning of "school" and I have since wondered about it. She was an understanding person, could put herself in someone else's position and see their point of view, yet it had apparently not occurred to her, or anyone else for that matter, that as I  had spent the first five years of my life as an only child, living on a remote farm more than a mile and a half from the village which I had visited infrequently, "school" and everything that went on there was shrouded in mystery.

Mother had lived within a stone's throw of a village school and maybe that was the reason she did not comprehend my total ignorance. She had grown up in the neighbouring village of High Bickington and lived just along the road from the school. From her earliest moments she would have been aware of the school and the daily routine. She would have heard the bell marking the passage of the day, and she would have seen and heard the comings and goings of the children (about a hundred at the beginning of the century). After completing her own education, she stayed on to train to be a teacher and then she had spent the next fourteen years teaching in local primary schools. There was no doubt that school life was deeply ingrained in her psyche, and maybe she had assumed it had transferred itself to me through some invisible osmosis. There was no doubt in later years we were telepathic, but at five years old the reality of school had not been conveyed to me by any means.

Except that was not strictly true, because I had visited Roborough School – twice, on each occasion to have an injection. During those war years when the doctor and nurse came to the school to give injections or provide routine health check-ups, the parents of babies and toddlers in the parish were notified and asked to attend with their little ones, so they could receive any necessary immunisations. There were no health centres in those days and no one had transport, so it was a sensible arrangement to use the school as a central base. I could remember both occasions all too clearly.

The school consisted of two rooms, "Big Room" and "Little Room", and apart from the lavatories and two small cloakrooms, that was it. This meant that the doctor had to use the "Big Room", in other words the juniors' classroom, as his surgery. I found the whole experience alarming and I am sure all the other little toddlers did as well. We certainly did a lot of crying. The whole ordeal took place at the front of the classroom, as the doctor and nurse used the teacher's desk. Our parents must have all been asked to attend at about the same time and so they formed a line, and one by one we were given our injections. It was a disturbing experience, and even at that young age I felt that it was not very dignified. It was not just the pain of the jab but the fact there was no privacy. The immunisation was not even done discretely in the arm, but was delivered in the top of the thigh, or a jab in the bottom. Of course, the schoolchildren were all supposed to be working but

I could tell that they weren't. They kept glancing up from their desks, watching and smirking.

My mother explained to me the importance of immunisation and how it stopped me from catching terrible diseases such as diphtheria like her little sister Betsy, who had died from diphtheria when she was only seven years old. Now that was something she did communicate to me – her fear of diphtheria – and although it was not rational I worried about it for many years.

So, it was with a mixture of misery, fear and wariness that I walked the mile and a half with my mother to the village school, at the beginning of the summer term in 1943 when I was just five years old. I was told that I was going to school because I was a "big girl now". I assumed that meant that I would have to face up to the doctor and nurse and the jab all by myself, without my mother being there.

Roborough School about 1900. Nothing had changed when
I began school there in 1943. This photograph was in Aunt Leah's
collection. I assume it was taken with a pinhole camera.

It didn't occur to me to say anything, because this was obviously the reality of life and what "growing up" was all about, and of course my parents had no idea what was in my mind.

*

I was told that I would learn to read and write at school, and the idea of being able to read certainly did appeal to me. However, the thing that I really, really wanted to be able to do was to knit. I had noticed that people did not sit around idly unoccupied; maybe it was because it was the war years and there was extra knitting for the war effort, but my mother, her friends, my aunties and everyone I knew were producing socks, jumpers, baby clothes, scarves, squares for blankets and even dish cloths in an endless production line. To me, knitting was a symbol of adulthood, but more importantly I found it intriguing that this persistent clacking of needles soon produced useful items, and I wanted to be able to do the same – perhaps make some clothes for my dolls or even for myself. My mother could knit at the speed of lightning without even looking at what she was doing. She had knitted herself skirts and dresses, and there was even a photo of her wearing a hand-knitted bathing costume. It surely could not be that difficult and when I enquired about learning, I was told that I would be taught to knit when I went to school.

That was the carrot that lured me along the road on that first miserable morning, a little glimmer of hope amongst the gloom. When we arrived and I entered the Little Room (the infants' classroom) there was no one there that I knew or recognised. I did have two cousins in the Big Room but they might as well have been on another planet as far as I was concerned, it was all very bewildering. I must have been a trial to my teacher that day for I think that I probably cried most of the time.

I knew that the doctor and nurse would arrive at some stage, and when we returned to our classrooms after the dinner playtime and Mrs Blackmore put some coconut mats on the floor explaining that we were going to have a little sleep, I knew instantly that was the moment they would appear. I made certain that they would not catch me unaware; I curled up on my mat and positioned myself so that I could keep an eye on both doors: the one that opened to the road and the one that led to the juniors' room. I dutifully closed my eyes when asked, but nevertheless I kept watch, determined not to sleep. To my relief no one turned up and eventually – much later – when the door did open and my mother stood there with all the other mothers I could not believe my luck, and so I survived my first day at school.

Like all the other children over the hundred years or so that Roborough School was in use, I entered the "Little Room" at one end of the building at five years old as a relatively empty vessel, and eventually emerged from the "Big Room" at the other end, filled with a motley collection of information, some transferred by teachers and some gleaned from peers. By this time, we were all able to read and write and do arithmetic with varying degrees of efficiency. We knew our tables, could do long multiplication and division, add up and subtract in pounds, shillings and pence (not forgetting the farthings and ha'pennies). We knew our weights and measures, could parse a sentence, write a composition and were in possession of a smattering of poetry. As it was a church school like so many other village primary schools, we also knew our Bible stories, could recall the Ten Commandments and recite our catechism. As a girl, I had learnt to sew and had several chair-back covers and tray cloths to prove my skill and knowledge of various stitches, and Hallelujah, I could definitely knit.

This last skill I have to say was the result of my mother's instruction and not the teacher's. As my fear of the doctor and nurse receded into the background I began to wonder why I was not being taught how to knit – after all it was the only reason I was still going to school. According to my mother, after I had been attending school for several weeks and Mrs Blackmore still had not taught me how to knit, I began to pester her and reluctantly she gave in. I can still remember the uphill struggle now and I am sure that it was engraved on her mind for the rest of her life.

My feelings about learning to knit at five years old were much the same as learning to use a computer at sixty years old. I wanted to be able to do everything immediately, and my frustration at all the snags and difficulties, and lack of knowledge and skills was overwhelming. In my sixties, I was just able to resist the temptation to stamp my feet, throw the computer across the room, and scream and shout. However, at five years old I had no such inhibitions. It was a fraught time, and Mother and I fell out regularly. Gradually though, over the ensuing weeks and months my struggles with the wool and needles, and constantly muttering to myself, "In, over, out, off", all began to pay off. One day I realised that I was knitting row after row and all was going well. By the time Mrs Blackmore did begin to teach us to knit, which was not until we were near the end of our days in the Little Room, I felt that I was an accomplished knitter. I could do plain and purl, I could cast on and cast off, and I could increase and decrease. Moreover, I was able to help my friends as they struggled with difficulties and dropped stitches.

Mrs Blackmore was my only teacher during those primary school years. When I was in the Little Room she was the infants' teacher and when I moved up to the Big Room at seven or eight years old, she was promoted to the position of headmistress and moved up with me. There were only four children in my school year, so all four of us would only have had the one teacher until we went to secondary school.

The school was well run under Mrs Blackmore's watch as far as I can recollect; discipline was good and she was fair. I think that we all found the school day boring at times but in those days children were not expected to be stimulated or excited by education. We were there to learn to read and write, become numerate, gain some general knowledge – enough to get a job and carry us through life. It was not necessary for it to be interesting or enjoyable. Looking back, I believe that Mrs Blackmore did her best to liven things up and broaden the curriculum from time to time, and the parents and managers had confidence in her, for she regularly managed to get a reasonable number of children through the selection exam and into grammar schools.

The school day always began the same way with an assembly. The whole school squashed together in the Big Room and we sang hymns and said prayers. "All People That on Earth do Dwell", "Jesus Bids Us Shine" and "All Things Bright and Beautiful" were three hymns that I remember singing quite lustily. "Onward, Christian Soldiers" was another of my favourites. Then we always had a scripture lesson, which meant bible stories. After the religious aspect of the day was over, it was English until playtime. After playtime it was arithmetic, which in the infants' room was called "sums", and this lasted until dinnertime. Every morning was exactly the same for the six years that I attended the school, although the afternoons were more varied and consequently more enjoyable.

I always enjoyed nature study lessons, and sometimes in the summer we would go on nature walks around the local lanes. That was always a popular afternoon. In the Big Room I think that someone came to take the boys for woodwork while we girls did sewing or knitting. We all did quite a lot of weaving, and I seem to remember making many raffia mats and teapot stands, and I also enjoyed painting. Strangely I cannot remember doing any painting in the infants' room, unlike these days when young children are encouraged to express themselves with paint from a very early age. We had plenty of crayons but no paints. Watercolour boxes were a privilege reserved for the older children, but as most of us had had little experience of using them, the results were rather amateurish. I think that during those war years and after, there was probably a shortage of materials and there was a lot of "make do" in schools as well as at home.

The two classrooms were very basic. I believe that the building had originally been a "poor house" and had been converted into a school sometime towards the end of the nineteenth century. The ceilings were high and the lower portions of the walls were covered in wainscoting. A round black "tortoise" stove heated each room and we jostled for a position by the guard during the cold weather. There was no electricity in the village and brass oil lamps with white glass shades hung from the ceilings. They were not often lit but were sometimes necessary in the afternoons of dark winter days, and they did cast a cosy glow over the classrooms. The lavatories for the girls were at one end of the school and the boys' lavatories were at the other end. There was no mains water or piped water supply, so they were bucket lavatories, which had to be emptied every night. Most houses in the village had their own well and pump, and there was a communal one set in the hedge opposite Scottington Hill. The water for the school was supplied by a pump, and I suppose we must have washed our hands from time to time. I vaguely remember a roller towel in the little scullery/cloakroom where Mrs Squance or Mrs Madge washed up the dinner plates, but hygiene and hand washing were not high on the list of priorities. Our dinners were cooked at Beaford School and brought over in metal containers in a truck. The village of Beaford was electrified before the war so they were lucky. The national grid had reached that far but it all came to a halt when war broke out, and the programme was not reinstated until the early 1960s.

These days, primary school classrooms are interesting and colourful places with children's work displayed prominently, but I cannot remember very much being pinned on the walls during those war years. There was one picture in the Little Room. It was a sepia print and showed a young child with curly hair dressed in what looked like a white nightdress, walking beside a lion and other animals following behind. The caption read "A Little Child Shall Lead Them". In the Big Room there were two pictures, one of the King and one of the Queen, and there was a plaque commemorating the individuals and trustees who were responsible for setting up the school.

What I do remember though, were the jam jars full of wild flowers that were placed on the windowsills during the summer months. That was the colour that brightened our young lives in the two otherwise dreary classrooms. The windows were set too high to see anything other than the sky and the tops of the hedges but I clearly remember the ledges being crammed with flowers. We brought them to school in the morning and we picked more during the day at breaktimes.

Snowdrops, daffodils, primroses and celandines were the first to appear in the spring, and then during the summer term there was a riot of hedgerow flowers: red campions, bluebells, buttercups, Whit-Sundays (stitchwort), Queen Anne's lace, herb Robert, dandelions and many others. They were stuffed into jam jars, which were interspersed with little meat and fish paste pots, full of daisies and bird's-eyes (speedwell).

I cannot remember not knowing the names of flowers, for like everyone else I was roaming the fields and hedges from my very earliest days and was told by adults what I could pick and what was taboo. My mother told me that anything with bright red berries was poisonous, and we knew to avoid bryony and cuckoo pint, although hips and haws were fine. There was no taboo on foxgloves, although I have heard since to be careful. Foxgloves were amongst the most spectacular of the summer flowers. We loved to pick off the flower heads, pinch one end tight and blow into them, making them go pop, rather like blowing up a paper bag. I can also recollect collecting foxgloves for the war effort. I think it was the seed heads that were needed. We were told it was to help people with bad hearts, and we collected them and took them to school.

Our little village school lacked a playground – not that it worried any of us children at all. I have read some early twentieth-century inspectors' reports about the school and they certainly bemoaned the fact there was no playground, however we all enjoyed our playtimes immensely exactly how things were. There were two small recesses, one at either end of the school and we made use of those: we drew hopscotch squares on the ground, we played skipping games, we sat in a corner and played "five stones", or used Miss Lugg's garden wall to hide our eyes to play "What's the time, Mr Wolf?" The boys tended to play more rushing-about kind of games and they used the recess at the other end of the school. There was no necessity to remain in those two recessed areas though, and we also played Hopscotch, skipped, played ball, Tag, and a wild running-about game called Rescue, up and down the road in front of the school. In fact, the only suitable place to play a ball game called Donkey, was next to the road, using it to form a line, while we threw the ball against the wall of the school and jumped over it. Like all the children who had attended the school before us, we considered the road to be part of our play area.

During those war years, as far as I can recollect, there were only two people in the village who were issued with petrol coupons and were likely to drive by. One was Mr Frank Allin, who ran a taxi service, and the other was Mr Jack Rockey, who, with his wife, Hilda, ran the village post office and shop and needed a vehicle to deliver the post. Mr Rockey also did a small amount of taxi work. I expect there were several other farmers, like my father, who had a car in their garage but were unable to use it because petrol was strictly rationed and only issued for tractors and farm machinery. It meant that the roads during that period were relatively free of traffic, and it was only occasionally that someone shouted, "Car coming!" and we all stood back and waited for it to pass by. One of the teachers stood in the classroom doorway while we were playing and kept an eye on us, but most of the time we were left to our own devices.

There was a playing field across the road opposite the school, which had been donated to the parish and was used by the school as well as for parish events, such as sports or the Revel. I remember spending many happy playtimes there, but of course it could only be used during dry weather in the summer. There was a sturdy chain link fence around the field which was ideal for doing handstands against. We would tuck our dresses into our knickers and practise headstands or handstands, and dangle our legs over the fence and hang upside down. The grass was kept short at the school end of the field, and we

were able to play ball or swing the rope for skipping games. One of the greatest pleasures during the hot summer weather was to sit in the grass making daisy chains, and when the bell rang for afternoon lessons we would return to the classroom with garlands of daisies around our necks and wrists.

Probably, because the field was only used during the warmer weather when there was no need to rush around to keep ourselves warm, we occupied ourselves with quieter games and interests. There were benches inside the gate, and during the morning break we would sit and talk, drink our milk or eat a snack. Like the adults though, it was not often that we sat around doing nothing, and there was usually a pastime or "craze" which kept everyone busy. Sometimes we would bring our knitting to school. Another popular hobby which captured everyone's interest was "cat's cradles", and we would spend our playtimes making intricate patterns with wool or string around our hands. "French knitting" with a cotton reel and four small nails in the top was another "craze" which lasted for many weeks, and we chatted to each other as the little rope of knitting appeared out of the bottom of the cotton reel and grew longer and longer.

The sun always seemed to be shining when I think back to those happy playtimes of long ago. I suppose it wasn't really but they were carefree times with much more freedom than children can expect these days. During our dinner hours, we often wandered along the road past the nearest houses, and Mrs Harris and Mrs Leverton would come out and lean over their garden gates and chatter to us. We also enjoyed ambling down the nearby lane which led to Cliston Farm, or along the road towards Parkyns looking for birds' nests or picking flowers.

I also regularly visited Aunt Leah and Uncle Jack, for by the time I began school they had left the farm and retired to Norhill Cottage in the village. After I had eaten my school dinner, which during those years I remember as being truly dreadful, I would walk down through the village to their cottage and often had another dinner. I loved Aunty's stews but the real treat during the summer term was raspberries. There was a sizeable patch of raspberry canes in the cottage garden, and although we had a good fruit garden at Wansley there were no raspberries. During the season Uncle always had a bowl of raspberries ready for me. I would sprinkle them with sugar, pour on some milk and then mash it all up into a delightful pink gooey concoction. I still remember how delicious they were, and there is little that I have tasted since as good as those summer raspberries. Aunt Leah and Uncle Jack stood watching me, obviously pleased because I was so happy, and I have always associated raspberries with warmth, affection and love.

Sometimes during the dinner hours instead of visiting Aunty and Uncle I would call on my cousin Rachel, who lived in the village and always went home for dinner. I am afraid I was sparing with information and did not tell Mrs Blackmore, so she would have thought I was with Aunt Leah and Uncle Jack. Rachel and I were good friends and close in age. She lived at Newcombes Farm with her brothers and sisters, my Aunty Gwen and Uncle Chesney and my grandfather, William Henry.

Norhill Cottage and Newcombes Farm were my two bases in the village. These were two places where I felt that I could walk in without knocking on the door and know that I would be made welcome. Rachel and I would play around the house, or sometimes out in the yard and in the fields at the back of the house. Nevertheless, we were always conscious of the time and listened out for the school bell (hung in the porch roof) and made sure that we were back in time for afternoon lessons.

As far as I was aware, it was permissible to wander anywhere in the village during the dinner break, although most children stayed near the school. I think that I usually asked Mrs Blackmore if I could visit Aunty and Uncle, but I am not sure that it mattered very much, as she would have known where I was anyway. However, I do remember some boys being caned for wandering too far. They had gone down to Great Wood, which I suppose was a good half-mile from the village. They had obviously lost track of time and were about fifteen or twenty minutes late for afternoon lessons. They were certainly in deep trouble, and had to line up and were caned in front of the class. It was not a quick hands-out job but a bend-over-the-chair punishment which was reserved for the most serious misdemeanours. All boys wore short trousers to school then, and the backs of the legs were a tender target. Even so, I still thought the caning was for being late and not for wandering so far. I always thought that it did not matter where you went, provided you returned to school in time. I must have been wrong in my assumptions, as Mrs Blackmore could not possibly have been happy with her pupils wandering off to Great Wood, and she must have been very worried.

The freedom of the village during playtimes was not something unique to Roborough School as I discovered when reading the High Bickington School logbook, and they did have a school playground. Mr Walter Ham, the headmaster, wrote on 20 March 1924:

> *A fat bullock rushed at Elfreda Squire during the mid-day interval, and either tossed her or knocked her down. She was much frightened, but only seems to have received a few slight bruises.*

Much later, in 1929, a new headmaster, Mr Pitman, was obviously concerned about the children wandering in the village. Two days after taking up his position as headteacher on 10 April he wrote:

> *Children told to stay in playground during playtime and not stray about the village, and to gather there before school.*

*

So, that was how those precious childhood school days gently unfolded. Despite the war and its aftermath there were no great dramas or crises; our excitements and disappointments were relatively low key. We all relished a change to the routine, and there were a few events to mark the passage of the school year. May Day was always looked forward to, certainly by us girls. A May Queen was chosen, and we roamed the hedges picking flowers and greenery to make a garland to crown her, and to decorate her throne.

Oak Apple Day also occurred in May, I think that it was on 29 May, and we sometimes called it "Chick-Chack Day". Everyone wore a sprig of oak leaves to school and woe betide anyone who forgot, because the penalty was a pinch. We all fervently reminded each other the day before, and most of us turned up in the morning with our green sprigs. The boys were always on the lookout, hoping there was someone who had let it slip from their mind, and if a friend did turn up unprotected, we scoured the hedge opposite the school to find a small piece of oak. The custom grew up in connection with King Charles II, who escaped from his enemies by hiding in an oak tree. I doubt whether there is any commemoration of the day now, also very few people even who can remember it from their youth.

There was a sports afternoon in the summer with traditional races. I certainly did not excel at running races but we all had a chance with the egg and spoon race, three-legged race or sack race. There were some team games which were enjoyable, and the afternoon certainly made a welcome break from routine. There was not a lot of emphasis on physical education; it was not really necessary, as most of us had walked quite a distance to school. Every so often we did what was called "drill", but I can only remember doing it in the field in the summer. We lined up in teams with different coloured bands around our chests and did what I can only describe as exercises.

I suppose then, as now, the biggest celebration of the school year was Christmas, and one of my happiest memories of school was making paper chains. At the time, we made our own paste from flour and water, although Mrs Blackmore had some carefully guarded squares of brightly coloured, glue-backed paper. We also cut up old magazines to festoon the walls. In more recent years since becoming a teacher myself, I have always had a paper chain afternoon. Children enjoy making them now just as much as we did then, and it has always brought back happy memories.

Probably the highlight of the school year was the Christmas concert. This was when I realised that I was not destined for the stage. I remember coping with my lines without too much trouble in one or two plays, even quite enjoying myself, but the crunch came during my last Christmas at the school, when I had to sing a verse of "We Three Kings". I was the last king, the one with the myrrh. We each of us had to walk along the right side of the stage, across the front and back down the left side while we sang our verse and Mrs Blackmore accompanied us on the piano. Well, the first two kings managed beautifully, and the gold and frankincense were ceremoniously borne to the correct place. As soon as it was my turn and the piano began, terror took over and my mind went completely blank. I could not remember a single word. My legs could still move though, as I walked up the right side, across the front and down the left side in complete terrified silence. Mrs Blackmore stopped playing and asked me to do it all over again, no doubt thinking that all would be well the second time. No such luck! I was like a rabbit trapped in the headlights of a car as I repeated the whole ghastly episode. I was aware of everyone watching me, and I was also acutely aware that I was letting down the school, letting down Mrs Blackmore and letting down my parents who were sitting in the audience cringing with embarrassment. From that moment, I knew that I was never ever going to set foot on a stage again if I could possibly help it.

*

Roborough School was not the only school which I attended during those primary school years. It was a long walk to the village and I was often ill, especially during the winters. My mother worried about my education because I was away so often, so one winter it was arranged that I should live with an aunty at High Bickington and attend the village school there. I was quite happy with the arrangement as I loved visiting High Bickington. It was a bigger village and much more exciting than Roborough, and I considered it to be my second home. I had been there on holiday, staying with my grandparents on several occasions, and they always made a fuss of me. I had five aunties living in the village as well as numerous uncles, although at the time all of them, apart from my uncles Dion and Peter, were away in the forces.

So, that was how I came to spend two terms living with my Aunty Dot and her mother-in-law, Mrs Gill, at the Golden Lion Inn. Uncle Ken was away in the army, and his mother and my aunty were running the pub, which was the only one in the village at the time. I soon discovered it was very different to living on a farm, and, oh dear, I missed everyone so desperately. It was my first encounter with homesickness – perhaps not a bad thing for it did prepare me a little for boarding school life, four years later. I know that Mrs Gill and Aunty Dot did all that they could to help me settle in, and despite missing my parents, the farm and all the animals, I have some pleasant memories of that period.

I was given a little bedroom above the bar, and if I needed anyone after I was put to bed, for they were both serving in the bar, I was given a stick so that I could bang on the floor. Actually, it was very comforting listening to the muffled buzz of noise from down below, and I rather enjoyed the ability to summon someone by banging on the floor with my stick.

"The maid's banging," someone would shout if my aunty or Mrs Gill did not hear me, and one of them would appear to see what I wanted.

According to the logbook I was admitted to High Bickington School in September 1945 so I would have been seven years old, and I soon discovered that I was a little chicken in a much bigger hen house. As one of the older children in the infants' class at Roborough, I was used to being one of the helpful children, trusted to do jobs around the classroom. When there were questions to be answered my hand usually went up and I was expected to know the answer. It was very different at High Bickington. It was a local farmer's daughter who was at the top of the pecking order in the infants' class. Tall, confident and self-assured, she knew everything and could do no wrong; there was no way I was ever going to make an impression.

I also soon realised that certainly in arithmetic, High Bickington children were slightly ahead of Roborough children and had been taught the mysteries of subtraction with decomposition – in other words, "taking away and borrowing". My heart sank as I gazed at the sums on the board, and wondered how on earth I was going to juggle the figures and hopefully produce the correct answers. Miss Newbery did briefly run through the process, but the group had obviously done it all before and I was the only one who did not have a clue. Predictably when I took my efforts out to be marked at the end of the session they were all wrong, and I was told that I had to spend my playtime redoing them. It was not quite as bad as it could have been, as it was pouring with rain and everyone was indoors. It just meant that I had to sit in my place and redo the sums instead of reading comics and playing with toys – the shame of it all, for I was not used to such things.

My knight in shining armour was an unlikely source. He was a quiet boy that I had barely noticed called Billy Laramy. He did not dash up on a white steed, but sidled up clutching his milk bottle and sucking on a straw.

"I know how to do those," he said, casting his eye casually over my book with all the red crosses and rubbings out.

"Really?" I whispered, for indeed I was a damsel in distress.

"I can show you how to do them," he offered, still pulling on the straw.

I was not sure whether it was allowed, but I knew a rescuer when I saw one, so I shuffled along, and he sat down beside me.

Dear Billy Laramy, he was as good as his word, for he did not do them for me but he showed me how to do them – which is completely different. By the time playtime was over and I had reached the bottom of the page, I could apply the process and work them out for myself. Unsurprisingly I have never forgotten him, and other than my cousin John, he is the only boy from High Bickington School that I can still remember.

Although I felt homesick from time to time and missed everyone from Roborough, in many ways life at High Bickington rolled along quite nicely. At weekends, in between opening hours, I was able to use the bar as a playroom. I had brought some of my toys with me, and Mrs Gill had some interesting books. They were a sort of cross between encyclopaedias and almanacs but there were many interesting bits and pieces. It was at this time I became acquainted with Rupert Bear, for they had a daily newspaper, which was a novelty to me. I quickly became a fan and shared Rupert's adventures in Nut Wood. My aunty must have realised this and about Christmas time a *Rupert Annual* appeared, which gave me many hours of pleasure.

My cousin John lived just down the road at the post office, and there were opportunities to visit and play at weekends. My mother told me many years later that John's mother, my Aunty Kathleen, dreaded me coming because I apparently instigated what she called "boisterous games", and John often ended up with an asthma attack. I believe she was quite relieved when I returned to Roborough.

Gradually I got to know the "regulars" that frequented the pub. One in particular that I still remember fondly was Leonard Murch from Umberleigh. He was a contractor with a threshing machine business, all run by steam engines. He used to come to Wansley to do the threshing and reed combing for my father. Many years later, after I had left school and was working at home on the farm, he still came on threshing days, although his health was not good by then. He visited the pub every night and always briefly came into the sitting room to say goodnight to me.

"Sixpence for a kiss," he used to say.

Well, I was willing, and by the time I returned to Roborough at Easter, I had a large pub ashtray full of sixpences.

Apart from missing my family and the farm, the only other cloud which marred my stay at High Bickington was the fact that I was frequently late for school. This really seems inexcusable, as the pub and the school are so close. Looking back in later years, I realised that my aunt and Mrs Gill were not used to getting up early and sending a child off to school in time. They were always late to bed because after closing time they had to wash the glasses and clear up, and consequently they were used to lying on in the mornings. Quite often I would arrive at school partway through assembly. I was always reproached for it which I felt was unfair, as it was not really my fault, but what really annoyed me was that I often arrived late with another girl called Melanie Harrison. She lived near Burrington village, and having walked all the way, she arrived at High Bickington with rosy cheeks glowing in her round face, blonde hair peeping out from under her pixie bonnet, looking a picture of good health and eagerness.

This was the first time I had come across the name Melanie. At Roborough there was a surfeit of Marys and other names such as Alice, Ann, Elizabeth and Jane, although there was a family with pretty flower names. I suspected that she looked like a melon, but never having seen anything so exotic I could not be sure. Incredibly, she was always praised for being late.

"You see Melanie has walked all the way from Burrington," they used to say, "and you have only had to walk from the Golden Lion."

I wanted to scream out, "Yes, but when I lived at Roborough I walked all the way from Wansley and I was NEVER late." Of course,

I did not say a word and just gazed sullenly at my shoes.

Suddenly, just as I was finding my feet and making friends, my brief stay at High Bickington came to an end. Mother came over to fetch me in Mr Rockey's taxi, and within an hour I was transported back to my old life at Roborough. As the car drew up at Wansley back door, there was Father just walking up from the pond. I ran all the way down the track to meet him and as he whirled me around with a huge hug, my happiness was complete. I did a quick exploration of my old haunts and my favourite trees and play places.

That night I lay in bed listening to the owls, and the next morning as I awoke to all the familiar sounds – the milking machine engine putt-putting, the clang of a milking bucket, a calf calling, a cow lowing, the poultry waking up and the dog barking – then the hollow, aching place in my heart faded away, and I knew that once again all was right with the world.

(Top and middle) Mother in her hand-knitted costumes by the River Taw near Kingford. It was a favourite bathing spot for the locals.
(Left) Mother could knit at the speed of lightning. Here she is in a hand-knitted skirt and jacket.

The Golden Lion in the 1930s. Mrs Gill is on the right, Uncle Ken is in the centre.

(Above) Cousin Rachel.
(Right) Cousin John beside his father's Austin Seven.

Out and About

During the weekends and holidays when I was not at school, the farm was my playground and the centre of my world. Like all farms it was a little kingdom of its own, insular and surprisingly self-sufficient if necessary. The fields, trees and woods cradled the farmhouse, making it for me a haven of happiness. It was the place where everything of importance happened: it was busy, there was a routine, people came to work, visitors and neighbours called and it was the reality by which I gauged everything else.

Aunt Leah and Uncle Jack retired and moved to the village when I was about four years old. Uncle moved their furniture and possessions with the horse and cart, and I certainly accompanied him on one journey, for one of my earliest memories is sitting beside him on the cart, with the horse clip-clopping all the way to their new cottage in Roborough – both of us feeling expectant, happy and content in each other's company.

In those days, it was the custom to go for a walk on Sunday evenings when the weather permitted. This was after tending to the animals and finishing the day's chores. Although this was only a walk around the farm and the roads in our part of the parish, everyone put on reasonably smart clothes, maybe not Sunday best but certainly not working clothes. Aunt Leah, Uncle Jack, my parents and I usually set off walking down the lane, heading towards the pond and Little Wansley.

Farm business, crops, people and parish affairs were discussed by the adults as we made our way down the track and across the fields towards the old barn at Little Wansley and the Ebberly road. Once we had reached the road we turned right, and made our way back towards Burridges Wood, and then on to Ten Oaks Farm. Although we were walking along an insignificant road in a sparsely populated parish, I seem to remember that we usually met other people also out for a stroll, and the adults of course would stop to have a conversation which I found extremely boring.

In those days Ten Oaks Farm was a partially thatched cottage, and in Great-Great-Great-Uncle Frank's time Hezekiah Quick, known to all as Kiah Quick, lived there. He worked on the farm for Uncle Francis, but was a good friend as well as an employee, and Uncle Francis left him a little legacy in his will. I understand that at the time, Wansley was about 200 acres and Ten Oaks was the farm cottage. When the Ebberly estate was sold, probably after the First World War, Uncle Jack and Aunt Leah bought Wansley as sitting tenants. It was all rather too much financially, so later they sold Ten Oaks with fifty acres to the county council.

When I was young, Tommy Newcombe and his wife, Flossie, lived at Ten Oaks, but they moved into Torrington when I was about eight years old. Then the Pethericks moved into the farm and became our very good neighbours. After passing the time of day we would make our way up to the top of the hill to the main farm entrance, and then along the rutted track and back home.

The old Ten Oaks farmhouse, which was partially thatched.

Mr Sid Petherick and Mrs Alice Petherick.
Both photographs courtesy of Carol Petherick.

My horizons broadened when I began school and had to walk the mile and a half daily to Roborough. It would have been further if I had walked all around the road, but that was unnecessary, as there was a shortcut through a field and wood. I walked the gentle slope up the lane to the high ridge, but instead of turning right and following the lane along the ridge, I opened a gate and walked or ran down over the field called Burridges Hill. I then crossed the little road and made my way down through Burridges Wood. This route cut a big slice off the journey.

The path was well defined and is marked on all the old Ordnance Survey maps. Not only did I use it daily, but Mr Marles who lived in the farm cottages at the bottom of the wood also used it – twice daily for him, as he always went home for one o'clock dinner. Anyone who walked to the farm from the village used this shortcut through the field and the wood, and this included friends and my grandfather. Very few people had the use of a car in those days, and most people walked to see us. For much of the year when the grass and undergrowth were likely to be wet I wore my wellingtons and took my shoes in my satchel. On reaching the road at the bottom of the wood I changed into my shoes, tucked my wellies under a thicket of brambles, upside down, so that no rain or drips would get into them, and then I was ready to trudge up Molland Hill towards the village.

It was at this point that I met Mary Waldron. She lived nearby in Burridges Cottage which was along a lane tucked under the woods. She was a little older and so was delegated to look after me, which she probably found a trial at times. We were much of an age though, and good friends, and as well as sharing the journey to school we often played together on Saturdays. We were the only two children, other than some evacuees for a short while, who lived at our end of the parish, and we were referred to as "the Two Marys".

I always enjoyed my journey to school, and come rain or shine, summer or winter, I cannot remember ever finding it boring, tedious or tiring. In fact, quite the opposite: I considered that walk in either direction to be one of the best bits of the school day and, unlike my brief sojourn at High Bickington, I do not believe I was ever late.

Mother always aimed to set me on my way by eight o'clock, and Mary's older sister Ruth helped. Ruth had left school at fourteen, probably about the time that I began school, and she helped Mother in the house for a few years before taking another position in Dorset. Ruth reckoned that getting me off to school was like setting a ship off to sea. Mother would give my face a lick with the flannel from a bowl of water placed on the end of the kitchen form. When I was a little older I washed myself with a bowl and ewer in my bedroom. If it was a good morning and the open fire had lit with no problem and the big black cast iron kettle hanging on the chimney crook was "singing", the water would be warm, otherwise, if the wind was in the wrong direction, or the wood was damp, or for any other reason the fire had been difficult to light, then it would be a bowl of cold water. Likewise breakfast: a good morning denoted porridge, or maybe toast, and a bad morning brought shredded wheat (which reminded me of straw), or cornflakes, and cross and irritable adults. Breakfast did not interest me very much, and my recollections of it are hazy, but I know Mother used to worry because I did not have a big appetite and I was little and skinny.

I was not very co-operative in the mornings. It took two of them to plait my hair, one each side. Some sandwiches for mid-morning break and my shoes were placed in my satchel, coat and pixie bonnet were thrust upon me and I was pushed out of the back door. Although we were never late for school I am afraid that sometimes I used to linger in the wood, much to Mary's exasperation. I always found Burridges Wood fascinating. After crossing the little road, I plunged into a cool whispery world under the tall fir trees, and then walked down under a green tunnel of laurels. This is where I used to dawdle and play until I suddenly remembered that Mary was waiting for me; then I would dash down the zigzag path between the hazels and oaks, cross the track that led to the old quarry and almost roll down the final steep path under more firs to the lane, and my waiting friend.

Molland Hill was very steep but we were used to trudging up under the trees, for in those days the whole of the valley was wooded. If we felt that we were running late then we would have a "run, walk" morning. After we had negotiated the steepest part of the hill we would run to a gateway and then walk to the next. By running and walking to alternate gateways we made our way to the village quite speedily. It was not often we met anyone, either on our journey to school or home again. The only person we were likely to meet in the mornings was Kit Harris with his horse and butt. He lived in the village but had some fields down Molland Hill way. There was a lane which ran from the sharp corner on the steepest part of the hill, along by his fields and then under Great Wood, and came out onto the Barlington road near Roborough Mill. This lane was known as Kit's Avenue, and Mary and I found it very interesting. We often played there and explored on Saturdays or in the holidays.

Our walk to school on Friday mornings was always rather more serious, as we had table and spelling tests every Friday. We took our books home on Thursday nights to revise and then we tested each other as we made our way to school on Friday. We each had different things to learn, for although we were in the same classroom we were in different year groups.

Usually there was not time to linger on our journey to school but it was a different matter on the way home. Quite often we walked straight home but not always, particularly in the summer. Sometimes we walked the fields instead of the road, for we knew which fields interconnected with gates or a convenient gap in the hedge. During our school days Molland Hill and all the hillside opposite Burridges Wood was also wooded, and instead of walking down the road, we walked down through a field called Pondclose and through the woods to the valley at the bottom. Then of course there were the delights of the brook, and much time was spent turning over stones and finding creatures in the water.

The hedges in those days were not neat and clipped as they are now, but were tall, overgrown, blowzy, beautiful and bountiful, for there were wild raspberries and blackberries to be gathered in season. Hazel bushes hung over the road and we always impatiently began to eat the nuts too early, before the kernels were fully formed. The wide banks of Molland Hill which basked in the afternoon sun were a secret treasure trove of goodies; for hidden under the vegetation were wild strawberries, so sweet and tasty, and in the autumn the greatest treat of all: whortleberries. It was the only place that I knew where they grew.

It was one afternoon on Molland Hill that I had my first close encounter with an adder. I had just spotted a little cluster of delicious red strawberries, and as I was putting my hand through the vegetation to pick them I was suddenly aware of two little hard, black, beady eyes staring at me. In an instant I realised that my hand was about two inches from an adder, and I managed to whip it away just in time. I was quite shaken and much more careful after that.

I was always aware of adders and overall not too bothered by them. I knew that they lived near the path that I used every day which went down over Burridges Hill. It was south facing, and there was an uncultivated strip of land the other side of the hedge in Cow Field; it was full of bracken, gorse and brambles and was an adders' haven. During hot weather Mother insisted that I use a walking stick. I was told to bang the ground in front of me with the stick, and was assured the vibrations would scare away any adders. I kept the stick by the gate at the top of the field, and in the mornings I banged my way down. I then left it by the bottom gate, and in the evening I banged my way back up again.

There was one adder though, that I did not scare away with my stick. He was always there in the afternoons on sunny days, lying on his stone near the bottom gate. We eyed each other with respect, and I did not bother to bang with my stick. He did not move, and I made a detour around his stone, although we kept our eyes on each other the whole time. Without doubt, he was the King of the Castle, and I did not start banging again with my stick until I was a respectful distance away from him.

The only times I walked home around the road were during the short, dark days of winter. School did not end until four o'clock and by the time I reached the wood it was already dimpsy and I did not fancy walking up under the trees alone in the dark – for there was no doubt that the wood changed character at night. I would say goodbye to Mary, collect my boots from the bramble patch, and then trudge up Ten Oaks Hill around the outer edge of the wood and then up the field. Just occasionally I would walk the long way around and in the rutted farm lane.

Although it was wartime or the aftermath, life in our secluded and isolated part of Devon was very safe; there were no strangers and no one was concerned about where we were, or what we were doing, or what time we arrived home. Only once can I remember my parents being worried. Mary and I must have lost track of time, like the boys who went to explore Great Wood during the dinner break. It was one of those lovely summer evenings and we walked back through the fields instead of along the road, and I believe we ended up in Kit's Avenue and lingered there to play. When it was six o'clock and I had not arrived home, my parents contacted Mr Jack Rockey and asked him to drive from the village and look out for us, while they walked down through the field and the wood. Of course, no one found us, and they drove back to the village and back to Burridges Wood again, and were wondering about searching the old quarry. We had always been warned not to go near it, but naturally we did. I think that Mary's father, Mr Waldron, had joined in the search by then. Luckily, we appeared through a gateway just as they were driving past. I was astounded to see Father sitting beside Mr Rockey in the car and Mother in the back with tears running down her face. We were admonished for our tardiness, and we were both contrite and rather shocked that we had caused so much trouble and worry. Certainly, for some time after that we were careful to arrive home within acceptable time limits.

Saturdays and holidays brought glorious freedom. Quite often friends from the village came over, especially my friend Alice who was the same age and also my cousin Rachel. Father always referred to me as "the Maid", and when friends came over he called us "the Maidens". He loved having children around, and would enquire of Mother where we were and what we were doing. It is a delightful old-fashioned term which is not used so much now.

I did have one constant companion on the farm and that was my very own dog, Bruce. He arrived into my life when I was about eight years old, and became my friend and playmate. He was one of a litter of puppies that Lassie produced one spring night in the chaff house in the barn. Father said that he would have to find homes for them but I could have first choice, and it would be my very own dog. I know from time to time I had complained about not having any brothers or sisters so maybe it was their solution. The choice was not very difficult, as Bruce was the biggest, fluffiest and cuddliest one of the bunch, and we fell in love with each other immediately. Goodness only knows who the father was. Lassie was a black and white Welsh Border Collie, a good worker with all the instincts of the breed. Bruce did not resemble her one iota. He had thick luxurious white fur with patches of brown; he was big and handsome and he knew it. He was a born playboy, with no intention of ever rounding up a sheep or following a cow.

I called him Bruce after Bruce Woodcock, the boxer. It was very difficult to have heroes or heroines or idols of any kind in those days, there was no celebrity culture at all – well, certainly not at Roborough. We did not have a daily newspaper; there were no magazines other than *Farmers Weekly* and the *Radio Times*. I never visited a cinema or theatre, and of course there was no television. There was just the wireless, and that was our window onto the wider world of entertainment and culture. Father enjoyed listening to a bit of boxing, and Bruce Woodcock had been in the news quite a lot at the time. I believe that he had won a championship. Father thought highly of him and that was good enough for me. I decided that Bruce was a masculine and highly desirable name to confer on my beloved new puppy.

He fulfilled his role as companion and playmate admirably, and we were constantly together. He instinctively knew how to play games, and could play hide and seek as well as another child. We both of us loved rabbiting, and we would go down over the meadows or out into Rushy Plat around the hedges and bramble bushes. Bruce would go one side and I would creep around the other side of a hedge and we would try and flush the rabbits out. We never caught anything, but we had the most wonderful time.

Bruce also did some more serious rabbiting with Mr Marles's little terrier; this was often when I was at school. Now and again the terrier would come visiting, and call on Bruce, and the two of them would lurrup off for a day out. Down the lane towards the pond they would go – side by side, the little one and the big one, tails wagging, anticipation and happiness etched on every sinew, and smiles on their faces. No matter how much Father or Mother called or whistled neither of them took any notice, and they would be gone for the day. When they returned, they were always covered in mud and Bruce would then spend the evening cleaning and washing himself all over. He was very vain and licked and preened until his neck fur stood out in a beautiful white ruff, and he was once again his handsome self.

I think that in the beginning Father had hoped that he might train Bruce to do just a little part-time farm work, but it soon became apparent that Bruce had no intention of doing anything at all. He knew that his role in life was to provide fun and pleasure for others. Eventually when Lassie became elderly, Father bought another Welsh Collie, Judy, as a work dog and Bruce continued with his fun-loving life.

Bruce was not my only companion during weekends and holidays. As Mary Waldron and I were the only children who lived in that area of the parish, inevitably we spent a lot of time together. Mary lived in a thatched "chocolate box" cottage, which was situated in the valley under Burridges Wood. It was approached by a secret lane which ran alongside the brook, and was surrounded by woodland. I am not sure whether there actually were roses around the door, but Mr Waldron loved his garden, and it was full of vegetables and flowers. There was an orchard and several little plats, and the brook gurgled and bubbled alongside the property. I loved to visit, and often on a Saturday it was our base. We would spend most of our time outdoors, briefly return at dinnertime for sustenance and then off we would go again.

The brook was the predominant attraction, and we could happily spend hours wading through pools and eddies, turning over stones, investigating under banks, and pushing and hacking our way through brambles and undergrowth, especially if we were going upstream towards Combe Farm, as the brook visibly narrowed. If we followed in the other direction, downstream towards Roborough Mill, the brook rippled and chattered over stones and pebbles as it made its way between steep grassy meadows, and babbled underneath Ten Oaks Wood as it hastened to meet its companion, another brook which flowed from the Owlacombe valley, under Great Wood. We usually carried jam jars where we placed our trophies, mostly nymphs, and occasionally a small fish. Mostly though, we enjoyed splashing through the water and exploring. We always returned home with wet wellies, wet socks and wet feet, but happy and satisfied, if tired.

We also enjoyed exploring the woods, and once again we were spoilt for choice. Burridges Wood was our favourite though, with the added benefit we were not trespassing, although such matters did not trouble us much. Burridges Wood was part of Wansley and covered about fourteen acres. It adjoined Combe Wood, which was probably about the same size, and the boundary was marked with a hedge and ditch. It was all on a slope, gentle at the top and very steep near the bottom. The ground rose steeply immediately behind the Waldrons' cottage, and trees overhung their house. There was a path directly up from the cottage, and as we scrambled up, it would have been possible to throw a stone down the chimney. There were several paths through the wood, and in those days all of them were used and maintained. One path ran the length of the wood and was a shortcut towards Ebberly.

Woods can have a presence or atmosphere much like some houses. On Wansley, there was one small triangular section of woodland at the bottom of the field known as Brake. It always gave me an uneasy feeling. It felt unwelcoming and there seemed to be a brooding presence so I never lingered very long. It had a boundary all around, even where it adjoined our own land, Wansley Copse, and I felt that it just wanted to be left alone.

No such feeling in Burridges Wood though. It seemed to welcome everyone with open arms, and invited us children to share its delights and secrets. Maybe it was because there was a regular human presence in the wood and the paths were well trodden, but I always felt happy and secure there, whether I was on my own or with friends, usually Mary. There was one sweet chestnut tree at the far end of the wood, and we would gather the chestnuts as a treat for Christmas. Not far from the chestnut tree was the bluebell patch, in late spring a sea of blue which gladdened the heart and lifted the spirit. The bluebells were swiftly followed by the rhododendrons which grew near my daily path to school, and in the flowering season we would pick them and put them in pots around the house. The last time I gathered rhododendrons was for my wedding day as decorations for the church. There was torrential thundery rain all day, and as I stretched up to cut the flowers, the water cascaded down my arms, ran inside the sleeves of my coat and soaked me.

The only part of the wood which was supposedly taboo was the quarry. It had not been used for a long time and was already overgrown when I was young. There was a track that led to it which was also overgrown, but it was still possible to walk along to the bottom of the quarry. As the quarry was cut into the steep hillside it was perfectly safe at the bottom. The danger lay at the top, as it was difficult to judge where the cliff-like edge began because of brambles, nettles and scrub. Mary and I had on several occasions dared each other to look, and had crept carefully and slowly on our hands and knees towards the edge and peered over the dizzying drop.

From time to time we explored Great Wood as well. This was further away on the other side of the hill, so we did not go there often. Nevertheless, we were quite familiar with the area. To reach Great Wood we strolled along Kit's Avenue, and this was where we usually lingered, as it was one of our favourite places. It was a track which joined the two public roads, and it nestled between high Devon banks which were covered in moss and flowers and topped with trees and shrubs. It ran along the top of a field, and then we climbed a gate as the lane continued alongside Great Wood between the trees, and eventually crossed the Owlacombe Brook via a little wooden bridge and emerged onto the road near Roborough Mill.

Miss Frances Bright who lived at Roborough Mill told Mother that when she was a child there was a house on Kit's Avenue near the wooden bridge, and a family with several children had lived there. She said that at the time about twenty children walked daily to the school from Roborough Mill. We both found this amazing, as there were only about thirty children in total at the school in our day. We searched for the vanished dwelling and found the remnants: the remains of a stone wall and a fireplace, mostly covered with moss and ferns. We would not have noticed it at all if we had not been aware that there could be some ruins in the vicinity. I tried to imagine what the house had looked like and what it would have been like to live there, but found it difficult to conjure up a picture.

One of the best bits of Kit's Avenue was the secret orchard which ran alongside the lane. It seemed mysterious to us that there should be an orchard in such a tucked-away place in a wood, and we had no idea what it was doing there or to whom it belonged. Probably though, it had belonged to the long-vanished property. One of our autumn delights was scrumping apples from the orchard. No matter that there were three perfectly good, legitimate orchards to choose from – two at Wansley and one at the Waldrons' – the forbidden fruits were best. We loved the thrill of scrambling over the hedge into the secluded orchard and wandering around the ancient and crooked moss-covered trees, searching for a tasty apple. Mostly the apples were small and blemished, but no matter, it was the tingle and excitement of danger, and we frightened each other by pretending we could hear someone coming. Then we would scramble back into the lane and run down over the field to the brook where we considered ourselves to be on our own territory.

It was not our own territory literally, but we played there so much we felt as though it belonged to us. The flat areas on either side of the brook flooded during periods of excess rain, and these marshy tracts were covered with flags (irises) which turned the landscape a vibrant yellow in the early summer. The steep hillsides on either side which rose from the valley bottom were ringed with horizontal ridges. These had been created by sheep treading the same paths over many years, and the whole area was surrounded by trees and woods.

Ten Oaks Wood, which hovered over the valley, covered an interesting, almost conical-shaped hill, and we played there from time to time. This hill overlooked our valley, and from the other side it looked down onto Roborough Mill and the confluence of our brook and the Owlacombe Brook. This hill was known as "The Camp", and running all around the top under the trees was a wide, shallow ditch or depression. The bottom of the ditch was thick with leaves and provided a soft, sheltered play area. It was easy to pull a few scrubby branches down, cover them with leaves and ferns, and create a cosy and secluded den, offering hours of fun and play.

These steep, secluded hills and valleys tucked away in our part of the parish created an attractive landscape. It was not a rugged scene but more intimate. It was pretty and had a cosy, homely feel about it. It was the sort of scene where no one would be surprised to see a Hobbit or two appear and go about their business. In fact, I discovered that Hobbits of a kind had once lived there, for my mother informed me that our shallow ditch where we made dens and played so happily was the site of an Iron Age hill fort. I wondered then, and I still wonder now, when there was only a handful of humans living on this earth, how those ancient people managed to find such a remote, isolated area in a far-flung corner of England.

Bruce, my beloved puppy and friend.

Mary Squire and Mary Waldron with Mary's dog, Jock.

Walnut Trees and Others

Whenever my mind drifts back to the old days at Wansley I think of the walnut trees. There were two of them, already past middle age when I was born, and to me they have always seemed an intricate part of the landscape. They grew on the south side of the old house on slightly higher ground, and stood like two sentinels guarding the ancient Barton. In the summer the sun shone through the leaves, providing a dappled shade and gentle movement in the rooms on that side of the house. During the summer months, when we heaved and pushed open the sticky sash windows, they brought a soothing rustle to accompany the daily chores.

The leaves arrived relatively late and then fell quite early compared with other trees, indicating that walnut trees are not native to this country. Neither did the leaves depart in a flurry of glorious colour; for a brief while they hung softly yellow, but soon turned a dismal mud brown. However, autumn signalled the arrival of the fruit itself and we all cast our eyes up from time to time to watch the green cases forming high up in the branches. When the first of the autumn winds began to blow them down there was a frisson of excitement as we rushed out to gather them in and taste the first offerings.

Fresh walnuts straight from the tree taste completely different from the wrinkly brown ones on sale in the supermarkets at Christmas time. Despite our desire to sample the new season's fruit, patience was needed. First, the green outer case had to be prised off to reveal the inner shell. When this was cracked open, there, hiding inside, was the delicate creamy kernel. We still had to restrain ourselves, as the thin skin which covered the kernel had to be carefully removed as it was bitter. I can remember impatiently scratching the skin off the curves and convolutions of the kernel until at last I could sink my teeth into the nut and savour the subtle delicate flavour.

Our two trees must have been slightly different varieties, as one always produced much larger nuts than the other. We stored the nuts for Christmas, and collecting them was a daily job often given to me. My main competitors were the pigs, usually a sow or two which were allowed to wander around freely.

Removing the outer green casings of the walnuts was a messy chore, as they contained a powerful dye which stained the skin a yellowish brown. Scrubbing did not fully remove the stain, and during the walnut season I had hands which looked as though they were stained with nicotine, which to me seemed rather splendid and daring, as smoking was still considered to be sophisticated. After the nuts were dry they were put into large Huntley & Palmers biscuit tins which were stored in the cool of the dairy until Christmas. It was very satisfying at Christmas time eating our own nuts, although it never occurred to me that most people do not gather their own. Of course, by then our nuts looked and tasted just like the walnuts from our local grocer.

Those two trees are now long gone but for about a hundred years they watched over the Squire family's comings and goings. Our photo of Great-Uncle Bob, taken in the early days of the twentieth century, shows the two sturdy trees in their prime, so I guess they were probably young saplings when Great-Great-Great-Uncle Francis took over the tenancy in 1870. They were flourishing when Queen Victoria died, and stood sturdy and strong during two world wars and five succeeding monarchs. They mark the passage of time in photographs of my own life: from a little toddler in a summer bonnet sitting in the leafy shade, through the winter of 1947 when the boughs were laden with ice, to my wedding day in 1968 when once again the leaves were unfurling ready for summer. By then they were elderly and not producing much fruit. We left the farm in 1970 and they were probably taken down not long after that.

*

If the walnut trees kept watch over the house, the guardians of the Lower Court were the two enormous elm trees which stood in Lower Rushy Plat on the high bank and towered over the lane and old linhay. I would think that they were older than the walnut trees, and had been there for some time before the Squire family took up residence. I was fond of those old trees, and like the walnut trees they were woven into my life. It was possible to scramble up the elm nearest the linhay and onto the lowest branch. This huge gnarled limb hung over the slee roof of the shed which was attached to the old thatch building. The linhay was two-storeyed with a tallet above. I could drop onto the roof of the shed and then tuck myself against the cob wall of the linhay near the roof, and there I would be perfectly hidden, secluded and safe among the elm branches with the tree towering above me and the security of the cob walls behind me. No one could see me but I could survey the world. I could peep through the leaves and branches towards the Ebberly high ridge and keep an eye on distant fields; close at hand, I could look down on the lane as cows or tractor and trailer and men passed below, all unaware there was a watcher in the trees.

This was my favourite writing place for I loved to scribble stories and poetry, and on warm summer days I usually found inspiration in my leafy nook. It was a good strategy to go prepared with a bottle of water and maybe one or two of Mother's nubby cakes and of course my exercise book and pencils. Then I would be set up for several hours of enjoyable story writing.

(Left) Uncle Bob standing under the trees, early 1900s.
(Right) The winter of 1947, when the trees were covered in ice.

Sitting under the trees with Ruth, early 1940s.

(Left) Feeding the lambs, about 1960. Mother planted bulbs and spring flowers around the trees.
(Right) Uncle John sitting under the tree, 1940s.

Our wedding day, 3 June 1968. The leaves were just unfurling. L–R: Denise Lugg, Rachel Stevens, David Stevens, Jean Hookway, Barbara Davey, Lionel Hookway.

There was no doubt that the protector of the animals and the Higher Courtyard was the great oak tree, which grew sturdily and steadfastly in the nearby grassy area. All animals and humans gravitated towards its powerful presence and welcoming shade. The pigs snuffled and snorted as they searched for acorns, and we children loved to collect the acorns as well and the little "pipes" that they sat in. The grass grew sweet and juicy in the shade, and the cows would grab a few extra mouthfuls as they strolled in to be milked. It was where the horses grazed as they waited to fulfil their duties, and the area was always full of movement and life.

One of my earliest memories is lying on the ground under the old oak tree, and gazing up through the rustling leaves at the blue sky. I remember thinking how beautiful it was and what a loss to chop a tree down. It was Father who arranged for the two elm trees to be taken down. He said that they were getting old and dangerous, and he was worried they would come down in a storm and damage the old building. He was probably right but it was a sad day when they went, for suddenly the landscape seemed bare and denuded. It was not many years before we left the farm, and I suppose they would have succumbed to the elm disease which swept across the countryside a few years later.

I also missed the stand of fir trees which once lined the track towards the pond. They were there during my early years but I am not sure whether they were removed because they were dangerous or whether they were used as poles when the telephone was installed. I always liked them and wished that other trees had been planted in their place, but everyone always seemed to be too busy or have other more important priorities. I think these days, farmers are more aware of landscaping and management of the countryside. The 1940s were grave times and even into the '50s the emphasis was on producing food, and not much thought was given to beautifying the countryside or amenities. There was no doubt though that someone in the Victorian era had done some thoughtful landscaping at Wansley. The pond had been created and they had gone to a lot of trouble to make the area around it pleasing. Many trees had been planted, and this is why the area from the back door down to the pond was so attractive.

*

There was one other tree which gave me much pleasure and provided endless hours of play. It was a tree that I had never actually seen. It was the bole of what must have been a huge ash tree, which at one time grew in the bank of the Mowstead at the point where the lane squeezed between the Mowstead and the pond. Here there was a gate which could be closed to contain animals in the Lower Court, and in its heyday the ash must have towered over the gate and pond. The bole was completely hollow inside, pleasingly smooth and shiny, with little ledges and nooks and crannies – in other words, a perfect playhouse. It still grew as a coppiced tree producing long whippy branches with leaves, making it a secluded hideaway. I kept a few toy cups and plates and tin lids inside, and would take my dolls there to have tea parties. It was my imagination though which provided the most fun. I was a great fan of Enid Blyton, and my ash bole easily transformed into "The Faraway Tree". It was there with Moonface, Saucepan Man and the children I went on exciting adventures and escapades to the magic lands at the top of the tree.

All those trees have now disappeared for one reason or another, and they only exist in my mind. I suppose I am probably the only person left in the world who can still remember that landscape clearly – walk the fields, pick the flowers, climb the trees, lie in the shade and listen to the birds which long ago sang their last song.

There is one tree though which has survived and thrived through the years. It was tall and strong when I was a child and is still flourishing today. It is not at Wansley but stands proud and tall on the road to Roborough. It was, and still is, a landmark. "Beech Tree" was always a beacon, and I passed it every day on my journeys to and from school. It stands alone in the landscape and I am surprised that it has never been struck by lightning. It is a survivor and makes my heart glad every time I see it. I always acknowledge it with a silent cheer and salute.

Domestic Affairs

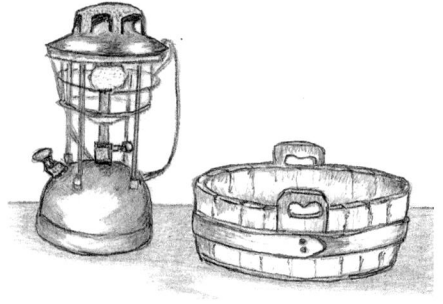

At the beginning of the century, when Uncle Jack pondered about what could be done to make life easier for Leah should she become his wife, there was very little that he could change to ease the burden of housework. Eventually, Jack's solution was to make sure there was plenty of help in the house so that Leah was spared the brunt of it all. As mistress of the house she supervised the daily round of tasks, while enjoying breakfast in bed and an afternoon nap. When my mother came to Wansley in 1937 not much had changed. There was still no electricity, no running water, no telephone, and the big, old, open fireplace with the chimney crooks and bread ovens was the main source of heat and comfort. Any changes towards modernisation dripped in very slowly over many years, and for most of my childhood I lived in the Victorian era as far as domestic mod cons were concerned. Like everyone else I had never known anything different, so domestic life for us all in the 1940s and into the 1950s was remarkably like what everyday domestic life in rural areas had been for the past century.

It was true that the lighting had upgraded slightly and we used Tilley lamps in the house instead of the old Aladdin lamps. The Tilley lamps vaporised the paraffin under pressure, and they burnt with a gentle hiss. This gave a much brighter light than the old oil lamps, and there were no wicks to trim. We had a modern chrome model for the kitchen table, which we considered to be quite stylish. It was taller than the lanterns and spread the light further, so that it was possible to sit near the fire and read a book in the dark winter evenings. Even so, it was still a better light at the table, and it was a toss-up: good light or warmth. During the winter, two lanterns were lit for use in the shippens, and whoever was doing the milking would carry them around from shippen to shippen. The Tilley lanterns behaved themselves well in windy and rainy weather, and could be relied upon on dark nights when checking the sheep, especially during lambing time.

There were still two old-fashioned storm lanterns around when I was very young, but the light they gave was very dim in comparison. Aunt Leah and Uncle Jack still preferred the soft light of the Aladdin lamp, or maybe they were apprehensive of the modern innovation which hissed and had to be pumped up regularly to maintain the pressure. I do remember how cosy and restful it was sitting around their table at Norhill Cottage having tea on a winter evening, bathed in the soft glow of the Aladdin lamp.

Oiling all the lamps was a daily chore and, after I left school, usually my job. It was tedious, repetitive and one of my pet hates but it had to be done, day after day after day… Oiling and lighting ate into the best part of an hour every day. It seems unbelievable now – all that time and effort just to produce light. I shall risk a description of this monotonous chore.

Newspaper was spread along the kitchen form (long bench) and the lamps were lined up. By then there were seven Tilley lamps to fill with oil, as we used them for the hens in the deep-litter houses as well. During the winter months we extended the daylight hours with artificial light to encourage the hens to keep laying eggs. The paraffin for the four deep-litter house lanterns had to be measured, so that they gradually dimmed and then went out on their own. This meant that as the lights became dim, the hens would go to roost naturally. As well as all the Tilley lamps there were also several night lights and small lamps with wicks to fill with oil, as these were used for carrying around the house when we needed to go to another room or go to bed.

I was quite knowledgeable about Tilley lamps and their foibles, although conversely, I am still ignorant about all aspects of electricity and cannot even wire a plug. I could change a vaporiser, put on a new mantle, and I was adept at lighting at least three at a time. Firstly, the vaporiser had to be warmed, and this was done by clipping on a lighter which had been soaked in methylated spirits. Four little glass jars of meths with their lighters soaking were kept on the end of the kitchen table, ready for the evening light-up. While the vaporiser was warming, about six or seven pumps of air were enough to create a little pressure so that when the knob was turned to release it into the burner, the mantle lit with a gentle glow, and was then ready to be pumped up fully to create quite a good light. I suppose that in many ways it was like a Primus stove and we had one or two of those as well, and of course a selection of good old faithful candlesticks. What a chore it all was compared with the simplicity of flicking a switch.

During the war all the windows were fitted with blackout blinds, and woe betide anyone who lit a lamp or walked into a room with a light without first pulling down the blinds and drawing the curtains. I think Mother was convinced there was always a German plane hovering over Roborough waiting to drop a bomb on any chink of light. I would be told off quite forcibly for being careless. In actual fact, there was a period when German aircraft did pass over regularly on their way to bomb towns in South Wales. I would lie in bed and listen to waves or droves of them flying over, and sometimes Mother would take me downstairs into the big cupboard under the main staircase. Even now the drone of an aircraft at night gives me goose pimples and makes all my ridge hairs stand on end.

As the song said, we had to "Keep the Home Fires Burning" and the big open fireplace in the kitchen was still the nerve centre of the house during my primary school years. Much energy and time were expended in keeping the flames alight. It was the only fire which was lit daily and consequently the only source of heat in the huge rambling house. We used our own wood from the coppices, woods and hedges on the farm. Faggots of wood were kept in the "hood rick" (or "wood rick") by the pigs' houses near the back door. The faggots were bundles of brushwood, often built into a rick for storage. Larger branches were stacked up by the wood-horse ready for sawing into logs with a cross cut, and an axe was always somewhere handy ready to split some of the logs for lightings. If anyone had half an hour or even a few minutes to spare, they knew that they could make themselves useful by chopping wood or splitting logs. A supply of dry logs was always stacked in an outhouse near the back door, and kindling wood was kept in one of the old bread ovens in the chimney breast.

The first job of the morning was to light the fire. I was too young to be involved with that, and usually it was lit and the kettle was singing before I came down. I knew that the ashes from the night before had to be scraped out, new kindling and logs laid with paper and a fire lighter, and then it was all gently coaxed into life with a big pair of wooden bellows. That open fire was a temperamental creature and needed vast quantities of air to breathe and live. We had to keep the door to the passage open all the time so that it could "draw". If we closed the door the fire would sulk and the smoke would billow out and fill the kitchen, making us cough and our eyes sting. This meant that we lived with a constant draught swirling through the kitchen.

There were several occasions when the chimney caught fire, bringing pandemonium. The stirrup pump was never far away, and one person would pump like fury while everyone else fed them with buckets of water as fast as possible. Another person manned the pump at the pump trough, and of course when eventually the fire was put out, the kitchen was awash with swirly, dirty, black water.

When I was very young I remember a settle by the side of the fire which cut off the draught from one corner. When I was a little older Mother used to drape a wooden clothes horse with old blankets to cut off the draught and make a cosy corner where I could play. Despite the ashes and dust which were constantly being created, everyone did their best to keep the fireplace as clean and attractive as possible. The bricks on either side were brushed off regularly. The grating in the front where the ashes dispersed, and the fire dogs which held the logs in place, were kept shiny and black with "Zebo" black-lead – another chore which I believe was usually Ruth's lot.

The big black cast iron kettle which hung on one of the chimney crooks was an extremely important piece of kitchen equipment, and other than "washing day" it was the main source of hot water. It was constantly being filled and was hopefully always either singing or boiling. There was a mechanism which allowed it to be tilted to pour water safely. All the saucepans and pots which either hung from chimney crooks or were placed on a brandis (trivet) over the flames were made of cast iron, and there was a huge cast iron frying pan with a handle which could be used on a brandis or hung from a crook.

The only methods of cooking on the open fire were boiling, steaming or frying, and when Mother needed to do some baking, she had to light an old black stove with an oven, which was situated in an outhouse. This was lit once during the week for "baking day" and on Sundays for a roast dinner, although I do not believe we had roast every Sunday. It took a lot of time and effort to produce cooked food, and there was never anything fancy. Everyone was grateful for what was on their plate.

The lack of running water in the house also made life laborious and tiring. In later years when electricity and mains water eventually arrived in rural areas of North Devon (it was the 1960s before both these modern innovations were commonplace), I remember my grandmother and aunties discussing which had made the most difference to their lives, the water or the electricity, and if they had to choose between them, which they would choose. A water supply with hot and cold running water in the house won hands down, and they all agreed it had made the most difference.

Our only supply of water was from a well which was situated just outside the back door. There was a pump and rather splendid big slate pump trough. Every drop of water we used for ourselves or the animals was pumped by hand from that well. A slee roof covered the area, and it was where the hand washing for everyone and most of the face washing for the men took place. Two planks of wood were placed across one end of the pump trough, with an enamel bowl for water and a dish with green soap. A roller towel hung on the back wall. Whenever I needed to wash my hands or felt like a glass of water, I was sent outside to use cold water pumped from the well.

A galvanise bucket of water was always kept in the kitchen and jugs of water for filling the kettle or saucepans. There was nothing as modern as a sink, and the washing up was done in a large enamel bowl placed on the end of the kitchen table, or on the end of the form. Afterwards the water was tipped down a drain situated in a corner of the room, which I now remember was another source of draughts. During the milder weather and summer months the washing-up bowl was often carried outside, and the dishes and pots and pans were washed on the pump trough, although a pan of hot water had to be carried out as well. There certainly was no such thing as washing-up liquid; I seem to remember flakes of green soap being put in the water to help dissolve the grease. Later there was a jam jar filled with clothes washing powder (Tide, Surf or Omo) and a dessert spoon, so a spoonful of washing powder could be put in the water.

Bath nights happened infrequently and were a real treat. I have heard other people reminisce about a weekly bath but I cannot remember bath nights coming around that often. It took a lot of time and effort to organise a bath, beginning with heating extra water in pans over the open fire. The bath itself was a rather superior model, not the ordinary galvanise tub that most people had. It was a handsome affair in brown and white enamel, with a high back and arm rests. It was usually kept in the unfurnished room that I used as a playroom and had to be carried into the hall, down the passage and into the kitchen, where it was placed in front of the fire. While the kitchen was transformed into a bathroom, everyone had to occupy themselves elsewhere in the house or find work to do outside in the farm buildings. This was no problem in the summer, but when it was cold everyone was longing to be allowed back into the warmth of the kitchen again. Consequently, I was not encouraged to linger too long but it was very pleasant sitting in the bath in front of a roaring log fire. Usually there were one or two cats around, and it was very cosy and great fun splashing around in the water. Everyone would take it in turns to have a bath while it was out, and the water would be topped up. I always had mine first, and then I went to bed while the adults had theirs. Afterwards the water had to be scooped or tipped out and the bath cleaned and put away again. No wonder it was an infrequent event.

Most of our daily ablutions were done in the bedrooms, for every room had a washstand with a china bowl, jug and chamber pots, and the big spare room had two washstands. When I was old enough to wash myself, Mother would bring a jug of warm water when she came to wake me in the morning. During the winter months we all used the water from our hot water bottles, for this would still be warm. The hot water bottles were not soft cuddly rubber ones that are in use now but were made of stoneware with a screw stopper in the middle. When filled with hot water they were far too hot to be placed against our feet, so they were always wrapped in an old thick sock. However, they did retain the heat for a long time, keeping warm until the next morning.

*

How cold it was back in those far-off days, and we were grateful for every vestige of warmth on offer. On winter mornings I would hurriedly wash myself as quickly as possible, shivering, and with my teeth chattering after leaving my cosy warm bed. In the depths of winter the bedroom windows would be covered with ice on the inside, and such wonderful patterns would be on display. Despite shivering with the cold I always stopped to admire them.

I learnt the poem about Jack Frost at a very early age because it really meant something to me. I was sure such intricate and delicate images could not occur naturally and must be created by some little sprite or elf. After washing I would squash myself into a small space between the chest of drawers and a chair, where all my clothes were placed ready to put on. For some reason I thought that it was warmer jammed into this small space. It would have been an illusion, for if Jack Frost had painted such wonderful pictures on the inside of the windows, the temperature must have been below freezing in the bedrooms. Even when the weather was not so extreme the bedrooms were very cold and no one lingered longer than necessary.

Oh, what a boring ritual dressing was, especially during the winter months. I often wore dungarees around the farm but on school days I had to dress "appropriately", and no girls, absolutely none, would dream of wearing trousers to school. During cold weather it would have been warmer and more practical, but women did not wear trousers in those days, and even boys wore short trousers to school and did not begin to wear long ones until they were in their teens. I always felt aggrieved that Mother insisted that I wore long Lyle stockings for much of the year. I hated them, they were always saggy at the ankles and wrinkly at the knees; how I envied other children who were allowed to wear knee-length socks. Mother dressed me in long stockings because I was frequently ill and she wanted me to be as warm as possible. Repeatedly being ill was another nuisance which vexed me.

When dressing, there were several layers that I had to struggle with before I reached my top clothes. After putting on my woolly vest, I fought with the garment I really disliked: my liberty bodice. It was a sleeveless garment that went on top of the vest. It did up the front with little buttons, and dangling from the bottom were the dreaded suspenders – four on each leg, to hold up the hated Lyle stockings

– and then my knickers went on top of that. It was all very fiddly, especially trying to do up the suspenders when shivering with the cold and with fingers that did not seem to be working properly. There are definitely some things about the old days that I do not miss at all.

Aunt Leah of course always wore "combinations". This was a woollen garment that covered her from neck to knees. The top part was like a vest with sleeves and the bottom half fitted closely down over her thighs. Fortunately there was a flap so the wearer did not have to strip off every time they needed the lavatory. I suppose it was a sort of Victorian onesie. Thank goodness Mother did not expect me to wear anything like that.

The coldest winter of all was the winter of 1947. Ordinary life ground to a halt while everyone struggled and improvised to retain some semblance of normality and keep humans and livestock fed and watered. The snow was thick and heavy and prolonged, and the farm, the parish and great swathes of North Devon were cut off from the rest of the world. There was a twenty-foot snowdrift at the end of our lane which eventually froze solid. Father, Jack Marles and Wilhelm, a German ex-Prisoner of War who was living with us, managed to hack and cut a narrow channel through the drift, just wide enough to push a wheelbarrow. The milk lorry did not get through for nearly six weeks, and the milk was used for feeding the animals. Mother made extra butter and cream but there was a limit to how much we could use, and the surplus was thrown away. It was a struggle to keep the poultry, cattle and sheep fed and watered, although in those days farmers were fairly self-sufficient. Father had plenty of hay and straw, and he ground his own corn in the mill to provide meal for all the stock. There were mangold and turnip clamps under the hedges in the fields, and they dug through the snow to find them. All the wildlife was struggling as well, and birds and animals must have died by the thousand. The red deer came down from Exmoor, and their hoof prints could be seen around the poultry houses in the morning.

One morning when we woke up, the world was a magical, sparkling, fairy wonderland. It must have rained briefly during the night and then froze again immediately. Every twig, leaf, branch, blade of grass, in fact everything in the whole world was covered in a sheath of ice, and it sparkled and glittered like the Ice Queen's kingdom. Even the adults said they had never seen anything like it.

I did not go to school for six weeks, mainly because the roads were impassable, but also because inevitably I was ill and confined to bed for much of the time. The larger bedrooms had fireplaces which could be lit if someone was ill but my little room did not have one, so Mother lit an oil heater to try and keep the temperature up, and she had a stroke of genius to try and keep my spirits up as well. She and Father turned the area outside my bedroom window into a feeding platform for the birds. It was relatively easy to do as my bedroom was above the hall, and the porch roof jutted out beyond. They laid planks across the roof and then put an old door on top, creating quite a large feeding area. I have never forgotten all the birds that flocked to feed, pecking and jostling and squabbling. I watched them for hours. As my bedroom had a huge wide windowsill due to the thickness of the wall, sometimes when I felt well enough I would wrap up in a rug and sit there to watch, just the other side of the glass.

There was another winter with severe weather and heavy snow in 1963, but that did not create the feeling of isolation and sense of living on the edge that we all felt in the winter of '47. One dramatic

Mr Jack Marles standing near the oak tree. The white on the branches is not snow, but ice. Mother's Brownie camera was unable to capture the glitter and sparkle, but it is a record.

change by 1963 was the advent of mains electricity to the parish. Although we had only been electrified for about eighteen months, many modern conveniences were already installed. It is impossible to feel really cast adrift, or to invoke the pioneer spirit (as in 1947) with electric light, a washing machine and a television. During the '63 severe weather, helicopters from RAF Chivenor daily flew over Wansley taking fodder to ponies on Dartmoor. Nothing like that happened in 1947 and the ponies must have been decimated. We had a car in 1963, and although the roads were impassable by car it was still possible to travel if absolutely necessary. I had to return to Bedford Teacher Training College, and our neighbour George Down who lived at Whitsleigh Barton took me to Portsmouth Arms station (about five miles) on his tractor. No cosy cabs on tractors in those days, we had to face the elements. I can't remember what happened to my suitcase, I expect it went in the link box. Father had a tractor, of course, but it was not taxed to drive on the road, as our farm was almost self-contained and there was no need to ever go on a road.

During the 1947 winter there was absolutely no way of getting about, and it was the simple everyday things of life that began to run out, such as bread, flour and sugar. We relied on a fortnightly delivery from our grocer, White's Stores of South Street, Torrington, about six miles away, but of course they could not reach us and neither could the baker or the butcher. We still had no telephone at that time which was another difference from the bad winter of '63, so we were unable to communicate with anyone at all. Our only link with the outside world was the wireless, but even that gave up the ghost after about a week or so, because we could not recharge the accumulator. This was a large acid-filled glass battery necessary to run the wireless. There were two accumulators and one was always in Plucknett's shop in Torrington being topped up. Mr Plucknett swapped them over every week.

After being cut off for nearly four weeks, a message came that a van with chains on the wheels was going to try and make the journey along the main road from Torrington to Beaford and bring badly needed provisions. I am not sure how the message arrived, probably via George Squire the builder, who had a telephone. A gang of men from our side of Roborough met up, and walked to Beaford across fields and on top of hedges to meet the van, and stock up with badly needed bread, yeast, sugar and flour.

*

The deprivations and struggles of that winter were seared on the minds of everyone who lived through it, so maybe that was the reason that during the following year in 1948, there was a life-changing event at Wansley. At long last the huge, ancient, draughty, kitchen fireplace was abandoned, bricked up and replaced with a smart, modern Rayburn.

Oh, the joys that it brought with it. It could be kept in overnight with coal, and therefore did not have to be lit in the morning. The kitchen became a cosy, warm refuge and we were able to close the door to the passage, so for the first time ever there were no draughts swirling around our legs. Belching smoke became a thing of the past and dust levels dropped considerably. The big cast iron kettle sat in pride of place on the Rayburn hot plate, gleaming, simmering and boiling, as though fully aware of its new elevated status. Mother was beside herself with excitement, as she now actually had an oven in the kitchen and no longer had the weekly chore of lighting the old black stove in the shed. We all admired the shiny temperature gauge on the oven door and wondered at modern technology.

This was only half the story though, as the advent of a Rayburn meant a back boiler and hot and cold running water in the house. There was still no mains water supply in the parish, but we piped the water from our well outside the back door and then pumped it by hand to a tank in the attic. This was a rotary pump and different from the up and down action of the old-fashioned pump at the trough outside. The rotary pump went from side to side, and pushing the handle and swinging from left to right was marvellous exercise for ensuring a svelte waist. It took 200 strokes to fill the tank, and this

1947. The morning when the whole world seemed to be covered in ice. Mary Squire, Bill Squire and Jack Marles.

1963. Wansley in the snow.

no 19.

Torrington, September 30th 1948.

Mr. Squire, Wansley, Roborough.

To Eastmond & Son,
REGISTERED PLUMBERS,
Furnishing & General Ironmongers,
PAINTERS, GLAZIERS, GAS FITTERS,
Copper, Zinc, and Tin Plate Workers.

Date	Description	£	s	d
June 30	To Goods.	5	14	11
July 15.	" 1 Hammer 5/3 a 3/9. 1 Hacksaw. 4/3 6lb Nails. 6 Batteries		19	3.
Aug 19.	" 1 Tin Caustic Soda 1/9. 1 Tube Durofix Sept 7th 3 Hack Saw Blades.		10	3.
Sept	Labour fixing Rayburn Cooker etc.,	21	12	0
	1 No. 2 Rayburn Cooker Complete with Plate Rack, Towel Rail & Thermometer & Smoke Pipe	39	15	0
	1 Copper Cylinder 36+18. 1-100 gal. Tank 4'x 2'x 2' 9.4.0	14	4	6
	1-5'6" Light Bath Complete + Set. 1 Basin 1 Set & Brackets 14.14.0 3.15.6	18	9	6
	1 CI Flush Tank £2. 1 P. Closet Pan 22.0. 2-1¼ S. Lead Traps. 8.6.	4	10	6.
	1-22+16 +10 Sink. 3.11.6 1 Aluminium drip 1'.14.0. 1 Belfast Waste 7/-	5	12	6.
	1 No. 3. Semi Rotary Pump. 1-1¼ Retaining Valve	5	3	0
	116' of 1" Copper Pipe. 50 of 1" Copper Pipe 110 of ¾" Copper Pipe	25	14	8
	56' of ½" Copper Pipe 2 Brackets 9 + 24. 1 Dog Screws 3"	3	1	3.
	1 Cistern Head 5/9. 6' of 2½" C.I. Down Pipe, 1 Damper 22lbs Lead 15/-	1	12	5
	4' of ¾" Lead Pipe 16/= 2-9 + 5/16 Bolts 1-10 x ⅜ Bolts		17	8
	20' of 4" Asbestos Soil Pipe. 1-3½ Asbestos Junction. 3lbs Putty.	4	5	8
	1-3½" Lead Bend. 1 Bakelite Seat. 3-3½ Clamps. Screws & Coach Screws.	3	0	1
	Copper Fittings etc., Brass Nipples Taps. Tees. Boiler Couplers Metal Couplers. Elbows. Stop Taps. Tap connections Tap Holders	16	5	1.
	15 1 Kettle 24/= 1 gall Flat White Paint ½ gall Grey. 1 Brass Bolt.	4	11	6.
		£144	5	9.
	By Cheque July 23rd	5	14	11
	TOTAL	168	4	10

Eastmonds' bill for installing Rayburn, kitchen sink, bathroom and all associated plumbing.

was a nightly task which was usually shared. No one minded the chore however, for the benefits it brought were truly mind blowing. A gleaming white china sink with attached aluminium draining board sat astride two brick pillars in a corner of the kitchen. I gazed in wonder at the two shiny taps that delivered hot and cold water so effortlessly, and marvelled when the waste water gurgled away down the plughole and disappeared as though by magic. The draughty drain in the corner of the room was no longer needed and was filled in.

Perhaps the biggest transformation was the bathroom upstairs. *A bathroom at Wansley!* I had come across a bathroom before – two actually. There had been one at the Golden Lion. Aunty Dot washed my face there at night but I cannot remember having a bath. I believe the water was pumped from a well. I rarely used the toilet, and made use of the chamber pot under the bed as I had done all my life. I regarded the room with awe and would never have dared venture in on my own, anymore than I would have stepped onto the flight deck of the *Starship Enterprise* (if it had been around at the time). There was also a bathroom at High Bickington Post Office where my cousin John lived. The water was supplied via a 600-gallon rainwater tank, which my uncle had installed in his workshop. I had peeked around the bathroom door and expressed my admiration at this technological wonder. Now however, unbelievably, we were to be proud owners of this modern innovation.

A small bedroom was converted. Presumably this room had once been one of the servants' rooms, for a bell hung there ready to summons or wake them. There were other rooms that had bells when I was young, although I cannot recollect that they were ever used. They were left over from another era. This room was now transformed into a bathroom and was a delight to behold, a vision of black and white. Mother had chosen black and white tile-effect lino. Along one wall stood a white metal bath with black surround, there was a white wash basin with shiny taps and, perhaps the most welcome necessity of all, a flush toilet, complete with tank and chain and black seat. Until now there had only ever been one lavatory at Wansley, and that was situated across the little courtyard opposite the back door. Like our school lavatories it was a bucket under a wooden bench seat and had to be emptied regularly. This lavatory was also updated to flush, and as a final flourish to underline our modernity, a little square box with Izal toilet paper was fitted beside each lavatory to replace the cut-up squares of the *Radio Times* or *Farmers Weekly*. An indoor, upstairs bathroom was indeed revolutionary and most welcome. How stylish we all felt. At last the chamber pots were tucked away in cupboards, and everyone was glad to forget all about them and the daily task of emptying them.

Mother always had eye-catching ideas, and whether it was decorating, dressmaking or anything else creative, she always put her own stamp on it. She considered that our new bathroom seemed cold, as indeed it was, as there was no heating. It was on the north side of the house so she decided to paint the walls pink, which certainly brightened the room and gave it a warm glow. She then had the really wacky idea to paint a frieze of mermaids and fish around the top of the walls in gold paint. It was a great idea, and we both agreed that no one else would have a bathroom with gold mermaids and fish and maybe even some seaweed. Mother spent a lot of time drawing and cutting stencils out of cardboard, and I watched while she went to work with the gold paint. Unfortunately, in spite of initial enthusiasm the project was doomed. The gold paint never really dried properly on the cold walls where there was usually condensation. She finished one wall, but the mermaids and fish forever dripped and drooled down over, and eventually she had to confess she was beaten.

The advent of electricity at Wansley came after I had left boarding school, worked for six years at home on the farm and then left again to train as a teacher, so I never really enjoyed or benefited from all the advantages and labour-saving devices that came with it. I must say that lack of electricity did not bother us very much and we did not feel hard done by. After all, no one else had electricity either. There were a few farms that had their own generator, and I was a little envious of a friend on a neighbouring farm who had an electric mixer.

I thought of all the arm-aching time it would save when making cakes and sponges, or beating royal icing for Christmas cakes. They had a television set as well which I realised would be a welcome addition to our own lives, but the item I really coveted was the mixer.

However, we managed as people had managed for centuries before us, as all the food was stored in the dairy. This was a large room situated on the north side of the house which was cool all year round. Cold slate slabs at waist height ran all around the walls, with brick arches underneath. The large window only had glass in the middle section; the two side sections were covered with a wire mesh with minute holes to let in air but keep out flies. There were shutters which could be pulled across if necessary, but usually they were left open and the winds and draughts blew in. There were two safes with wire mesh doors, one for meat and one for other food products such as cakes and pastries, so it was possible to keep food cool and mostly hygienic and uncontaminated. The pans of milk and cream were placed on the cold slabs, and the butter was wrapped in greaseproof paper and placed on the slabs as well. We managed perfectly well without a refrigerator, as did everyone else, in fact we did not know anyone who had a fridge. The main drawback with storing all the food in the dairy was the distance from the kitchen. The dairy was on the north side of the house and the kitchen was situated on the south side, and there were two long passages to negotiate in between. Mother's solution was a trolley which we rattled up and down the flagstone and slate floors, illuminating the shadowy passages during the long winter evenings with a candle or a Tilley lamp perched on the top deck.

It was a very hard-working kitchen, for in fact it was more like a living room than a modern kitchen. There were no units for storage. It was the only warm room in the house, and there was a sofa and fireside chairs. The table was pushed back near the wall and the middle of the room was kept clear. There was very little storage space apart from a cupboard in the wall where the everyday crockery was kept, and a drawer in the end of the scrubbed table for cutlery. All food, utensils, pots and pans or crockery connected with cooking were stored in the dairy or one of the pantries on the way to the dairy. Even in later years when electricity was installed, unbelievably no one thought of putting the fridge in the kitchen. As a matter of fact, Mother did not buy a fridge until 1967, just three years before leaving the farm, although a television and washing machine were purchased in 1961 almost immediately after electricity was installed. When she eventually did buy a fridge, it could not go in the dairy as there was no space with all the slabs around, so it was put in the salting house which was as far away as it possibly could be from the kitchen. As one of my aunties once wryly commented,

"This is the only house I know where you have to walk half a mile just to fetch a jug of milk!"

*

Mondays always brought washing day: steam, soapsuds, Reckitt's Blue, wet floors, puddles, indignant cats, harassed humans and cold meat dinners. During Aunt Leah's time the copper under the slee outside the back door would have been lit to boil the water. This was a brick, purpose-built copper with a place to light a fire underneath. This however had been abandoned before I was born, and I remember a huge copper like a witch's cauldron being hauled into the kitchen, hung on the chimney crooks and filled with water. Of course, life was much easier after the Rayburn was installed and we could use hot water from the tap.

These days it is difficult to imagine life without a washing machine, and actually we did have one. We were very proud of it, and I have never seen another one the same (even in a museum where many of the household utensils in use during my childhood now seem to reside). We called it "the washer", and it lived in the second pantry which was a little room near the dairy. Every Monday it had to be hauled along the passages to the kitchen. It was a circular tub about two feet in diameter made of blue galvanised metal. It stood on four legs and had a drainage tap. The lid had paddles on the underside and a handle on the top. When closed, we pushed the handle over and back, and the paddles swooshed the clothes around and washed them. A smart mangle with rubber rollers was attached to one side, so as we finished washing or rinsing we could put the clothes through the mangle. Then as we turned the handle the clothes fell neat and flat into the big wicker clothes' basket.

There were usually three loads of washing. The first load was light colours, followed by dark or coloured garments, and these two loads shared the same soapy and rinsing waters. Finally, when the water in the copper was really hot we began again and washed the sheets and all the white linen. This was finished with a few swirls of Reckitt's Blue in the last rinse. The cube of blue was neatly tied in a piece of cloth, and the blue water made the whites appear whiter. The amount of blue had to be gauged just right though, as too much turned the washing a depressing grey.

Everyone breathed a sigh of relief if it was a dry and preferably a breezy or sunny Monday. Then the wicker clothes basket with all the wet washing was carried out into the vegetable garden where there was a long clothes line running the length of the garden near the hedge. Someone in the past must have given a lot of thought to the needs of the washer women of the house, and a bank about three feet high and three feet wide had been built alongside the hedge, so we could walk along and hang the washing on the line without stretching or straining. I always enjoyed hanging the washing out on sunny summer days and still do. There is something very rewarding about seeing newly washed clothes flapping against a blue sky. The lilacs grew in the hedge behind the washing line, and in the early summer their scent mingled with the freshly washed smell of the clothes.

Washing day chores did not end when the washing was hanging on the line. All the splashing, sploshing, filling and emptying left wet and messy floors which had to be mopped or scrubbed. During the summer when the weather was kind we would often put the washer on the cobbles in the little courtyard outside the back door. Although it was further to carry buckets of hot water to fill, it certainly saved all the mess indoors and the great advantage was, we could just turn the tap to empty it and let the water splash down over the cobbles into the drain.

If the weather could not be trusted then the smell of wet washing permeated the house. The clothes horses were brought out, and clothes were hung around the kitchen and spare bedrooms. It was a rare Monday that we could say, "We have washed, dried and ironed," but it did happen occasionally. Usually though, ironing day was Tuesday. Most people look at me aghast when I say I enjoy ironing, but as I became old enough to be useful I discovered that ironing was a relaxing and soothing occupation. I loved the warm smell and neat piles of freshly ironed clothes.

In the days before the Rayburn, the flat irons were lined up on the grating near the glowing embers of the fire. Flames licking the irons were no good, as it made them smutty and sooty, so hot glowing wood was what we aimed for. At least three irons were necessary so there was one in use and two heating up. Mother would pick up the iron with the iron holder, wipe it with a cloth to ensure there was no smut on it and away she would go. Then as it cooled down it was replaced by another iron. A pretty embroidered iron holder was always a welcome present to give aunties or grandparents, and the stitches would be much admired. We always used the end of the table as an ironing board and ironed on top of the folded sheets.

When I became old enough to help with the ironing, the only part of the day that I disliked and found a nuisance was starching Uncle Jack's collars. Robin starch was mixed up in a basin, and the collars dipped in and then ironed so they became stiff as boards. Uncle Jack then did them up with studs front and back.

Life was easier when the Rayburn was installed, as then the irons could be placed on the hot plate and there was no problem with soot and smut. We did have a Tilley iron for a while which hissed and glowed like the Tilley lamps. Mother and I were never entirely happy with it, and eventually it ended up at the back of a cupboard.

My mother was never particularly interested in housework or keeping things spick and span. She was not one of those farmers' wives who delighted in running a house where everything was scoured and scrubbed and gleaming and glowing. She kept it fairly hygienic but took the line of least resistance. She always had someone in the house to help, and even after she retired she had someone for a few hours a week to clean. She just could not see the point of endless tidying and cleaning, and if we were pressed for time she would say, "Do the bit in the middle where it shows," and I suppose that was her motto.

To be truthful, trying to keep Wansley spotless and gleaming was rather like trying to hold back the tide. Everyone walked into the kitchen and up and down the passages to the dairy with muddy boots. Dogs and cats wandered in and out, and if we were not careful curious hens would venture in to have a look around. Downstairs most of the floors were brick, slate or flagstone, and linoleum covered most the bedrooms. When I was young only two bedrooms had squares of carpet and the floorboards around the carpet were varnished. There was an upright Ewebank cleaner for the carpets, and once a year they were taken out and put on the clothes line to be beaten with a carpet beater. Otherwise all the cleaning was done with mops and dusters, and of course the scrubbing brush.

Just occasionally Mother's conscience would get the better of her, and she would make a concerted effort to have a blitz on a room. Not long after the war she decided that the first pantry needed sorting out. It was one of the small rooms just off the dairy passage where we kept all the cleaning equipment – polishes, saucepans, frying pans, and other cooking utensils. Harvest baskets and egg-collecting baskets were stored there. There were hooks on the walls where bills and receipts were placed ready for the annual trip to the accountant, and behind the door in a recess there were shelves laden with unknown boxes, tins, old veterinary bottles and many other miscellaneous objects.

"We really must sort this out," Mother said to Ruth one day. "Goodness only knows what there is on these shelves, it must have all been here since the Ark."

They steadily worked their way up the shelves starting at the bottom and eventually reaching a large, mysterious box on the top shelf. By now Ruth was standing on the steps as she carefully passed the box down to Mother who was waiting, arms outstretched and cigarette in her mouth as usual. It was quite heavy so they put it on the floor, lifted the lid and peered in. It did not take Mother very long to realise what was in it, and she nearly dropped her cigarette in amazement. Thankfully she didn't, as it was Great-Great-Great-Uncle Frank's gunpowder.

"Good heavens," she gasped, "if a bomb had dropped on us during the war, we would all have been blown up!"

Mother was partial to brass and copper ornaments. She loved going to sales and often returned with yet another piece of brass to be cleaned. It was not often she cleaned it herself because she always had someone to help in the house, and when I left school that was me. I think that the worst job was cleaning the brass stair rods. Thank goodness it was only once a year.

Great-Great-Great-Uncle Frank's gunpowder and shot flasks.

Sometimes I think Mother wondered how she had me, as I was completely opposite to her in so many ways. Even as a little girl I liked things to be orderly and neat, and I was always tidying up. I was never thanked for it, in fact I think that it irritated her and I would hear her exasperated voice say,

"Mary's been tidying up again and now I can't find anything!"

One thing she was very particular about however was bed making and everything had to be just so. All the beds had feather mattresses which she insisted were turned over (yes, actually turned over) and plumped up every day. The bed in Mother and Father's room was a large mahogany affair, and I discovered many years later, it was the bed in which Father had been born. A Tudor rose adorned the footboard, and on each corner there was a tall post which had been rounded off on the top. It had almost certainly been a four-poster at sometime, and Mother said that when she came to the farm it was a half-tester, which meant that it just had a canopy over the top half of the bed. She had the canopy removed and inserted into the back to create a headboard. The bed was very high and made even higher by the addition of three mattresses. The feather mattress sat on another mattress, which in turn sat on a straw palliasse. It was not a question of getting into bed it was a matter of *climbing* into bed. One foot had to be placed on the wooden bed frame, which was wider than the mattresses, then it was a case of heaving oneself up onto the top. It would have been a very good bed for testing princesses.

It takes a lot of effort to turn a double feather mattress. It involves much tugging and heaving, walking around the bed and pulling and pushing, and sometimes when I was making the beds, I would just plump up their feather mattress without turning it over. I was sure they would never know the difference. Not being a princess, my mother would not have been bothered by a pea, but there was no doubt that she could always tell when I had not turned the feather mattress and I would be in trouble the next day.

"To Reap and Sow, and Plough and Mow"

And be a farmer's boy,
And be a farmer's boy.

I suppose that if I had been a "farmer's boy" I would have been much more knowledgeable and precise about everything that went on around the farm. I would have known all about crop rotation and been able to name varieties  of corn and other seeds planted. I would have known much more about animal husbandry, breeding and veterinary matters. I would have had first-hand knowledge of farm machinery, and of course I would have been more aware of farm finances and the cost and expected returns on everything. I was aware of all these things in general terms, often listening to farming matters being discussed by adults. However, it was all a long time ago now, and many of the details which may have been interesting are hazy with the mists of time, so I will stick with the jobs and memories that have remained clear down through the years.

There was no doubt that the poultry on the farm was always the domain of the farmer's wife, and consequently as a farmer's daughter I was involved from an early age. My mother might have been a teacher but she did have some knowledge and experience of rearing hens. Her parents kept quite a lot of poultry and Mother helped at weekends.

In the early years at Wansley, Mother hatched her own chickens in an incubator which was set up in a small outhouse across the cobbles, opposite the back door. I would think the incubator could hold about sixty eggs. Heat was provided and regulated by paraffin heaters, and during the periods when the eggs were incubating, the first job of the morning was turning them. When a broody hen is sitting on a clutch of eggs she instinctively regularly turns them, so that all areas of the eggs have contact with her warm body. Naturally, in an incubator it had to be done manually, and to be sure that we had turned all the eggs, they were marked with a cross on one side and a nought on the other. When the door of the incubator was opened and the tray containing the eggs gently pulled out, it was important to turn the eggs as speedily as possible, as there was a loss of heat, and that was why it was one of my jobs to help.

It was a task that I was quite happy to give a hand with, and I was able to be gentle with the eggs as I thought of the little chicks growing inside. A chick takes three weeks to incubate and it was always exciting when hatching day drew near. Mother was very busy for the next twenty-four hours, as the incubator was regularly checked, and the newly hatched chicks were gently removed and placed in a nearby shed with more paraffin heaters. It was fascinating watching a new chick tap its way through its protective covering to freedom with the little egg tooth on the top of its beak. It could take some time from when the first crack appeared until the scraggy bird emerged exhausted and bedraggled. It was not long though before the warmth of the incubator transformed the ugly newcomer into an endearing ball of fluff, and it was surprising how quickly they were self-sufficient in looking after themselves, and feeding and drinking.

Many years of rising early and going out to the shed to turn the eggs before breakfast had given my mother an aversion to eggs which she was never able to overcome. I must admit it was a hot, rather addled, sort of smell, not very pleasant, and Mother never felt able to eat an egg again for the rest of her life. I also developed an aversion, not to eggs, but to milk. It was for the same reasons though. Early morning trips to the shippens, especially in the winter when the cows had been in all night, put me off milk for ever more. My reluctance to drink milk during those formative years is probably one reason why I suffer from osteoporosis now.

Shortly after hatching, Mother liked to segregate the chicks according to sex, putting the cockerels in one house and the pullets in another. As far as I know her method was unique, although she must have gained it from somewhere. I wish now I had taken more notice of the process. She placed each chick on her lap and dangled a needle on a thread over the little bird. It was all according to how the needle swung. I cannot recollect now whether it was round and round, or over and back, and which denoted female and which was male. She did it year after year with roughly a hundred birds, and she was always about ninety-eight percent correct. There were only one or two birds that were ever in the wrong house, and then sometimes it was obviously a transvestite who had not quite decided which it was. I was so used to Mother determining the sex of the chicks with a needle dangling on a thread, that it never occurred to me whether the method or ability might be a little unusual.

While I was at primary school, the poultry was truly free range. There were poultry houses scattered all around the vicinity of the farm buildings, both Lower Court and Higher Court, and the hens wandered anywhere they fancied. Feeding and egg collecting took place twice a day, early morning and mid-afternoon, and of course they had to be shut in at night or they would be victims of the fox. Probably about three quarters of the hens went to roost obediently and happily in the intended places inside the poultry houses, but there was always a minority who were obstinate and free thinking, and preferred the lower branches of the trees. When it was dusk they flew up onto the branches and settled down for the night. They had to be brought into the houses, for if left to their own devices they would fly down in the early hours of the morning – four or five o'clock in the summer before we were up – and they would be easy targets for Mr Reynard's breakfast.

Shutting up the poultry was the last chore of the day, and it was easier if two people did it. There were long poles left against the trees around The Plantation, Rushy Plat and the Top Orchard, where they were likely to be roosting in the trees. We knocked and shook the branches with the poles until, squawking indignantly, the hens fluttered down. Even then they resisted entering the little hatches of the poultry houses, and it took two people to round them up. They were driven into the houses every night, and every night they seemed surprised by what was happening, and appeared to have no idea what to do or where to go. We did have one sheep dog, Lassie, who instinctively helped to round up obstinate hens and guide them into the correct place. Nevertheless, it was an exasperating job to round off the day, particularly during the war years when it was Double Summer Time (known in our family as "Bloody Double Summer Time") as the nightly round-up took place nearer eleven o'clock than ten.

After many years of incubating and hatching her own eggs, Mother decided to buy in "day-old chicks". They arrived in sturdy boxes and we had to fetch them from Portsmouth Arms station. I was probably about ten years old when this began to happen; it was about the time Father acquired an Austin Seven. I remember it was great fun sitting beside him as he drove to the station to collect the boxes full of little cheeping birds. They were loaded onto a carrier on the back of the car, and there were many anxious glances out of the back window as we slowly and carefully drove home. They arrived as day-old pullets, so they had been sexed by some means or other. Whether it was by a needle dangling from a piece of cotton or by some more scientific method I have no idea.

Any profit from the poultry was considered to be the farmer's wife's spoils, and when the Egg Marketing Board was set up after the war, it soon became obvious that egg production could be quite lucrative. Mother began to expand the number of birds that she kept, and more poultry houses were acquired. These were not the traditional houses that one might expect, but incongruously were buses that had reached the end of their life with the Southern National Bus Company, and were being sold off. They did not blend in with the surroundings at all, so to try and keep them from standing out too conspicuously they were tucked away by the hedges at the bottom of Six Acres and Easter Field. They may not have been beautiful to look at, but they were very practical and made excellent homes for the poultry. There was plenty of room to store grain and mash inside as well as the poultry. We even had a double-decker at one time with residents on both floors. The top floor was home for the little day-old chicks until they were old enough to be transferred downstairs and let out into the run. All this time the poultry was still free range and we always kept Leghorns. They were white hens – prolific layers and a relatively healthy and trouble-free breed.

During the 1950s thoughts about poultry rearing began to change, and more intensive methods began to appear. Mother read about deep-litter houses and thought that she would give it a try. The stable block at the end of the Higher Court was still underused, so it seemed a good idea to convert it into a deep-litter house. Mother thought it would be worth the gamble, so the stable was gutted out and the stalls and loose box vanished for ever.

The litter consisted of wood shavings, straw and in those days peat, although I doubt whether that would be used now. It was a good thick layer, probably nearly twelve inches, and in fact it proved to be a very good method of keeping poultry. Father built nest boxes and roosts for the ladies, and they all settled in remarkably well. They scratched in the litter and their droppings were broken down naturally by microbes. Sometimes if the surface became a little caked or slimy we would dig it off and rake it over, but by and large there were few problems. The roosts and nest boxes were disinfected from time to time with Jeyes Fluid, and it was necessary to keep the windows open and a good flow of air to keep it fresh, as ammonia would build up. About once a year the men would dig the top off the litter and replace it, but they always left a working layer underneath, and it made good compost and manure for the garden.

It was all so successful that Mother and Father decided to build another deep-litter house across the open end of the Higher Court, and so enclose it. This was really a rather ugly structure built of concrete blocks and not at all in keeping with the lovely old stone buildings around the rest of the court. However, financially it made sense as eggs were paying well. We sold them to Cobbledicks of Torrington, and on Wednesdays Mr Stormer or Mr Heal would come to collect them and pay Mother. It was very impressive watching the five-pound notes being handed across. They were large, white and crisp, with wonderful swirly black writing. There were usually four of them, occasionally five, which was quite a sum of money in the 1950s.

When Mother decided to change to the deep-litter method of egg production, she also switched breeds from Leghorns to Rhode Island Reds. For some reason, the general public had the notion that brown eggs were more desirable than white eggs, maybe even more nutritious and healthy. We knew this was untrue, it all depended on the breed of bird laying the egg. Rhode Island Reds had beautiful rich brown plumage and laid brown eggs, and Leghorns had white feathers and laid white eggs. We gave the public what they wanted though, and it was probably a good move to put Rhode Islands in the deep-litter houses, as they had a quiet contented character and were probably more suited to a confined space.

Like most farmers' wives Mother kept poultry destined for the table, mainly at Christmas time. When I was young she kept turkeys for a few years, but these were problematic and prone to diseases. Every year she had to inject them against a particularly virulent disease called blackhead. I think that it was a disease of the liver. Although I was not very old I remember having to hold the young birds while Mother injected them. She knew absolutely nothing about administering an injection, which she freely admitted, and we were both a bit worried. However, to our great relief the birds seemed none the worse for their experience.

After a few years, she decided to abandon rearing turkeys and concentrate on the other poultry. The young cockerels, which she had separated from the pullets at a young age, were fattened up and sold off when ready. I am not quite sure about the outlet, but my grandmother had a stall at Barnstaple Market and I think that quite a few went regularly to our local butcher, Mr Squire of Torrington, and were sold in the shop. She kept a few ducks which she fattened up for Christmas, and we usually had a duck for Christmas Day, and later when I left school I kept geese. I bought the eggs from a friend and hatched them out under a broody hen. Hens make excellent mothers, and never seem particularly puzzled when their offspring turn out completely different from them and exhibit strange habits.

All the poultry for the table had to be killed, plucked and drawn. Mother killed the birds by slitting their throats with a sharp knife. They were then hung upside down by a cord tied around their legs and strung along the wall of the little courtyard outside the back door, while the blood drained away. Many years later when I left school I went to classes organised by the Young Farmers' Clubs, and learnt how to kill hens and larger birds by breaking their necks. It was no use being squeamish, it was a deed that had to be done. I did occasionally pluck the birds but I think I was often at school and Mother had a circle of ladies who could be called upon. Miss Frances Bright was a seasoned and reliable plucker, and Mrs Hilda Rockey was called upon as well, also my Aunty Audrey, my mother's sister who lived at High Bickington. She would come if really needed and my uncle brought her on the back of the motorbike.

The ladies all donned overalls and headscarves, and tied a sack around their middle as they prepared for action. They sat in a circle in the outhouse across the back yard, with galvanise bathtubs in front of them to collect the feathers, and then they set to. At Christmas time there could be several days of plucking, and at the end of the day there were usually sore and sometimes bleeding fingers. When they emerged for a brief respite, a cup of tea or a bite to eat, they would be covered from head to toe in fluffy white down which clung to their eyebrows and eyelashes like fine snow.

After the birds had been plucked Mother did the drawing and this was usually done in the cool of the dairy on one of the slate slabs. She always smoked while she was doing it – well, she always smoked anyway, but this was one occasion when it could be justified, as it did disguise the smell. When this was completed she singed off any stray feathers or down, and the birds were trussed up with the giblets safely inside. It was very satisfying seeing rows of plump birds lined up on the slabs all dressed ready for the table, waiting for their customers.

While Mother was busy expanding the poultry side of the business, Father had not been idle. During Uncle Jack's time the emphasis had been more about beef production, but then herds were not separated so distinctly into beef or dairy as they are now. The Milk Marketing Board had been set up before the war, and Father felt that the future for him lay with milk production. He only had a handful of cows for milking and they were of indeterminate breed. I guess some were Dairy Shorthorns and most of them were of a colour that I can only describe as roan, which was a mixture of pinkish brown, heavily interspersed with grey and white. Some of them were quite pretty, and one or two looked exactly like the picture in my nursery rhyme book – The Cow with the Crumpled Horn in *This is the House That Jack Built*.

Father must have been reading *Farmers Weekly* and other journals and decided that he would buy in some Ayrshire cows; they were brown and white and noted as being good milkers. He probably saw the advertisement in *Farmers Weekly* and decided to buy six cows direct from Scotland as a nucleus to start his new herd.

The lorry with the cows arrived in Roborough village about three o'clock one winter afternoon. It was the school afternoon playtime and we were all milling around and charging about up and down the road. The cattle lorry drew up, and the driver leant out of the window and asked Mrs Blackmore if she knew where Wansley was.

"Why, Mary Squire lives there," she said. "It's near the end of the day, she can show you where to go."

"Mary," she said to me, "go and get your coat and satchel and you can jump up into the lorry and show the man where to go."

Well, I was delighted. I soon grabbed my belongings and clambered up into the lorry. I sat there feeling like a queen looking down on her subjects. The whole school gathered around, all the other children looking up at me with envy, partly because I was going home early and partly because I was having a ride in a cattle lorry. A ride in anything was a rare event in those days.

My goodness, how innocent and trusting everyone was back then. It did not cross anyone's mind that maybe it was not a good idea to put an eight-year-old child in a lorry with a complete stranger and wave goodbye to them, but that was exactly what happened. We waved at each other and away we went, through the village and along West Road, heading for the sunset.

My parents were a little surprised to see me in the lorry when we arrived home but agreed that it was a good idea that I should "show the man where to go". Anyway, they were much more interested in the cows and their welfare, for the poor creatures had had an exhausting journey. It had taken two days and a night's stopover to travel from Ayrshire to North Devon in what can only be described as a boneshaker. The poor wee driver looked totally done in as well, even I could see that. He'd had to tend to the cows and make sure they were fed and watered as well as negotiating the roads of 1940s Scotland and England. It was all quite a responsibility, and there were certainly no motorways then. After settling the cows into their new home, he was fed and watered as well before crashing out in one of the spare bedrooms for the night.

Poor Father, his first venture into increased milk production was not a great success, although it did not become apparent until a few years later. It was about this time that the government was promoting Attested Herds and introducing testing for bovine tuberculosis. The programme was introduced gradually, and Scotland must have been ahead of the game. The canny Scots obviously unloaded all their reactors down south and sold them to unsuspecting English farmers. A few years later, when testing for bovine TB was compulsory and the programme was being rolled out here in Devon, every one of those six cows was a reactor and had to be destroyed. They were the only reactors on the farm. I suppose in the very early days of testing it was still legitimate to sell the cattle on to areas where it did not matter.

Father had calved the cows in, more than once, and their progeny were free from disease. By then of course the big news in the world of milk production was Friesian cows because of their heavy yields, and Father had enlarged his milking herd even further by buying Friesians. Nevertheless, he always kept a core of Ayrshires descended from the "Scottish Six" and these helped to keep the butter fat content up, as their milk was richer than the Friesian milk.

Dairy herds in those days were small compared to the vast herds that are seen now. We milked between twenty-one and twenty-four cows, which was a good-sized herd then for a mixed farm of 150 acres. We could not accommodate any more in the shippens anyway. I was not very involved with the cows until I left school. Occasionally I helped with the milking, and sometimes I would help carry cattle cake or swede to their troughs or turn the handle of the mangold cutter, but mostly I left the cows well alone; they were big and I was not keen on them close up.

After I left school I took over the milk recording, as a record had to be kept of each cow's yield, and I also saw to the milk cooling, which was necessary for the evening milking during the summer months. The milk cooler was set up in a room by the kitchen door, and water was pumped by hand from the well to a small tank. It then flowed through the cooler and back into the well. It was a job that involved Mother and me because the milk had to be carried in pails from the yard to the house, also the water tank had to be topped up regularly with the rotary pump, so one of us was pumping much of the time while the milk was cooling. After the cooling was finished and the cooler and receptacles, buckets and strainer had all been washed, then we turned an online tap and pumped again for twenty minutes to fill the attic tank for the Rayburn. It was certainly all go.

There were no milk tankers in those days. All the milk was put into ten-gallon churns and after the morning milking these, and the churns from the evening before, were loaded onto the trailer and taken out to the milk stand at the end of the lane. From there it was collected by a lorry from Torridge Vale Dairies. This was a thriving business which served a large area and was one of the main employers in the district. It was inconceivable at the time that one day it could disappear, and even now it is unbelievable how it happened.

Whoever took the milk out to the milk stand always checked the drainpipe at the end of the lane to see if the post had come. If not, then it was my job if I was not at school to walk out to the end of the lane later in the day and fetch it. The dogs always liked to accompany the tractor and trailer; it was about a quarter of a mile to the road and they ran along yapping noisily. When I was young I also remember a sow that enjoyed the daily trip and trotted along happily beside the tractor.

As Father increased his dairy herd during the 1950s the water supply increasingly became an issue. Until then, the well under the pump trough outside the back door had been the only supply of water for the whole farm, for man and beast, although the animals had always used the pond. There were several long hot summers during this period, and the well was under severe strain. It was becoming obvious that another supply was needed. Father was also aware that a modern dairy herd needed a water supply in the shippens with drinking bowls for each cow.

Well, what to do about it? That was the question, and Mother as usual came up with a wacky answer. She would try her hand at water divining. Her brother, my Uncle Arty, was a stonemason, and he had found water with a hazel twig and had dug wells for local farmers on several occasions. Mother reckoned that if Arty could do it, so could she, so off she went out into Rushy Plat and rummaged around in the hedges until she found a suitable piece of hazel that could be fashioned into a Y shape. After being satisfied with the size and shape of her hazel apparatus, it was then necessary to do a test and establish whether indeed she had "the gift".

It was decided that she should test it by standing over a drain where we knew there would be water, and we followed her into the yard as she placed herself strategically over the drain. We all stood around fascinated, but sceptical, as Mother tightly held the two ends of the Y over the drain. I do not know who was the most surprised as the stick twisted violently towards her and pointed down. She was holding it so hard that some of the green bark rubbed off onto her hands and she was so alarmed that she threw the hazel twig onto the ground. We were all amazed but elated. There was no doubt that Mother was a natural, and could find water.

The next problem was to find a good reliable source of water which could be brought into the shippens, so over the next few weeks Mother traipsed around the fields testing and honing her skills. She discovered that the process was very tiring and she could only do so much in one day. Naturally, the rest of us wondered whether we could

Bringing in the cows.

My father on the tractor.

There was usually a sow and piglets wandering around when I was young.

(Above) Father in the yard, clearing out the open linhay.
(Left) We are off to drench the sheep.
(Below) I came at the very end of the horse era. The only one that I can really remember is Bobby.

also "divine" water and we all had a go. Sadly, but not unexpectedly, we were all useless, although the stick would gently turn if Mother put her hands over my wrists. The gift certainly runs in the family though, as Cousin John was also a natural, and many years later founded the Devon Dowsers.

Eventually Mother decided that the best place to try for water was at the far end of Grinding Stone Meadow near the hedge that separated it from Higher David's Plat. The men set to work digging, and eventually seven or eight feet down a good spring was found. Eastmonds of Torrington fitted a two-stroke pump, and the water was piped across the meadow to the shippens.

Milk production paid quite well in the 1950s and into the '60s, and Father thought that it had all been worthwhile, but it was a great tie. There was no getting away from the fact that the cows had to be milked twice a day, every day of the year. He always had someone to help him on the farm but he was ultimately responsible, and although it was arranged for alternate Sundays off, nevertheless it was quite a burden. My parents never ever had a holiday, as it was impossible to leave the farm for any length of time. Eventually I think that the milking did get him down, but of course the monthly cheque from the Milk Marketing Board helped and was gratefully received.

Although I was not very involved with the early morning milking I was needed and expected to give a hand with the calves in the morning. When they are first weaned from their mothers they have to be trained to drink milk from a bucket. It takes a few days to encourage them to bend their heads down rather than upwards, as they are used to nudging their mother's udder. The trick was to put my hand in the bucket so they could suck my fingers, and then eventually they drank unaided. Father always had a few calves, perhaps six to eight in the calves' houses opposite the back entrance, and the end house was always the home of the fattening pig. He also always kept about ten to fifteen steers or yearlings. They had the run of Grinding Stone Meadow and Higher and Lower David's Plat. These three fields were always meadow pastureland and I cannot remember them ever being ploughed up.

There was a shed in Grinding Stone Meadow which had been built against the back of the stable where the animals could take shelter and be fed. It was built of galvanise sheets and was a bit ramshackle, but it served the purpose. During the winters, the steers and yearlings were accommodated in the old linhay down in the Lower Court, and this provided very snug accommodation.

There were two other meadows, Higher Meadow and Lower Meadow, and they nestled down against the copse. They were in a sheltered position with trees all around the edges, and the dairy herd spent much of their time there. It was always wise to wear wellingtons when walking down over, as the ground was covered in cow flops and thistles. These fields were never ploughed either and were a good hunting ground for mushrooms in the autumn. There were also two hay meadows at Little Wansley. They were known as First Meadow and Second Meadow, and were not grazed until we had cut them for hay. None of the names were very imaginative, although I recollect from an old map that Lower Meadow had once been called Frogs' Hole. Very apt, as it was damp and shady with a small stream trickling around the edge.

My favourite animals were the sheep. I have always liked sheep, and Father had a flock of about a hundred, a mixture of Devon Closewools and Longwools. Sheep are very comfortable and friendly animals. People say they all look the same but I always thought that was so untrue. When I studied them, it struck me that each one had a different face and character and they were all individuals. I always enjoyed being around them and gave Father a hand from an early age, even if it was only to accompany him to the fields with fodder. During the winter months when the grass was sparse it had to be supplemented daily with hay, mangolds and meal and cake, and when we entered the field with the tractor and trailer or link box, they all came running.

I always associate lambing time with snow. The sheep began to lamb in February, and during the 1940s and '50s and even into the '60s it usually snowed during January and February. It was a busy and stressful time, with sleepless nights for both my parents. There would be a late-night round near midnight and then the alarm clock would be set for two or three in the morning for another check. If Father thought that a birth was reasonably imminent he would sit in the kitchen chair and doze, walking out with the lantern to check every half-hour. It was remarkable how many births occurred at night. Those ewes who looked as though they were due imminently were brought into sheds near the house. There was a large shed in the top orchard, and the barn and turnip house were used as well.

Many of the ewes lambed completely unaided but sometimes help was needed. A lamb could be born during the night or during the day and become cold and not feed, especially if born to an inexperienced mother. Then it would be brought indoors, wrapped in a sack and put into the bottom oven of the Rayburn. That warming oven saved the lives of many lambs. It was miraculous, and so rewarding and heart warming to see a lifeless scrap of skin and bone suddenly open its eyes, lift its head and give a bleat. Then it would be given a little milk from a bottle, and when it could wobble about it would be taken back to Mum again.

Naturally Father always hoped that a good proportion of doubles would be born, as later in the year the fat lambs were taken to market. Occasionally there would be a triple, and this was usually problematic, as most mothers could not provide enough milk for three lambs. The result would be a tame lamb, hand reared, and from quite a young age that would be my department. Sometimes my father had another ruse if a sheep had lost her lamb. All ewes can tell their own offspring initially by their sense of smell and it is useless just giving them a replacement lamb to nurse. They know it is not theirs and won't take it. Father would skin the dead lamb and tie the skin around the lamb he wanted the sheep to take, and this usually did the trick. The sheep would bond with the changeling and after a few weeks the skin could be removed.

I always enjoyed being involved with the sheep, even if it was just watching what was going on, and I enjoyed giving a hand with the drenching. Father would catch a sheep, sit it on its hind legs holding it firmly, while I thrust the syringe-like holder into the sheep's mouth and squirted the medication down its throat.

In the early days I recollect that Father and the farm workers did the shearing themselves with clippers. One person turned the handle to work the clippers and the other person did the shearing. It was very slow, hot work and labour intensive. The sheep were penned up in Rushy Plat, near the barn in the Lower Court, and were brought one by one into the barn to be shorn. Later Father paid contractors. There were several teams in the area and I believe he used a team from South Molton. They brought their own generator and used electric clippers and were unbelievably fast. It was fascinating to watch the fleece being peeled off so quickly and professionally. The adults were stunned by the speed as well, and there was no doubt the days of tiring, backbreaking hand clipping were over – it was a job worth paying for.

I always enjoyed the day in the summer when we went sheep dipping, although I doubt whether the adults looked forward to it very much. It would have been round about July, and in my memory it is always hot and sunny. Dipping was compulsory to protect the sheep from skin diseases, ticks, warble flies and other infestations. We did not have a dip of our own and always had to take them to a farm which did have one. My earliest memories are of going to our next-door neighbours, the Downs at Whitsleigh Barton. I was far too young to be of any use with herding the sheep, but Vera, who was the youngest of the Down family, liked having me there. She must have been in her teens and enjoyed having a little girl to look after and play with. I loved going to Whitsleigh and was always thoroughly spoilt. I can still remember the cherries. They must have had several trees, for there were many bowls of cherries placed on shelves all around the dairy where it was cool. I would be lifted to the high shelves near the ceiling and allowed to help myself.

I also liked Mr Down. He was a jovial man and used to toss me up into the air and catch me. He always seemed to be laughing and happy, and it seemed unbelievable that within a few years he was to die of tuberculosis. Even in the 1940s it was still a scourge and antibiotics were not readily available. I overheard adult discussions in hushed voices. Apparently, the residents of Ebberly House were visiting America, and had offered to try and obtain some penicillin and bring it back for him. The Down family were grateful for the offer but thought that it was far too late for any medication to help. My father walked into Whitsleigh every day during the last few weeks, and I recall him coming back and gravely shaking his head. It was all so sad.

At some point the Down family stopped dipping sheep, so then we drove our flock to Thelbridge Farm which was much further away. This was where we were still taking them when I was working on the farm after I left school. I have such pleasant memories of walking companionably with Father behind the sheep and lambs along the winding roads around Ebberly and Roborough, the verges already becoming dusty and full of swaying meadow grasses, and the hedges awash with blackberry blossom, elder flowers, red campion, yarrow and meadowsweet.

There would have been quite a flock with the lambs as well, somewhere between 150 and 200, I should think – all noisily bleating and baaing. Wilhelm went ahead to block off the junction near the Ebberly fishponds. Then we drove the flock past Coombe Farm, through the Moorpark's crossroads and then on to Thelbridge. The Prouse family lived at Thelbridge in those days, and Ann, who was the eldest of the three children, was a school friend and we visited each other from time to time.

The sheep-dipping schedule had to be well organised, as it would be chaos if two flocks met, so I think quite a lot of thought was given to the timing and the direction the flocks were being driven from. Luckily there was very little traffic on the country lanes in those days, so we did not disrupt village life too much.

The sheep dip was like a long bath set into the ground. Each sheep was pushed in at one end and then virtually had to swim along the bath in the solution. At some point, it was pushed under and totally submerged by Wilhelm or my father using a pole. Then it was hauled out at the other end, wet and bedraggled, shaking itself and bleating with indignation.

They were happy days and I was always grateful for those six years that I spent working at home on the farm, and glad that I made the decision to do so. I did have a pipe dream at the back of my mind, that one day I would have a sheep farm out on Exmoor somewhere. It would have a view of the sea and there would be no cows. Of course, it was only a dream and did not happen but we all need a dream or two to help us along.

Many other happy days were spent on the tractor. Wansley, like most farms in the district, was a mixed farm and quite a lot of land was arable. Father grew a range of crops and in my young years was almost self-sufficient. As the milking herd grew and Mother expanded the poultry side of the business, they needed to buy in cattle cake and poultry food to supplement the homegrown fodder. Nevertheless, they still grew a good proportion of what was needed. There were always several acres of root crops – mangolds, swedes and turnips – and Father also grew a few acres of potatoes. This was more than we needed for our own consumption so it was a cash crop which he sold to agricultural merchants Berrys. Mother jotted in her 1952 diary on 3 March that Berrys had bought 5-ton 15 cwt of potatoes. Unfortunately, she doesn't say what the price was. They also killed the pig on the same day and paid Mr Rogers ten shillings for doing it. I expect he enjoyed a glass or two of cider as well!

I helped with the potato planting and picking after I left school, but I think that I also helped in holiday time as well, certainly with the planting, as it would have been during the Easter holidays when I was home from boarding school. Round about Good Friday was noted as being the time for planting, and I remember it always being cold. The potato planter had three seats and could plant three drills at a time. It was usually Wilhelm and Mr Marles on the two outside seats, and I sat in the middle squashed between them. We dropped the seed potatoes down through the coulters into the soil, while Father drove the tractor. While they were at it they would also plant a few drills for Wilhelm and Mr Marles's own personal use.

In my mind, a brief cameo lingers of one moonlit night planting potatoes in Six Acres at Easter time. We had completed about two thirds of the field in the daylight before tea, but Father felt that he had to stop and do the milking and tend to the stock, so he sent Wilhelm and Mick, who were helping on this occasion, home to have tea, and asked them to come back again later in the evening. Wilhelm was a German ex-Prisoner of War who had remained with us after the war was over. Mick was a "Displaced Person" (we would now say refugee) from the Ukraine, and he had been with the Petherick family at Ten Oaks Farm since the war, and he stayed with them for the rest of his life.

About eight o'clock in the evening, after the stock had been tended to and settled for the night, we recommenced the potato planting. The Fordson Major tractor had headlights, which was helpful, but it was also the most beautiful moonlit night. It was very cold but clear, and the sky was full of stars and the moon bathed us in its light as we drove up and down the field dropping the potatoes. Suddenly Mick began to sing very softly. The cadences and timbre of the melody reminded me of Hungarian or Russian music, and I instantly realised that it must be a folk song from his homeland which he had learnt long ago, probably as a child. It was a magical few minutes that I shall never forget, wedged between two friends, a German and a Ukrainian, planting potatoes in a field in Devon, to a haunting melody in the moonlight.

Mick Drapan.
Photograph courtesy of Carol Petherick.

I always loved harvest time – hay harvest and corn harvest. Even as a young child I looked forward to those long, hot, sunny days in the fields with the men and the dogs. The bustle and fizz of anticipation as I helped Mother prepare the "drinking". This was what everyone called the sustenance that we carried out to the fields for the men. There was the morning drinking at about eleven o'clock, and a teatime drinking in the late afternoon between four and five. Everyone went home for one o'clock dinner. Two large wicker harvest baskets were each lined with a crisp white tea towel; the big brown enamel teapot filled with steaming hot tea and the milk and cups were placed in one basket and the food in another. Then Mother and I would carry them out to the fields. It was a long way to carry a heavy basket if the men were working at Little Wansley. We always shared the weight of the heaviest basket as we made our way towards the pond, then followed the track between the high banks under the tall elm trees. Carefully carrying our load we walked down over the meadows, through the little copse and up over the fields towards the old barn.

The men were always glad to see us, and gladly stopped the tractor and other machinery, found a comfortable spot usually against a hedge and settled down for a well-deserved picnic and break. I always stayed with them, although Mother would go back to the farmhouse. It was plain food but wholesome. The afternoon drinking consisted of slices of bread spread thickly with our own butter and there was always a pot of homemade jam. Mother would also put in her little nubby cakes. She made them every week and they were part of our staple diet. They were little buns with sultanas or currants in them, and they were kept in the dairy in large Huntley & Palmers biscuit tins.

For the morning drinking she usually made potato cakes known as "teddy cakes". They were delicious and enjoyed by all. They were rather like large flat scones but some mashed potato was put in the mix with the flour. She made two kinds, savoury and sweet. For the morning drinking she made the savoury ones. These were baked with a slice of fat bacon on the top and the fat oozed down through the cakes and made them very tasty. She sometimes made the sweet ones for teatime drinking and they had a little sugar in the mix and a few sultanas were added. Either way they were always eaten warm, and the sweet ones would be sliced and spread with butter. If she made teddy cakes for the afternoon break, then she usually sent out bread and cheese for the morning drinking.

*

One morning I am outside playing near the back door when a strange noise breaks into my consciousness; it is an unusual rasping sound. I listen intently and hear it again. It doesn't sound as though it is made by a human, besides it is coming from the direction of Easter Field and the men are still in the yard. I try it against my bank of known sounds, a miscellaneous accumulation over my four years of life. Well, it's not a bird and I cannot recollect ever hearing a fox that sounded like that. Baffled and curious I trot indoors to ask Mother whether she has heard it. Yes she has, and she informs me it is a landrail or corn crake. Ah, so I was wrong – it was a bird, but a bird with a voice like no other.

I heard it several times that summer and possibly for another season or two but I was never lucky enough to see a landrail and I know now that I was lucky to hear one, for they have long since vanished from these parts, and must have been among the last in North Devon.

*

The cornfields were always a delight, and sometimes I play back in my mind's eye those long sunny days spent in the fields when corn harvest and summer holidays coincided, arms turning brown at last and legs scratched with the corn stubble.

Hidden underneath the corn is a world of miniature flowers. I am not sure whether anyone else knows they are there or notices them except me. One of the joys of summer is creeping through the corn gently pulling the stalks aside, until finding a little place where I can sit completely hidden from the world. I know that I must not flatten too much corn or Father will have a few words to say. I gaze through the stalks at the blue sky and then turn my attention to the ground. A myriad of shy, unseen flowers form a carpet. Mother must know they are there as she has provided names so I can personalise them. My favourite are heartsease or wild pansies; there is an abundance of them, their creamy white petals with purple and yellow markings like little faces looking up at me. Almost as plentiful are the scarlet pimpernels, a joyful contrast clothed in bright orange. I am drawn into this small world and can sit for ages admiring petals, noticing small differences and following the journeys of ladybirds and beetles.

At last Father thinks the weather is settled and he is going to begin cutting the corn. Already Mr Marles has pared back the hedges around the cornfields, and the binder has been dragged out of the implement shed at the back of the linhay in the Lower Court and given its annual service. Excitement and anticipation are in the air. Grandfather and Uncle Jack have walked over from Roborough to give a hand to put the corn into stooks, while Father and Wilhelm man the tractor and binder. I am happy because Cousin Rachel has walked over with Grandfather and I know we are set for an enjoyable day. Rachel and all her brothers and sisters call him Granfer but I am not allowed to. Mother does not like the word and thinks it is disrespectful, but as far as I can tell he doesn't seem to mind and I rather wish I was not the odd one out.

The tractor revs up and away they go, the dogs barking, the binder clittering and chattering as the vanes turn and guide the corn stalks onto the blades and then over the canvases. The machinery whirls and clanks and the corn is bound into sheaves which are thrown out onto the ground. The men let the binder do a few rounds before they begin gathering the sheaves and putting them into stooks. Rachel and I imagine that we are helping and drag some sheaves over to make a stook. The stooks are six sheaves put together and the men can all carry two sheaves at a time. It is wise to wear dungarees when in the cornfields as the stubble and straw soon create cuts and scratches and play havoc with legs. After a while Rachel and I abandon our efforts of help and play amongst the stooks of corn. It is great fun crawling through them or hiding in the middle. Later we wander around the hedges and check for early blackberries.

The best bit of the day is near the end, as the binder reduces the corn to a small square in the middle of the field. We know that the rabbits will all have been driven into this little oasis and as it vanishes they will make a dash for the nearest hedge. All the dogs know as well, they remember from year to year, and begin to go mad with anticipation. At last the fun begins as the rabbits make a bid for freedom. The dogs chase them barking wildly, we children chase them and the men all shout and kick up a hullabaloo. Someone has usually brought a shotgun for it is a good opportunity to bag a rabbit or two for the pot. Despite the noise and frenetic chasing as far as I can recollect most of the rabbits get away.

Corn being cut with horses and a binder. This photo was taken by my mother's cousins who lived on a farm at Martinhoe near Lynton.

"Carrying" the corn was just as enjoyable, and with luck and no rain, took place ten days or so after cutting, although if the weather was unsettled it could be much longer. The tractor and trailer were driven from stook to stook, and the sheaves were pitched onto the trailer and taken to make a rick in the corner of the field. When I was young most of the ricks were made in the Mowstead, which was the rick yard opposite the barn, and this was convenient if Father needed to thresh some with the barn thresher. Riding in on top of a load of corn or hay was one of the treats of harvest time. Later, as Father began to rely more and more on contractors to do the threshing, the ricks were made in the fields.

Once again, we children would crawl in amongst the stooks of corn and hide. The men would pretend they did not know we were there and would come over to stab the sheaf with a pitch fork and we would run out screaming. Sometime in September as we finished the last field I would hear Uncle Jack shout,

"Yer 'tis."

There he would be with the last sheaf held aloft on his pitchfork. I suspect this little ceremony was important to Uncle, and was the remnant of a much older ritual.

I enjoyed harvest time just as much after leaving school when I was working full time on the farm. By then I was trusted to drive the machinery, although I must admit that I had been allowed to drive the tractor under supervision since I was ten years old. There was no legislation forbidding children from driving tractors during the 1940s and Father decided I could be useful when they were "carrying". I was permitted to drive from stook to stook while the men pitched the sheaves of corn onto the trailer. It saved one of the men from constantly having to jump off the tractor to pitch, and then jump back on again. I was overcome with happiness and pride when Father suggested it, although later when I went in to fetch the drinking and told Mother what I had been up to, she nearly had a fit. A precedent had been set however and no matter what her opinions about the subject were, from then on I was useful as a tractor driver in the cornfield.

We still had the old Fordson spade-lug tractor at the time, and the clutch and brake were combined as one pedal on the floor on the right of the seat; being very small and skinny and light, the only way I could operate the pedal to stop the tractor, was to swing off the seat and jump onto it with as big a thump as I could muster. My take-off was just as haphazard, as the choke had to be rammed in and out to rev the tractor up, while I let the pedal back up as smoothly as possible, cocked my left leg back over the seat and resumed my driving position. There was only one hard and fast rule: the men had to tell me when to move. This was so the person on the trailer could prepare himself and hang on firmly before I lurched forward. Mother never accepted that I should be driving the tractor; she always worried and could never bring herself to come out to the fields and watch.

After leaving school at sixteen my presence in the fields was accepted, although I was more likely to be operating the machinery than the tractor. Wilhelm and I made a good team and we enjoyed each other's company. He was usually the tractor driver and I followed behind on the implement. From then on, I rode the binder for corn cutting. It was an old Albion, meant to be drawn by horses, and had been adapted for a tractor. Lots could go wrong and usually did. Father tilled a lot of dredge corn which was a mixture of oats and barley. This was useful to put through our own mill as meal for the cattle. Some years he also tilled wheat as he needed the straw for thatching ricks. The binder rider had quite a lot to watch out for, it was no use just sitting back and admiring the scenery. If it was a little damp the cutting blades could easily clog up, especially if the corn had been under-planted with grass seed, ready to be a lay field the next year. The canvases could easily jam and the gear which bound the straw and tied the knot with the binder twine frequently gave trouble. I had to be alert and yell at the top of my voice to stop if necessary, and Wilhelm would sort things out.

Most of my tractor driving was during hay harvest, and how I loved it. I was always delegated to drive the sweep. This was an implement with wooden prongs which was attached to the front of the tractor and scooped up the hay. It was always dry and sunny, and the hay would have been tossed into rows by one of the men with the hay turner earlier in the morning. After dinner, it was my job to drive around the field and sweep up the hay and transport it to the elevator by the rick.

I have such happy memories of the hay fields; perhaps it was the sweet-smelling hay, perhaps it was the sunshine on my arms and legs, maybe the countryside itself, hedges and woods exuberant, lush and green, full of wild roses and honeysuckle, and the expectation of more abundance to follow, with sunny days stretching on into the future. I only left the sweep to help Mother carry out the drinking, then I would settle back into the soft sweet hay with the men and take my fill, knowing that I was a member of the team and had earned my refreshments. No matter how late we had to work we would finish carrying the field, and return to the house weary, but satisfied.

This was not the end of the day by any means, even if we were very late, as the milking still had to be done and the stock

attended to. As we followed the track back through the meadows, the cows would be standing clustered together by the gate waiting to be milked, their udders swollen and uncomfortable. They were longing to be let into the shippens. Father, Mother and I still had several hours' more work to do, as the milk had to be cooled, which meant lots of pumping with the rotary pump. During harvest time, it was not unusual for it to be past eleven o'clock and dark before we had completed all the daily tasks.

The only part of hay harvesting to beware of was the dreaded "hay sweet". As girls, we had to keep a wary eye on the men, especially when my friends came over to play and help. When we heard some surreptitious laughter and saw one of the men twisting some hay into a long roll, we knew it was time to watch out. They would try and grab one of us girls around the neck with the "hay sweet" and deliver a smacking kiss.

When I was very young the hay was carried to the top of the rick with a hay pole rather than an elevator. This was a very tall pole with a grab attached and the hay was swung across to the rick. It was not unknown for accidents to occur with the hay pole and I realised that this was another implement that my mother worried about, and she was always exhorting the men to be careful. She was pleased when the hay pole was replaced by the elevator as it was a much safer way of transferring the hay to the top of the rick.

It was always fun out in the fields, even when the weather was not so good, and Wilhelm and I usually turned our jobs into a game. Tilling the corn provided us both with some laughs; I was always the seed-drill rider and Wilhelm the tractor driver. After planting "the foreheads" (a few drills around the outside), we then planted in rows up and down the field. At the end of a row I had to swing off the seed drill, heave on the lever which pulled the coulters out of the ground, while Wilhelm swung around without stopping and drove back again ready for the next row. I had to catch him as he came by, jump back onto my seat, at the same time releasing the lever to insert the coulters back into the soil again; all this we did as fast as we dared

Hay harvest with horses and the hay pole in Barn Park.

without wrecking the machinery. Once again it was a machine from the horse age, which had been adapted for a tractor. Wilhelm tried his hardest to leave me behind and I did my best not to be caught out. Luckily, I was light and agile and not often left behind. At the end of the session I had won if I had managed to jump back on each time, and he had won if I'd missed.

Perhaps the only job which was not a bundle of laughs was potato picking. There was little that could be done to make such a boring, back-aching job more interesting. It was towards the end of the afternoon one October day in Billy Hill, that my grumbling appendix decided that it had had enough of being bent double and squashed against my other intestines, and fired up for one last revolt. That was the end of potato picking for me that year, and I enjoyed a calm and orderly stay at the North Devon Infirmary and a leisurely six-week convalescence.

I suppose my time spent doing farm work balanced evenly with time spent with the domestic side of life and helping Mother in the house. On the whole, I probably spent rather more time with the farm side of things, and it was certainly the most interesting. They were busy active days which did not stop when the work was finished, for there were many occasions after work when we would scrub up and then go off to a local village "hop" to spend the evening dancing.

I think that I was lucky with the years allotted to me to be a farmer's daughter, for those wartime years and into the 1950s, until 1960 when I eventually left for good to follow another career, were quite unique. The age of the horse was over, although I was surprised to read in an old 1953 diary that I had spent a day horse-hoeing turnips for Father with the Pethericks' horse in Barn Park. I was fifteen at the time and home from school on holiday.

We considered ourselves to live in a mechanical age, although it was nothing like what was to follow. The balers and combine harvesters might have been forging their way across the open flatlands of East Anglia and the rolling plains of Wiltshire but here in North Devon they were a rare sight and still a novelty. Silage was another innovation which was being gingerly tested. Villages were still relatively insular, and no one had figured out that tourists might like a holiday on a farm equally as much as one at the seaside, and there were new business opportunities for the farmer's wife.

Those far-off times and the people who inhabited them seem like a dream now, but all it takes is a smell, a song, a remark or turn of phrase to transport me back, make me smile, and remind me of when the world was young and anything was possible.

All the World's a Stage

As an only child living in such a remote and lonely place, much of my childhood was quite solitary. Not that I minded, I was always quite happy with my own company. Some of the time Mother, Father and I rattled around the old farmhouse on our own but often there was someone living in. Aunt Leah and Uncle Jack  moved to their cottage in the village when I was about four, although they visited frequently. The house was huge for just three people, but it was all that I had known and it did not seem big to me. Although I was often on my own and followed my solitary pursuits, there were however many people – relatives and others – who played an important part in my world, and several of them shared our life at Wansley.

The village was small, with only about twenty houses during the 1940s, then a few council houses were built after the war. Ebberly people considered themselves to belong to Roborough, and of course there were the outlying farms and cottages. I knew everyone and where they lived, even if I did not know them well. There were a lot of spinsters or "old maids" as they were sometimes called, their quiet and dignified loneliness and lack of husbands and family another consequence of the Great War of 1914–18.

Two such people were the Misses Bright, Bessie and Frances, who lived at Roborough Mill. They were sisters, industrious, God fearing and hard working. "Salt of the earth," my mother used to say. Bessie worked at Thelbridge Farm and walked the two miles there and back daily. Frances walked up to Wansley twice a week to help my mother in the house after Mary's sister Ruth moved to another position in Dorset. Frances had a sweetheart, Harry Harris, who also worked at Thelbridge Farm. It seemed such a shame that they had never married, but Frances had felt that she was needed to care for her parents when they became elderly, duty was very important, and she said there was not really any right time for marriage. My mother felt that was wrong, and she had sacrificed too much. When Mr Harris retired he moved into the cottage at Roborough Mill with Bessie and Frances, and the three of them lived together very contentedly.

I was taught to always address adults by their title of Mr or Mrs, and was never allowed to use their Christian names. Anything less was considered bad manners. This convention was deeply ingrained and extended to the adults as well. My parents referred to and addressed all their neighbours and friends by using their surname. The only exceptions being family or old school friends. It did not matter if they had known each other for fifty years, it would still be Mr and Mrs.

"Mrs Squire, you can't imagine the trouble I've had with my leg. The doctor says I mustn't put foot to ground for a week."

"Oh my goodness, Mrs Petherick, what a nuisance, how are you going to manage? What can we do to help?"

It was Mr and Mrs Rockey, Mr and Mrs Down, Miss Harris, Miss Bright, Mr and Mrs Squire, never Alice or Molly or Hilda. The nearest to familiarity that my father and Mr Petherick came was to call each other "Farmer", but that was as intimate as convention allowed, and I never heard the words Sid or Bill pass their lips.

It was the same in later years when Brian's family and my family met. Everyone got on well and our two mothers became good friends, for they had a lot in common. They were both country women who had spent much of their lives on a farm; they both enjoyed a smoke and neither of them were very bothered by housework, both felt there were better things to do. Nevertheless, they always addressed each other as Mrs White and Mrs Squire, never Kit or Molly, and that was how they both liked it.

I grew to know Miss Frances Bright well over the years that she came to help Mother, and I liked her. She was quite tall and thin and bony. She seemed stern, austere and unsmiling at first but this was because she was very deaf and missed most of the conversation unless spoken to directly. She was a good sport though and surprisingly good fun as I found out later.

I would never have imagined her cavorting about in the brook catching eels with a carving fork if I had not seen it for myself. For some reason I was at Roborough Mill and she told me there was a glut of eels and would I like to help her try and catch some. We armed ourselves with carving forks and a toasting fork and set out to wreak havoc on the eel population. It was great fun splashing about and lunging at them; Miss Bright was surprisingly good at it and caught enough for her supper and ours.

Miss Bessie Bright and Miss Frances Bright, in their garden at Roborough Mill.

Mother was delighted when I came home with the trophies, and she prepared them into cutlets and fried them. It was the first time I had tasted eel. It did not taste at all fishy, the flesh was sweet and really delicious.

Miss Bright was my saviour on another occasion. It was some knitting that caused the bother. As we neared the end of our time at Roborough School, we progressed to knitting with four needles and were expected to knit socks. Obviously, my knitting skills were not as good as I thought. I had spent the whole afternoon at school turning the heel which was the tricky bit, but Mrs Blackmore was not impressed with my efforts. It was pronounced not good enough, was ripped back and I was told to take it home and do it again.

I walked into the farm kitchen rather down in the mouth about it all. It was just about the time when Miss Bright was going home after her day's work. She looked horrified that I had to do the heel all over again and she grabbed it out of my hand saying, "I'll do it," and marched off home with my knitting in her bag. She was as good as her word, and when I woke next morning the sock was back with the heel expertly completed. It was so good of her for she not only had to walk home a good half-mile to the valley bottom and complete the sock, but she had to trudge all the way back up the very steep hill to return it and then walk home again.

I presented the sock to Mrs Blackmore when I arrived at school the next morning and she eyed it sharply. She must have realised that it was not my knitting but she made no comment.

Sadly, it was Miss Bright's deafness that contributed to her death. A relative was coming to stay and was arriving on the Exeter bus. A friend took her to meet the bus, and they waited in the car on the main Beaford-Torrington road, at the junction with Peggy Trigger's Hill. When the bus arrived, Miss Bright was so excited and eager to see her friend, she opened the car door and rushed out into the road just as a car was passing. She was seriously injured and died a few days later in hospital. It was so sad and so undeserved.

The church played a big part in her life and she had a deep faith. She had expressed a wish to be buried as near the church as possible and she now lies very close to the tower.

*

Various people from the parish worked on the farm from time to time. During the seasons there was often the need for casual labour as well as a full-time workman. Mr Percy Shaxton from Ebberly did quite a lot of part-time work, in fact when I looked at my mother's 1953 diary where she kept note of wages paid out, I was surprised at how often he had given a hand. He walked over from Ebberly (sometimes with a bunch of flowers which he presented to me with a coy smile).

He was certainly a hard worker and would tackle any task in any weather. He was known to fasten a piece of galvanise to his back to protect himself from the rain when working in the fields, especially for something like potato picking. I understand that, although very honest, he was quite tight fisted with the money. If he had some milk or eggs or potatoes from Father, he was unwilling to part with any hard-earned cash to pay but insisted on working it off. Apparently, he refused to waste money on oil for lamps and was even frugal with candles. This meant that during the winter months he and his long-suffering wife, Alice, went to bed at about half past four in the evening, and stayed there until it was daylight. It was rumoured that he gave doctors a wide berth as well, certainly in the days when the doctor had to be paid, and if feeling under the weather he would have a sip of Jeyes Fluid. Whether this was true I am not sure, but there was no doubt he was tough.

Apparently, Alice had a few tricks of her own, and managed to secrete an occasional luxury out of Percy's reach. I have heard that sometimes a kindly neighbour, when she visited Barnstaple, would bring Alice back a fruitcake as a treat. Alice always hid the cake in an old basket which was hung high up at the back of the pantry, in amongst the cobwebs, so that Percy would be most unlikely to find it.

Percy and Alice Shaxton, No Place, Ebberley, October 1975. Photograph by James Ravilious © Beaford Arts, digitally scanned from a Beaford Archive negative.

*

Another person that floated in and out of my life from time to time was Sammy Lake. He lived in a cottage on the edge of Pondclose Wood.

"Poor old Sammy is not quite all there," I was told.

He must have been considered to be completely harmless, as Mary and I regularly visited his cottage with groceries, milk and bread. Mary's mother, Mrs Waldron, used to get all the necessities that Sammy needed from the local delivery vans when they called on her, and then someone had to take them to his cottage. On Saturdays it was often our job to deliver meat and bread. There was no road into Sammy's house, there was just a rough track which went from the village road along the top edge of Pondclose field and into the wood. The cottage was also named Pondclose and when approached from that direction, it was clear that it was only just inside the wood.

We did not often walk all around the road though, as it was a longer route, and when we were at Mary's house it was more direct and quicker to walk up through the woods. Mrs Waldron would give us the basket with the goods and a note with the money owed, then we would walk through the Waldrons' two plats beside the brook, cross a little wooden bridge and follow a path up under the trees. To me it always seemed like something out of a fairy tale. I felt like Goldilocks finding the three bears' house, or Red Riding Hood going to visit Grandmother, for approached from that direction the cottage seemed to be in the middle of the wood. There was never any problem; Sammy was gentle spoken, he would give us the money and we would race back down through the trees to Burridges Cottage.

I suppose he would walk to the village once a week to collect his pension, but I can only once recall seeing him anywhere except his cottage. Mary and I met him one summer afternoon on the way home from school. We were slightly alarmed to see him "out of context" so to speak. He was holding an adder on the end of a stick. "I've just killed this," he said, "I didn't want it to hurt you." We thanked him profusely and walked smartly past.

We did hear him sometimes though, even as far away as Wansley, which was situated over the hill on the other side of the valley from Pondclose Wood. On beautiful moonlit nights as we stood in our yard, we would sometimes hear Sammy shouting to the full moon. Uncle Jack would shake his head sadly. "Poor old Sammy," he would say. Of course it is all gone now, not only Sammy Lake but the cottage and the wood. Now a vast grassy field covers the hillside – no hint of a house, a troubled old man, a wood, bears and wolves… It is as though none of it ever existed.

*

Recalling people and events from so long ago is rather like letting ghosts from the past whisper down the years. One of the ghosts from my past that never did materialise was my longed-for baby sister or brother. I definitely would have preferred a sister but a brother would have been better than nothing. Everyone at school had brothers and sisters, and as time went on I began to feel hard done by. My cousins in the village were a family of four when I began school, which later increased to six siblings. There was another family where there were twelve brothers and sisters. My mother, herself one of eleven children, assured me that it was not always easy being a member of a large family and in many ways I was lucky that I was an only child. I couldn't quite see why I was lucky, and I remember on one occasion marching home from school bristling with indignation. Someone at school must have had a new baby brother or sister and there had been much discussion about the new arrival. I felt that as far as my parents were concerned there was a definite lack of action and I was being left behind. I realised that I was going to have to do something about it. My mother dined out on my words for some time after, for apparently I stamped into the kitchen, slammed down my satchel and issued my ultimatum.

"Mother, if you don't hurry up and get a new baby brother or sister for me, I am going to get one for myself!"

I can remember the occasion clearly, and despite the bravado of my words and the fact that I had been brought up on a farm, I had absolutely no idea where babies came from. From an early age I had seen calves and lambs being born. I had been there when kittens arrived into the world; I had watched with amusement and awe as a newborn lamb struggled to its feet and shakily staggered to its mother to suckle. I had watched one desperate birth where a calf had been pulled from its mother with a rope and tractor, albeit I had watched from the dairy, peeping through the window, as I had been sent indoors out of the way. Nevertheless, I had never connected animals and humans.

Father said you found babies under gooseberry bushes. Well, we had plenty of those and I did consider the idea, but gullible though I was, I never felt that it was a likely explanation. When eventually I did find out, several years later – I cannot remember from whom but it was definitely not my parents – I knew instantly that it was the truth and I wondered why it had not occurred to me before. I tucked the information into the back of my mind and then forgot all about it.

*

I may have lost out in the baby stakes but in the "aunty department" I was truly blessed. I had seven aunties and they were all golden in their own way. They shimmied and darted in and out of my life like a shoal of dancing fish bringing happiness and fun. Five of my aunties lived at High Bickington. They were all younger than my mother, three of them considerably so, and that was one of the reasons why I thought it was such a terrific place to stay or live. The hub of the family was "Prospect", my grandparents' house, and during my childhood it was such a lively and fun place to be. It was bursting at the seams with people, dogs, cats and, alarmingly, ferrets, as the uncles usually went rabbiting at the weekends. There was always something happening and lots of talk and laughter. When I was young it was a cosy thatched cottage, and life there was bustling and busy. My grandmother and aunties turned out stews and hotpots, pies and cakes, and what seemed like endless goodies from the old black stove and hob, even during the hard days of rationing. There was a liveliness and energy in the house which was in complete contrast to Wansley, although I loved the place dearly.

There must have been about ten people living at Prospect when I was young, but they always found a space for me. As at Wansley there was no electricity or running water, and even I was aware of the workload, particularly on washing days. Monday washday was fraught at Wansley but at Prospect the logistics were like a weekly military campaign. The battle with the clothes took place in an outhouse. A boiler or furnace was lit, galvanise wash tubs were unhooked from the walls and the ladies went into action. The main drawback, of course, was no water. It had to be fetched in buckets from "Home Well" in the village. It was a marathon. What drudgery! Every drop to do that mountain of washing was carried up from Home Well. It made our pump and pump trough just outside the back door at Wansley seem positively slick and streamlined.

Two of the liveliest of my aunties were Dot and Audrey. They were always fun and game for anything. Aunty Dot, who lived at the Golden Lion, had a sunny personality. She was pretty with dark wavy hair and enormous big brown eyes. She was creative and loved flowers and gardening. She created a garden in a patch of waste ground at the back of the pub and packed it with flowers. She then sold them for a shilling a bunch and saved the money in a cocoa tin. She was a talented flower arranger as well and took part in local flower shows, and her skills were sought after at weddings.

My Aunty Audrey was also good fun and always had a twinkle in her eye. She had a ready wit, although she could be more caustic in her comments than Aunty Dot who always saw the best side of everything. Aunty Audrey spent her days at Prospect helping with work both indoors and out, as the family had a paper round business and kept a lot of poultry. Every night she walked up the road to sleep at her sister's, my Aunty Kathleen's house, which was the post office, as Prospect was so full.

Aunties Dot and Audrey were the two who always seemed to have the time and energy to have fun and take me places. One of my earliest memories is going to Barnstaple Fair with them. This was back in the days when the fair was held on the Strand. I think that it must have been in 1945, just after I began my winter stay at the Golden Lion. I have since read in the school logbook that a day's holiday was granted so pupils could attend the fair. I would have been seven years old then and it was the first time I had ever been to the fair. I am not sure who enjoyed it most, the aunties or me. We had a whale of a time and they took me on most of the rides. It all seemed wildly exciting, although I suppose the rides would have been much more sedate than present-day fair rides. There was a weekly bus from High Bickington to Barnstaple on Fridays so we probably went on that. We certainly would not have had any means of travelling by car, although we could have walked to Umberleigh station and caught the train. I can remember doing that on several occasions.

My visit to Barnstaple Fair was a one-off event but every year I looked forward to High Bickington Fair. It took place in May and was one of the highlights of my year, and I would not have missed it for anything. My parents were unable to be there in the daytime as they were always too busy with farm work, so the aunties took charge of me. Many of the events were in the playing field along Quarry Lane, and there were sports and football and a gymkhana, but best of all were the swing boats. Cousin John and I would have spent all day on them if we could. I just loved pulling on the rope and swinging through the air. The band and the music always made me feel excited, and the aunties taught me how to do the Floral Dance. We practised in Prospect sitting room, always called "Lower Room", because it was down a step from the rest of the house. "One two three hop, one two three hop" – it was not long before I had mastered it well enough to join everyone else and dance round the streets.

Fair week always culminated with a carnival and a dance. Dot and Audrey were always involved in some way. Aunty Dot was usually in charge of decorating the Carnival Queen's float, and in later years created wonderful costumes for her daughter Barbara. My Aunty Bunny, sister-in-law to the other aunts, usually dressed up, and all my cousins would go along as walking characters.

Everyone, young and old, went along to the church hall dance for the first part of the evening, then as our eyelids began to droop, us young ones would be taken home. By this time my parents would have arrived, all the milking and other chores completed. Until I was about eleven years old when Father bought another car, they always came in Mr Jack Rockey's taxi. Father and Mr Rockey would head for the Golden Lion and Mother would catch up with all the news and gossip with her sisters.

When I stayed at Prospect on holiday, Aunty Lorna was always in charge of me. She was the only sister who was unmarried, and she was the youngest of the five sisters. My grandmother had had her family over an extended period of twenty-five years; my mother was the oldest and Lorna was twenty-three years younger, in fact she was only ten years older than me. She was different in character from her siblings. All my other aunties were small, quick and lively, talkative, opinionated, creative and ready for a laugh. Lorna was taller than the others. She was quiet, staid and placid with not nearly as much to say for herself, although this did not mean that she did not have strong opinions about things, she most certainly did. She had a well-defined sense of her own self-worth and would not budge on issues she felt strongly about.

She certainly looked after me well, and I knew that I could depend on her and she would see to all my needs. I slept on a little iron bedstead in the corner of the room while Lorna and Granny shared the double bed. There was a lot of bed sharing in those days, it was the only way of packing everyone in. During my childhood when I was holidaying at Prospect, there were still eight people sharing three bedrooms, and nine when I was there.

By the time I had reached my mid to late teens Lorna and I had "caught each other up". She was only ten years older, so by then we would go to dances together, and in my early twenties we had several holidays together. We got on quite well, although she was a very self-contained person. I always felt in her shadow. She had stunning looks, and seemed to me to be a cross between Princess Margaret and Sophia Loren. She had good bone structure, enormous green eyes and long black curly eyelashes. She was taller than I was and had an hourglass figure which was so desirable in the '50s. She always dressed in good expensive clothes, even in the days when she was not earning very much. She carried herself in an aloof manner and created an aura of mystery about her. I have walked beside her along Barnstaple High Street and watched people turn and stare at her as she made her way down the street. She must have realised that she was creating an impression but she never let on.

She left school at fourteen as everyone did in those days and began her working life helping with the family paper round. It involved cycling to Umberleigh to collect the papers from the train, and then delivering to customers in Umberleigh, Atherington, High Bickington and Burrington – in total about twenty miles all done on the pushbike. After she had delivered the High Bickington papers she went home to have her dinner. She then delivered the Burrington papers, eventually finishing about mid-afternoon.

Later she trained to be a school cook and worked at Beaford School for six years. She cycled there every day in all winds and weather, a distance of seven miles, and arrived for work at eight o'clock every morning. I can remember her occasionally spending the night at Wansley when it was snowy weather, as Wansley was much nearer than High Bickington. She then became the cook at High Bickington School, which was very convenient, and she remained there for ten years. However, she finished her career as a cook by becoming travelling supervisor for Devon County School Meals (she had learnt to drive by then), so altogether she did very well for herself.

I never understood why she did not marry as she was so attractive; maybe "Mr Right" did not come along and there was no doubt she would never compromise, or perhaps she was just too independent. They were a close-knit family and the sisters always supported each other. During the years while Lorna was working, my other aunties, Dot, Audrey and Kathleen, all regularly went to Prospect to clean and cook and help my grandmother, as much of the time there were four unmarried men living there.

There were very few opportunities for children of my mother's generation. My mother was extremely lucky to have had the chance to stay on at school and train to be a teacher. Like everyone else, Mother's brothers and sisters left school at the age of fourteen, and except for Lorna and Peter, the two youngest, the only school they attended was High Bickington village school.

*

My grandmother was born in 1885 and was Victorian through and through. As far as she was concerned men did not do any housework;

men went to work and women ruled the house. Basically, her attitude did not change even in more modern times after the war, when women discovered that they were quite capable of holding down a responsible job, and housework and motherhood were not necessarily the sole purpose in life. When Lorna came home tired after a long hard day at work, she was still expected to look after and wait on the men of the family.

My grandmother had had a hard life. Her mother had died in childbirth when she was only eighteen months old. She was brought up by her father, Thomas Headon, who lived at Hill Farm, Burrington, and she also spent a lot of her childhood years with her maternal grandmother and family, the Shoplands, at Ditchett Farm in Creacombe, near Rose Ash. She married when she was nineteen and had eleven children over a period of twenty-five years, my mother being the oldest. One child, Betsy, died of diphtheria when she was seven. It was not a very happy marriage, but there was no choice in those days, and like everyone else she just had to get on and make the best of it. However, although there were tough times and grinding poverty in the early years, she lived to enjoy her children and grandchildren and enjoyed mostly good health, eventually dying only six months short of her hundredth birthday.

*

I came to know my Aunty Bunny well during a six-month period when she came to stay at Wansley during the war. Mother's brother Gerald was in the army, and Bunny and my little cousin Philip came to stay for a weekend. She enjoyed herself so much that the vacation extended to six months. I expect my mother enjoyed the company and I certainly did, for it was the only time in my life that I had a baby to look after and fuss over. It must have been during the spring and summer of 1945.

My cousin Philip learnt to walk at Wansley and I loved having a little toddler shadowing me around. However, there was one occasion when I tried to leave him behind and I regret it to this day. I had been asked to go into the dining room to switch off the wireless. I suppose the wireless was considered too trendy and modish to be kept in the busy working kitchen, so, gleaming and shiny it was kept in what was then the "best room", and connected to the kitchen through the thick wall with wires to a crackly, Bakelite loudspeaker. I hurried up the passage intent on my task, trying to leave my little shadow behind. I switched off the wireless and rushed out of the dining room slamming the big heavy door behind me to stop Philip entering the room. I did not see that he already had his fingers around the hinge side of the door, and of course they were caught and crushed. Oh, the pandemonium and noise! I was mortified and ashamed that I had hurt my dear little cousin. The adults rushed around with Dettol and cold water and dressings, and Philip howled and cried for what seemed like hours. We pushed him around in his pram to try and calm him, and wheeled him up to the vegetable garden to pick new green peas straight from the pod, his favourite, but all to no avail. Nothing could comfort him or assuage his pain. He still has a mangled top to one of his fingers to this day, but he assures me that I am forgiven. He says that anyway he is unable to remember it, but I have never forgiven myself.

Poor Philip, another occasion that sticks in my mind is when he jammed his head through the banisters. The two of us were going up the big wide staircase together and he was in front of me crawling up on his hands and knees. He turned the corner and began to ascend the second flight and we stopped to have a conversation. He stuck his head between the banisters to talk to me, on the lower flight. He put his head through the wide part and then his neck slid down into the narrow area. Then when he tried to pull his head out again, he was unable to. Neither of us had the wit to realise what had happened. I ran screaming down the passage to the kitchen to summon adult assistance, and Ruth and my mother came rushing to the rescue. It was a while before they managed to compose themselves enough to realise how to reverse the situation. My mother was pushing from the lower flight and Ruth was tugging from behind on the upper stairs, and I was convinced they were going to pull his head off. I provided sound effects by running up and down through the house from kitchen to front door, screaming at the top of my voice. Eventually my mother collected herself enough to tell Ruth to lift his head up to reach the wide part and then gently pull him back out.

*

Aunty Kathleen, or Aunty Kath as she was always called, was one of the quieter sisters. For many years I thought her name was Aunty Calf. I had an Aunty Bunny and consequently did not think it odd to have an Aunty Calf. It was not until my mother saw me write her name one day (when I was in my teens!) that she realised my misunderstanding. In my defence though, I have to say that the previous owner of the post office had been Mr Bull, and of course the district nurse was: Nurse Stear…

Aunty Kath did not have time to go gallivanting around to dances and socials and fairs like the other aunties. For one thing, she was married and had a small son, my cousin John, but mainly because she ran High Bickington Post Office, which was a full-time and demanding job. During the war years my Uncle Arthur was away working as an engineer for the Bristol Aircraft Company, so Aunty Kath had to cope on her own. She had had plenty of experience of post office work as she had worked there for ten years for the postmaster, Mr Bull. When Mr Frank Bull retired in 1936 Uncle Arthur bought the house and business for £400, and Aunty Kathleen ran it. Officially, she could not become the postmistress as women were not allowed, so my uncle applied for the job and became postmaster. Aunty Kathleen did not officially become postmistress until after the war when attitudes and regulations changed considerably.

Back then not many people had a telephone. It would have been mainly businesses, the doctor and the gentry. It was a manual exchange and when people needed to make a phone call Aunty Kathleen had to plug them in. She was used to dealing with all the plugs, and people were only allowed three minutes for a call. When their time was up, she had to say,

"Your three minutes are up," and then disconnect them.

Perhaps the most annoying calls were the night-time ones, as there was no time limit during the night and people could chat for as long as they liked. Often the Misses Barton who lived at Little Silver House would make calls after a dance or party. They would ring their friends after they got home in the early hours of the morning, to chat over the evening. They talked for ages and seemed to be oblivious to the fact that someone had connected them and was sitting there yawning and longing to go back to bed. Over the years Aunty Kath must have been privy to many secrets, but she was the soul of discretion and any nuggets of information or interesting titbits of news stayed safely within sealed lips and went no further.

Of course, sometimes the night calls were for an emergency. Aunty Kath remembered one night when there was an urgent call from Burrington. Someone in the village had gone into labour and Nurse Stear was needed as quickly as possible. It was a terrible night, windy with torrential rain. Aunty Kath flung a mac over her nightdress, grabbed a flashlight (no street lights in those days) and rushed out to wake Nurse. At the time, Nurse Stear and her aunt, Miss Evans, were living in rented accommodation at Little Bickington, which was a farm in the village. Aunty Kathleen ran down through the village and up the muddy lane to Little Bickington. Luckily Miss Evans slept at the front, as Nurse was quite deaf. However, hammering on the door did not wake anyone and Aunty Kath had to resort to throwing stones up at the window. Eventually she succeeded in waking Miss Evans, and shouted up that Nurse was needed at Burrington. Nurse Stear did not waste any time; she quickly dressed, grabbed her bag, jumped onto her motorbike and roared off into the night. Maternity services in North Devon have certainly changed since those days.

There were not many toys around during the war years and after, and none of us children expected very much. Cousin John was one

Nurse Stear on her motorbike.

of the lucky ones who always seemed to have a few special toys. I remember a Hornby train set and watching while John played with it, although under the supervision of my Uncle Arthur. I found it fascinating but would not have dared touch it. To my joy and delight though, I was allowed to ride John's tricycle. How I loved riding that tricycle around the village (so few cars back then). I would dearly have loved one for myself and dropped endless hints to my parents, but all to no avail.

The best times of all with my Aunty Kathleen, Uncle Arthur and John were the summers at Putsborough. They were magical and it seemed as if no one else in the world had discovered Putsborough. My uncle, aunty and cousin had enjoyed a few holidays in a caravan at Bream in Somerset and they thought that it would be lovely to have their own caravan. Uncle Arthur, being practical and inventive, decided he would build one himself and then it would be exactly as he wanted. It was built in his workshop and consisted of a mahogany frame which was clad in aluminium. He built it in the early 1950s, and during the summers it was kept at Putsborough. They spent weekends there, and during the summer holidays they lived there as much as possible. Aunty Kathleen saved up her holidays and I believe Aunty Audrey helped run the post office while she was away. My uncle worked in Barnstaple at Shapland & Petter and commuted to the caravan. Their reason was twofold: it gave them wonderful holidays and the fresh air was beneficial for John's asthma.

The joy for me was I was often invited to stay, and I have wonderful memories of Putsborough. We would drive there in Uncle Arthur's car and old Mr Tucker would be standing at the gate collecting money from day trippers, although there were very few compared with these days. Uncle Arthur referred to him as "Old Man Tucker" and I gathered that he was quite a character who did not suffer fools gladly. He seemed to get on well with my uncle though, and they always had a chat and cracked a few jokes together. During the week there might be a few cars in the field and even at the weekend there would not be more than a dozen. Our caravan was the only one there most of the time; just occasionally it would be joined by someone else. For much of the time the beach was ours, and often during the week there would be no one else in sight.

This was when I discovered the joys of surfing, although these days it is called belly boarding, or body boarding. It was very simple: we just waded out to catch a wave, tucked the wooden boards against our stomachs, stretched out, and then experienced the glorious feeling of being swept into the shore. I just could not get enough of it. The most exhilarating times were when it was nearing high tide and the waves were sweeping in close to the cliff. I can remember many evenings riding in on the breakers with John and no one else in sight anywhere. Aunty Kath would be up in the caravan preparing tea, ready for my uncle when he returned from work, and we would be down on the beach amongst the noise and the seagulls and the surf. As we rode in on the waves it seemed as though we were the only two individuals in the universe.

I think that access to the beach has been altered since those early days, because then the only way down from the field was a steep, narrow, zigzag path down the side of the cliff. When the tide was out, like so many North Devon beaches there was an endless expanse of flat sand, wonderful for running, ball games, sandcastles and searching for shells and flotsam and jetsam. As the beach curved towards Baggy Point it met the rocks and rock pools. At low tide these rocks and pools provided endless interest and entertainment. I felt like a mountain goat as we leapt from rock to rock playing out imaginary games, the rock pools providing many hours of happy exploration and foraging as we carefully pulled aside the fronds of seaweed, or lifted pebbles and discovered crabs, shells, shrimps, little fish and many other delights to hoard in our buckets. Once again, we were almost entirely on our own and rarely saw another person.

Quite often the day was rounded off by a walk around Baggy Point. My Aunty Kathleen was a lifelong walker and most evenings we either walked along the cliffs around Baggy, or walked along the bay towards Woolacombe Beach. It was a peaceful and relaxing way to round off the evening, chattering and reminiscing as the sun gradually headed across the sea towards the horizon.

*

About fifteen years later, when Brian and I were in the early stages of our relationship, we drove down from Bristol one weekend to spend some time in Devon and I decided that I would take him to this wonderful secret beach. I had been living away from Devon for nearly ten years and I thought that I would like to reacquaint myself with Putsborough. He said that he was a Wiltshire man and didn't much like beaches, and didn't like sand in his sandwiches. I told him that this beach was magical and he would be won over by it.

Disillusion began to seep in as we became stuck in a traffic jam on the way to Braunton. *Surely this could not be North Devon*, I thought to myself; it was nearly as bad as notorious Bridgewater. It was hot in the car and Brian looked cross and was muttering things about "waste of time" and "better to turn around and go home". I assured him it would all be worth it when we got there.

It all began to really go downhill as eventually we tentatively made our way along the little narrow winding road from Croyde in the direction of Georgeham and Putsborough. I could not believe the amount of traffic on the road, and every few seconds we were having to reverse or pull into the hedge while another vehicle scraped past us. I could not recollect that it was ever like that when Uncle Arthur used to drive us, in fact we rarely met anything at all.

By now the atmosphere in the car was murderously black and I did not dare say a word. I just hoped that all would be redeemed when we reached the idyllic spot. However, I knew that all was lost when we reached the final hundred yards, and I eagerly looked over the hedge to the field below where the caravan used to sit, so often in solitary splendour. To my horror, I looked down upon a sea of cars neatly parked in rows, covering the field from end to end. There was no doubt about it, Putsborough had definitely been discovered.

*

I had two other special aunties who were my father's sisters. Aunty Gwen lived in Roborough at Newcombes Farm and was married to Uncle Chesney, and they presided over a boisterous household of cousins, and I loved calling in to see them. My grandfather also lived with them and was always pleased to see me. "A chip off the old block," he used to say as he ruffled my hair. Aunty Gwen was kindly and welcoming and always made a fuss of me. I loved sitting around the farmhouse table for a meal with my cousins. It was so much noisier than our quiet mealtimes at Wansley; there seemed to be an abundance of food and Aunty Gwen bustled around making sure everyone was content and had all that they needed.

Aunty Doris lived at Dolton. She had never married but had devoted her life to bringing up a young cousin, Mildred, who was always known as Mid. Mid's mother had died of tuberculosis a few months after her birth, and there were two older boys left motherless as well. At the time, Aunty Doris was seventeen and working at Dolton Rectory. The family asked her if she would mind giving up her job to help Uncle Ern look after the baby. Probably it was only meant to be a temporary arrangement, or certainly Aunty Doris would have thought so. She was the sort of person who would want to be helpful, and after the trauma of the death everyone rallied around to do all that they could to help. Well, time passed by and the temporary arrangement somehow became the norm. Aunty Doris, kindly, hardworking and generous, made a wonderful housekeeper and surrogate mother for Mid and the two boys; it would be impossible to find anyone better.

Doris was pretty and had a happy, pleasant personality, and apparently young men called and wanted to take her out, but they were sent away, or she was told that she could not leave the baby. To a certain extent she probably did it all from a sense of duty, and I am not saying that she was unhappy with her position. Obviously, she was very fond of Mid, but in the end her chance of marriage and children of her own was sacrificed. Our side of the family felt quite strongly about it. She would have made a wonderful wife and mother. I remember my mother discussing it with me when I was old enough to question and understand such things. She thought that if Aunty Doris's mother had been alive she would not have let it happen, but my grandmother, Beattie, had died when Aunty Doris was about twelve years old and there was no one to stick up for her.

I always looked forward to visiting Aunty Doris at Dolton, and she was naturally delighted to see us. She made such a fuss of us all, particularly me, and laid on the most wonderful spread. She was an excellent cook and the table would be laden from end to end. I heard many years later from a friend in Roborough village that Aunty Doris's hospitality and good cooking were well known, and Roborough people and children were always made welcome at Higher Rosebank, particularly on carnival nights. It did not have to be a special occasion though, and I was told that you could always be sure of a welcome, even if you were just cycling through Dolton and needed a break.

Aunty Doris never forgot a birthday or Christmas, and her cards were special, as they were the only ones I received through the post. I knew that on my birthday the postman would be coming especially for me, and of course there was always some money inside. At Christmas she sent a present. I never spent the money, as there was nothing to spend it on at Wansley and we never went shopping. It was always put into my money box. This was a Post Office-issue box made of strong steel. It was green and could not be opened. It said, "Property of the Post Office," and I always had the feeling that once the money went inside, it no longer belonged to me. It had to be sent to the Post Office Savings Department, and then Savings Certificates could be

My grandmother and her nine children, 1968. L–R: Audrey, John, Dot, Gerald, Lorna, Granny, Peter, Molly, Arty, Kathleen.

My grandmother and her nine children, 1980. L–R: Gerald, Peter, Lorna, Granny, Arty, Molly, John, Audrey, Kathleen, Dot. Weddings became less formal during the twelve years between the two photographs. In the 1968 photograph all the women are wearing a hat; in the 1980 photo only my grandmother and my mother are wearing a hat.

(Left) Uncle Chesney and Aunty Gwen.
(Right) Uncle Bill Norman.

The caravan at Putsborough. Toilet tent in the background –
also the old Putsborough Hotel, which burnt down.

purchased. My mother sent it away on several occasions and I know that I did have Savings Certificates. It was all very boring though, and consequently money did not mean much to me.

The postman did not call every day, in fact he only called when there was some mail that he considered to be important – a registered letter, or a parcel, or an epistle that he felt was eagerly awaited. Usually the mail was left in the drainpipe at the end of the lane, and if it had not arrived by the time the milk churns were taken out and put on the stand, then someone had to walk out to collect it later in the day.

If we needed to post a letter it was relatively easy, as there was a post box at Ten Oaks. It did not take long to walk up the lane, and run down over the field and down the road to Ten Oaks. There was one collection a day, in the middle of the afternoon. It was also possible to post parcels without walking to the village. We just had to wait by the post box, then when the postman arrived he would take the parcel to the village and the next day Mr Rockey would tell us the weight and how much was owed.

I was always fascinated when Mother sent a parcel, as the process involved the use of sealing wax. There was nothing as useful as Sellotape in those days, and parcels were wrapped in brown paper and tied with string. She always kept a couple of bars of sealing wax in a tin on the mantelpiece and it was quite a ritual, as she heated the end of the bar with a match and slowly the hot wax would drip onto the knots. The waxy smell was pleasant – even addictive – and the soft wax quickly hardened around the knot to ensure that it was secure.

*

My uncles did not have such an impact on my life as the "aunties", who in later years called themselves "the Old Ants", and us, their nieces and nephews, "the Young Termites". The uncles played their role in the background and as far as I was aware were the supporting cast for the aunties. I am sure that was not how it was in reality, but to me they were always more shadowy figures. I was always a little wary of Mother's oldest brother, Arty. With his black hair, hooked nose and fierce gaze from deep-set eyes under bushy eyebrows, he was quite intimidating, and his gruff voice and brusque manner did not help. My own boys were also wary of him and called him "the Big Bad Wolf", even though his hair was grey by the time they knew him. Of course, being a Snell he was not big, and he certainly was not bad.

He was a man's man, and a countryman through and through. He loved hunting, farming and rabbiting and the countryside. He spent his demob money buying a few fields and helped his youngest brother, Peter, with the farming, although he worked as a stonemason all his life. During the First World War, while he was still a schoolboy, it was common practice to excuse the older children from school and allow them to work in the fields during harvest time. Arty recalled working in the fields with other boys aged between ten and fourteen. Their job was to gather the corn which had been cut with a reaper around the edge of the field, and tie it into sheaves by hand. The sheaves were bound with twists of corn which they made themselves.

During the Second World War it was not necessary for him to join up to fight, because as a stonemason he was in a "Reserved Occupation". Nevertheless, he felt that he should, and enlisted in May 1942 when he was thirty-six years old. He embarked for France on 26 June 1944 and served as a gunner throughout the war in North West Europe. Post war he was with the British Army of the Rhine. He did not speak much about his war experiences other than comment on the blissful silence when the guns stopped, and amazingly the birds began to sing again.

He would never have sent away for his medals as he was not interested. An old army pal who went to regimental reunions thought that he should and did all the paperwork for him. To everyone's surprise when the medals came, he had an extra one, the Defence Medal. Apparently, he had volunteered to rescue someone who was traumatised and wandering about in no man's land towards the enemy lines.

I always thought that Uncle Arty was a quiet, reserved man who did not socialise much. I was staggered to see the large crowd of people who turned up for his funeral. On making enquiries I discovered that as well as his involvement with hunting, he spent every weekend in Torrington at the Conservative Club, and he had a wide circle of friends. He enjoyed reading and had a good general knowledge, and consequently was often in demand for quiz teams. He also enjoyed evenings at the Golden Lion playing euchre. I obviously did not know him very well at all.

Fate dealt my Uncle Dion a cruel blow and his life was blighted by severe asthma. It was well before the days of cortisone and modern drugs, and he spent much of his life just struggling to breathe. There are not many photographs of him, but of the few we have, in almost all of them he is smoking either a cigarette or a pipe! When I commented about this to an aunty, I was told that no one realised at the time that smoking was a health hazard, in fact quite the opposite. Apparently, a doctor had even suggested to my grandmother that when Dion became old enough to smoke, a cigarette may do him good and be beneficial for his lungs.

When he was well enough he enjoyed watching a spot of horse racing, and friends would take him to Exeter or Newton Abbot. I remember him with admiration as he never complained, and he was so brave. He told me to get out and enjoy life, which was something he was unable to do.

Several of my uncles were quiet figures on the fringe of my life really. The men were the breadwinners and at work most of the time, so I saw less of them. I had more contact with Mother's brother John than most of the other uncles. He came to Wansley regularly, mainly for the shooting. The first encounter I can really remember was when I was very young, probably only three or four years old.

"Now then, Molly," I heard him say, "can she sing?"

They both looked at me expectantly and I was put on the spot.

"Well, she knows some nursery rhymes," Mother said dubiously.

I realised that for some reason this was important, and I was expected to be able to sing. I think I had a go at "Polly Put the Kettle On". I knew the tune well but I could not make my voice produce the notes that were in my head. Not much was said when I finished, but I knew anyway that it had been a poor performance. I was aware that all the family enjoyed singing and gathered around the piano at Prospect, and so it was obvious that I was expected to be able to hold a tune.

Many, many years later when John was giving me information for the family history book, I realised that the most exciting time of his life was the wartime years, and I suppose this must have been true for many other young men. They travelled, went places and did things that they would never have done otherwise.

John received his call-up papers in 1943 when he was nineteen, and had to report to Chichester Barracks. Until then the furthest he had ever been from High Bickington was to Taunton for a cricket match. He was involved with the Normandy landings a few days after D-Day. He fought with the American army at Cherbourg. He drove his jeep on the railway tracks across the flooded Netherlands. He was involved with the crossing of the Rhine, which was an operation almost as big as D-Day, and later he went to Burma.

All these events were still vivid in his mind and he had so many funny stories to tell. It was obviously a time of great adventure for him despite all the dangers, and I secretly wondered whether the rest of his life after the war was almost an anti-climax. He would never have done any of those things if it had not been for the war. How lucky we are these days to have the freedom and opportunity to travel almost anywhere in the world, safely and just for pleasure. Like many others, he did not bother to send away for his medals. I think he was pleased that he had done his bit and felt lucky that he had survived when so many had not. He said that he tucked the war away in the back of his mind and just got on with the rest of his life.

Another uncle who enjoyed the war was Uncle Bill Norman who was married to Aunty Audrey. He had already joined the Territorial Army, and when war was declared he was one of the first to be called up. He loved it all and made rapid progress through the ranks and became a sergeant. He was another uncle who came to Wansley quite regularly and I liked him very much. He had a go at teaching me how to shoot with an air gun. He lined tin cans up along the top of the half-door across the little courtyard by the kitchen. I stood by the pump trough and aimed at the cans. It was good fun and I really enjoyed it. I thought that my shoulder felt rather sore and later that night when I undressed, I saw that it was black and blue. Many years later he spent some time at Underhayes in Torrington with my boys, and they lined cans up along the wall across the garden. One of the main reasons for the uncles to visit Wansley was for the shooting, and rabbit pie and pigeon pie were part of everyone's staple diet.

*

Relatives, neighbours and school friends were not the only people who entered my life, for as a result of the war, many paths crossed unexpectedly. The turmoil in Europe and the consequent upheaval of nations and humans meant that people found themselves in unlikely places, and unexpected friendships and relationships were forged. The ripples spread far and wide and even the quiet backwater of Roborough did not escape.

Probably the first sign of change in my life was Dixie. She was our Land Girl and she entered my life when I was four or five years old. She came from Norwich and arrived one evening about six o'clock, just before my bedtime. Mr Jack Rockey had brought her in his taxi from Portsmouth Arms station. No one had explained much about the situation to me, but I gathered that Father needed some extra help around the farm. Mr Marles was quite elderly and he could not drive a tractor, and I was told that most young men were in the army fighting the Germans. A women's Land Army had been formed to help on the farms and grow food which was so badly needed.

Her real name was Edna Dixon but she was always known as Dixie. She was young and very pretty with bubbly fair hair, and she dressed with flair despite the restrictions of wartime clothing coupons. It did not take me many minutes to sum her up and I soon knew, with certainty in my heart, that she would be warm, dependable and good fun. I fell in love with her there and then, and always adored her.

Mother's reaction was rather different, although I did not discover this until sometime afterwards. I overheard a conversation and Mother was telling her sister about Dixie's arrival that evening.

"Well," Mother said, "when I saw her get out of the car in her high heels and stockings, and with all her makeup and nail varnish, I thought to myself, 'What on earth use will you be on a farm?' But I couldn't have been more wrong."

Mother certainly was wrong, as Dixie soon settled down and took to all aspects of farm work with good humour. She was willing to learn, asked if she did not know, and was ready to give everything her best effort. I believe one of her first tasks was getting acquainted with the cows and learning about milking, and it was not long before Father had her on the tractor and making herself useful out in the fields. I overheard quite a lot of adult conversation and I gathered that once introduced to ploughing, she seemed to have a natural eye for it. As she gained experience she could plough a pretty good furrow, and neighbouring farmers seemed to find a reason to pass by, look over the hedge and pass comment. Maybe it was not just the ploughing they were interested in, as Dixie was attractive. Father was quietly proud of his protégée and I heard him remark that if there had been any ploughing matches during the wartime years, she would not have disgraced herself.

I think there were several young men in the area who were sweet on Dixie and I doubt whether they were bothered if she could plough or not. I understand there was one gentleman who lived at St Giles who was quite heartbroken when she returned to Norwich, but in actual fact Dixie was engaged. She had a fiancé, Robin, who was in the RAF, and towards the end of the war she returned home and married him.

At the end of the war, after one more Land Girl who did not make much of an impression on me (no one could really replace Dixie) came the German Prisoners of War. I never found it strange or incongruous that one moment they were our deadly enemies, threatening our country and bombing our cities, and the next moment they were living in our house. For as long as I could remember my uncles had been away fighting them. Every playtime the boys at school played a noisy game which involved running around with their arms outstretched called "Bombing the Germans", and at night when we used the chamber pot which was kept under the bed, we referred to it as "The Jerry". We had cowed under the stairs as German bombers flew over to wreak havoc on towns in South Wales, and standing on the high ridge in Cow Field, my parents had watched the glaring red sky far away in South Devon, as Plymouth was destroyed.

Suddenly, there they were, in our midst and part of our lives, and I can only put it down to my parents' tolerance and understanding that I accepted them so readily. I knew that the war was over, and Mother explained that they were Prisoners of War and waiting to return home, and while they were waiting they were going to work and do something useful.

Once again, we were lucky and shared our home with someone we all liked and respected. Erich was quite old for a soldier; he must have been forty or more. He had a strong accent but could converse reasonably well in English. His parents were farmers, and Erich had been brought up on the family farm in East Germany. It was obviously a large farm and very modern and mechanised. Apparently the shippens, or their equivalent of shippens, were all tiled with white tiles and food to the cattle was provided by a system of conveyor belts.

Erich had worked on the farm but he wanted to join the church and when war broke out he was in a seminary training to be a priest. His brother was working on the farm with Father. It was not long before the brother was called up and Father asked Erich to come back to the farm to help, as he could not manage on his own. Of course, it was only a matter of time before Erich was called up as well. We do not know what happened to the farm and the family in the Eastern Sector under the Communist regime. My parents had Erich's address and would have liked to have kept in touch, but in the end they decided not to write, in case it caused trouble and difficulties for the family. They felt that if it had been fine to correspond he would have written first.

I always liked Erich and as with Dixie I instinctively knew from the very beginning that he was "OK" and trustworthy. He was like a kindly uncle. I always felt that in some small way I kept a link with him over the years. He left a religious leaflet behind. The text inside was written in German, which I could not understand, and on the outside was a coloured picture of the tomb on Easter morning with the rock rolled aside and an angel standing nearby. I kept it for many years as a marker in my bible until eventually it fell to pieces.

Heinz was the next POW to cross our path. He was very different and arrived shortly after Erich left. I guess he was in his twenties – handsome and charismatic. I felt rather shy of him to begin with, but before long we became good friends. He spoke good English when he first arrived, with only a slight accent, and it improved all the time. I overheard my mother remark that his English was very good and he had a wider vocabulary than Mr Marles. He was very fit and athletic, and amazed me by vaulting over some of our five-bar gates.

He made it his mission to train me up as a gymnast. Perhaps he saw that I had a flair for it, I was always upside down on my hands or doing headstands. When I went to Totnes High School for Girls a few years later I soon realised that gymnastics was the only sport for which I had a natural talent. I always loved the gym classes, and although gymnastics during the 1940s and '50s was not a big phenomenon like it is now, nevertheless I was always chosen to participate in displays. Although I was small I could jump well and had no problem with the box or horse, and I knew I could shine on the bar or floor work. Heinz soon had me balancing and walking on my hands. He taught me how to do back flips and cartwheels, and how to do the movements correctly without straining myself. He taught me quite a lot of intricate manoeuvres and how to link them together. I enjoyed it all immensely; it was much better than Mrs Blackmore's "drill".

Heinz was a very sociable person, and by now several of the farms had Prisoners of War living in. There was Franz from Combe Farm and Oegan from Owlacombe Farm (or maybe it was the other way round) and at weekends they would get together. Quite often it was at Wansley. They all seemed genial, pleasant and happy. I think that everyone felt a sense of relief and happiness that the war was over in Europe, and although there was still chaos and mess, at least all the dreadful fighting and bombing had come to an end.

I certainly felt relieved and happy, for although I had been sheltered from all the worst aspects of the war, it had always been the bogey in the background. I knew that it was a serious worry for the adults, and the only times I had ever really been shouted at and scolded was when I made a noise when the adults were clustered around the crackly Bakelite loudspeaker trying to listen to a news bulletin. My life had always been punctuated by the "guns on Dartmoor", for there was a firing range there, and from a very early age I learnt to distinguish between the guns and thunder. The searchlights were another manifestation of the war during those years, and as we crept home in Mr Rockey's taxi, along the little lanes around Ebberly and back to Wansley late at night from a visit to grandparents at High Bickington, we would watch them sweep across the countryside and sky. I suppose they were checking and keeping watch for enemy aircraft, but I always thought they were trying to find us and I found it quite scary and creepy, and was always relieved when we arrived home.

Probably the thing I disliked most about the war years was my gas mask. It was a Mickey Mouse gas mask and if that was supposed to endear it to me, it certainly did not work. I hated it. It was so claustrophobic, and when it was pulled over my face I thought I was going to suffocate. The only way I could be persuaded to wear it was to play "Bears", so all three of us, Mother, Father and I, would crawl under the tables and up and down the passages on our hands and knees playing "Bears".

During those war years I had learnt to read, and although we did not have a daily newspaper I came across newspapers in my relatives' houses at High Bickington, and we had various magazines from time to time, and of course there was the wireless. All news was about the war, even cartoons, there was nothing else at all. It was war, war, war. I remember asking my mother what was written about in the newspapers or on the news before the war, but she did not give me a very satisfactory answer. She seemed vague, as though even she could no longer remember what had made the news in those pre-war days.

After Heinz was repatriated Wilhelm came along and he stayed with us for many years. We always pronounced his name the English way, William, which was also my father's name, although he was known as Bill. Wilhelm decided not to return to Germany after the war. His father wrote to him and said that the country was in turmoil and there was no work, so if he had a job and was happy, stay in England. He lived with us for several years and then he married Mr Marles's daughter Winnie and they moved into the cottage next door to Winnie's parents. The cottages, known as New Buildings, were in the valley under Burridges Wood, and later my parents turned them into one property and renamed it Melland Hill. Wilhelm was good-natured and easy-going and looking back I realise he played a large part in my life until I left home to train to be a teacher.

There were some evacuees who came to Roborough village for a few years and they mostly integrated well. In fact, one or two still return to the village. These days the plight of the evacuees is viewed with pity and sympathy, but my recollections are from the receiving end and they are not all happy memories. There were two evacuees in particular who worried me. They were staying at New Buildings and walked home along West Road with Mary and me. They were two older boys who seemed very noisy, big and rough. At the time, there was a quarry along the road about a quarter of a mile from the village, where all the local rubbish was disposed of. There was a steep drop down from the road and they threatened to throw us over the hedge into the quarry. Mary and I tried our hardest to avoid them, so after school we would either hurry home in front of them, or linger until we thought they were well ahead. Luckily, they did not stay for long.

Those war years certainly were a melting pot and there were others who unexpectedly crossed our paths. There was a DP camp at Holsworthy. This was for "Displaced Persons"; these days we would say refugees. They worked on local farms and came to work every day in a lorry and were collected again and taken back to the camp in the evening. I believe there was a mix of nationalities, but for some time a Pole called Walter came to help out at Wansley. He was a big, tall, strong man and was a great help to Father on the farm. I gathered from adult conversation that the Polish nation was well regarded, and admired for its war efforts. Walter came regularly to Wansley for some time, and Mother would often relate the tale when Walter single-handedly held an awkward cow while Father drenched it.

Walter used to tease Mother about the kitchen clock because she always kept it half an hour fast. I think that she liked to look at the time and know that she was half an hour in front of herself. After the war, Walter settled in Birmingham and unexpectedly visited the farm sometime in the '60s. Mother saw a strange car pass the kitchen window and assumed it was another rep. It was summertime and the kitchen door was open. Suddenly there was a huge body filling the space and a familiar voice said,

"And I see the clock is still half an hour fast!"

So, that was how it was. During those years our lives entwined with unlikely people from unlikely places. The tentacles of war reached into every corner of the land, even the remotest of areas, and brought change that was permanent. For better or worse all our lives were affected from old to young, and nothing would be the same again.

Dixie in her Land Army uniform.

(Left) Dixie dressed in sacks and with a pitchfork,
probably as a "country yokel" picture to send home.
(Right) Holding hands with Erich. Mother must have been busy with the
dinky-curlers the night before. It always miffed her that I had almost
straight, straggly hair, while Cousin John had the most beautiful curls.

(Left) With Wilhelm.
(Right) Heinz.

Erich with the Fordson spade-lug tractor.

Food: Glorious and Not So Glorious

"Mary, do eat up! Just think of all those poor little starving children in the world who would love to have that."

I seem to remember those words or ones very similar being used quite a lot when I was young. Well, as far as school dinners were concerned those poor little starving children were welcome and I would gladly have given it to them if they had been around. I did not have a big appetite, but it was not the meals at home that I could not bring myself to eat, but meals when we were out, and that included school dinners. Our school dinners were cooked at Beaford School, put into metal containers and delivered to us by truck. How did they manage to make them so ghastly?

There was nothing that I looked forward to. The smell of the oil cloths that were spread on the tables instantly made me feel queasy and even now remind me of school dinners. It was mostly the same day after day. The potato sat on the plate staring balefully in various shades of grey, as though to say,

"Eat me if you dare!"

The cabbage was yellow and stringy, the gravy lumpy, and the minuscule pieces of meat tasted of nothing that I recognised. Even worse was macaroni cheese – a thick, stodgy, glutinous mass. I resisted delving into it too deeply for fear of what I would find. We had to eat the first course or make a very good attempt before being served our "afters". These overall were more edible, but only just: spotted dick, rice pudding, tapioca, sago, and prunes and custard. The one that I really struggled to eat was semolina. It was the texture, I just did not know how to get it down, and sometimes I would sit there with the bowl in front of me until afternoon lessons began.

Suddenly, school dinners began to improve. Instead of the grey potato and sticky macaroni, we began to get cheese sandwiches. There is nothing wrong with bread and cheese, you know where you are with it. True, there was no spread on the sandwiches but I was not used to marg on them anyway. Even though we made our own butter we never put butter or margarine on sandwiches, it just seemed excessive and over the top.

Initially the sandwiches did seem to cause the two teachers some concern, and after a huddled discussion Mrs Blackmore stood on a chair and delved into the emergency cupboard high up in the wall. She brought down packets of crisps and then a few packs of biscuits. Wow! Bread and cheese, crisps and biscuits; school dinners were definitely improving.

Sadly, this wonderful state of affairs only lasted for a few days. I overheard Mrs Petherick, who had connections and family at Beaford, telling my mother that the cook had been sacked.

"Mrs Squire, he was selling all the kiddies' food on the black market. He didn't care what they had to eat, all he was concerned about was making himself a bob or two. Did very nicely, I expect."

I was not quite sure what the black market was, but I had heard a lot about it and I knew that anyone involved was up to no good.

It was not long before another cook was found. I think that we had to take a packed lunch for a short time and then the meals were once again delivered from Beaford – exactly the same as before. The recipes for glutinous gunge, grey potato, stringy beans, yellow cabbage and inedible semolina must have been passed on from cook to cook.

As I became older and was allowed to sit at a desk to eat my dinner there were unexpected benefits. The ruse was to sit at the back next to the wall. There were holes in the wainscoting, almost certainly dry rot, and it was possible to surreptitiously dump spoonsful of unwanted food, and so feed the mice. I hope they grew to like semolina.

*

Like any true Devon Maid, I was brought up on junket, yeast cake, parsley pasty, hog's pudding, rabbit pie, stew, home-cured ham and bacon, brawn and clotted cream. Everything was fresh and grown or made on the farm. It goes without saying that the best food of all is what you grow or gather for yourself, and although I suppose I was a fussy eater, I always enjoyed fruit, especially apples either raw or cooked. We had two orchards. The older of the two was Top Orchard, which was situated on slightly higher ground near the walnut trees. This orchard contained mostly cider apple trees. The main orchard was larger and adjoined the vegetable garden on the west side, opposite the main frontage. This was packed with a variety of apple trees – cookers, eaters, a few cider apples – and one Victoria plum.

I liked the orchard, it was a pleasant place, and the moss and lichen-covered trees were mature and laden with fruit most years. They were old varieties. I remember the Newton Wonder with its deep red skin and the pink colour extending into the flesh. It was a dual-purpose apple, suitable for cooking or eating. The Listner tree bore small green apples with little black blemishes. They were good eaters, tangy and sharp. Then there was the Cornish Gillyflower, the Worcester Pearmain and the Russet but my favourite was the Blenheim Orange. Apple varieties all taste so different and it is difficult to become bored with them.

I was always free to sample fallers or any that I could reach, and I soon discovered that the very best way to enjoy an apple is to sit in

one of the trees while eating, preferably with a good book. There was one tree at the bottom of the orchard, which grew at an angle not far from the ground. It was easy to clamber along the trunk and reach a fork in the branches and lean back in comfort against the mossy boughs and contemplate or read.

At some stage during the autumn, Father and Mother decided that it was time to gather in the ripe apples from the trees before the autumn winds blew them down. The ladders and big baskets were brought out, and the men climbed the ladders, carefully picked the apples and placed them gently in the baskets. The women stood at the bottom of the ladders to steady them, offering advice and pointing out any apples they had missed. It was always a pleasurable and satisfying task. Then the heavy baskets were carried indoors, upstairs to the apple room. This was a long room about twenty-two feet in length, although not very wide. It was accessed by a small door from the little bedroom which eventually became our bathroom. Two rows of wide shelves lined all the walls. These shelves were covered in newspaper or lining paper, and the apples were carefully placed on the paper in neat rows, all the same varieties together. The room was on the north side above the dairy and was always cool. From here the apples were used during the coming months, and some varieties lasted well into the following year.

During the dark winter months when I was little, I was enticed to bed with an apple. My night-time treat, and a ritual for many years, was to go into the apple room with Mother and choose an apple to eat in bed. Together we would walk up the wide shadowy staircase, into the little bedroom at the top of the stairs and lift the latch of the small door into the apple room. The sweet smell of apples would assail our nostrils and Mother would hold the candle aloft while I searched in the shadows along the shelves to find the perfect one. "Nenom" Orange (I was unable to pronounce the word correctly) and Russets were my favourites. Then it was off to my bedroom and I would snuggle into the feather mattress, pull my eiderdown up to my ears, cuddle my toes against the sock around the stone hot water bottle and munch my apple while Mother placed the candle on the shelf and told me a story. As a teacher she had a vast repertoire of stories, everything from "Brer Rabbit" to "The King of the Golden River". She always made me say a prayer before I got into bed, but in the chilly winter months I rattled through it as quickly as possible before hastily jumping into the warm, welcoming bed.

I cannot remember many apple pies during those early years, but that was probably because we did not have an oven in the house. The old black stove in the shed was not lit that often and I think that it was more of an ordeal than a pleasure to use, but there was always plenty of stewed apple and everyone loved apple suety pudding. It was easy to boil things over the open fire, and suety puddings of all kinds were part of the staple diet.

All desserts were accompanied with lashings of Devonshire cream, and like everyone else we made our own clotted cream. The milk was poured into large white enamel milk pans which were placed on the cold slate slabs of the dairy. They were then left for the best part of a day so the cream could gradually rise and settle on the top. Then the pans would be carefully carried and placed on a low heat and slowly the cream on the top would turn into a creamy yellow crinkly crust. It had to be removed from the heat at just the right moment, for if the milk began to boil the cream would be spoilt. When ready, the pan was carried back to the dairy and placed on the cold slabs again and left until completely cold. Then the thick crust of cream was carefully lifted and removed from the milk by means of a flat skimmer with holes in it. Any excess milk drained through the holes back into the pan and the folded crusty layers of cream were placed into glass bowls ready for use. The milk left in the pans was skimmed milk and we drank it in tea or coffee, or made desserts with it.

There was always a bowl of cream on the table at teatime which was round about six o'clock and was always the same. There was bread and butter and jam and Mother's little currant and sultana nubby cakes, and there was always the bowl of cream if anyone fancied some. Except for Christmas Day or some other special occasion, this meal was the same all the year round. The only slight variation was on Sundays, when the jam was replaced with Lyle's Golden Syrup. Bread and cream with syrup on top is out of this world and I always had it for Sunday tea. The cream was spread on the bread instead of butter (quite thickly) and the syrup or jam on top, likewise cutrounds which were a kind of yeast bun. It was not often Mother made scones.

We made our own butter as well. Mother only made enough for our own use and it was made once a fortnight. Standing in the middle of the dairy was the separator, and this was how we obtained the cream to make butter. The separator was a large piece of apparatus securely fastened to a plinth in the middle of the dairy floor. It was coated in red enamel and was quite smart looking. At the top was a large oval container, red enamel on the outside and white enamel inside. It was very heavy and was probably cast iron. It was big enough to hold a pail of milk. The cream was separated by centrifugal force. It was usually one of the men who operated it, as the handle had to be turned quite quickly. As the milk flowed from the container at the top into the centre of the separator, it was whirled around, and the cream came out of one spout, and the whey flowed into a bucket at the bottom. The whey was then used to mix up mash for the pigs and poultry.

Then it was the women's job to make the butter. We did not use a churn for butter making, as it was only a few pounds for ourselves. Mother had a round wooden butter tub. It had a flat wooden bottom and wooden sides about six inches high with handles. The separated cream was poured into the tub, and stirred and beaten into butter with two wooden butter pats. In the winter, it was cold enough for the butter to be made in the dairy, but as the warmer summer days came it had to be coaxed in the large slate pump trough outside the back door. We would block off the drainage hole at the end of the pump trough and pump up cold water from the well. Then we could stand the butter tub in the cool water while we leaned over the pump trough frantically beating the cream, willing it to "come". On bad days, usually sultry weather, it could take ages and everyone would take a turn to bash and beat; even when I was young I was expected to take a turn for a while. When eventually the lovely creamy golden ball of butter began to form, Mother would add a little salt, then take it to the dairy on a wooden board. Then she would pat it and beat it into half-pound blocks. The butter pats were plain on one side and ridged on the other. She always finished with the ridged side and then made the Wansley pattern on the top with the edges of the butter pats. Then the butter would be wrapped in greaseproof paper and stored on the cool dairy shelves. We made our own butter for many years and as I grew older I was entrusted to make it, although I preferred it fresher than Mother, and I put in less salt.

All the jam was homemade. There was a good-sized fruit garden adjoining the vegetable garden. We had gooseberries, blackcurrants and loganberries, and when the fruit was ripe everyone was expected to help pick. We each equipped ourselves with a chair, usually the low chairs which were kept in the shed for poultry plucking, then we selected a bush and worked steadily to fill the bowls and basins. Most of the fruit was used for jam, although some was stewed or made into pies. During the war years when there was rationing it was a problem obtaining enough sugar. No one was allowed sugar in tea or coffee, we had to make do with saccharine, and each year Mother saved as much sugar as possible for the jam-making season. She stored it in a high cupboard in the hall. This cupboard was above the door where there was a discrepancy in ceiling heights between the two parts of the house. She called it "Lord Woolton's cupboard" after the Minister for Food, and in it she kept her secret hoard of goodies, such as sugar, sultanas and any other scarce commodities. The jam was then stored in a large cupboard in the dairy. My favourite jam was the loganberry, it was delicious, although the fresh fruit was sharper than raspberries.

The fruits of the hedgerows were also used and I always looked forward to the blackberry-picking season. There were many places where the blackberries grew on Wansley but our favourite spot was David's Plat Lane. This was a mysterious lane which just led to some fields. It was not a poky, unpretentious lane but was wide and looked as though at one time it had been important. It connected to the main lane opposite the two elm trees in the Lower Court. It was so wide it needed fencing on either side of the gate, which was always closed to stop cattle and sheep from wandering along. It was not used very much by man or beast. The lane ran along beside the Mowstead and Grinding Stone Meadow and ended in a large mossy square area surrounded by trees; in the springtime this was covered with a carpet of primroses. Each year I picked the primroses under the trees, and strangely some of them were tinged with pink like garden primroses. Mother said that she had once found a garden rose struggling in the hedge; we wondered if once a cottage had stood there and perhaps someone named David had lived in it. There are no records to verify any of this but it was a theory that we both liked.

We also liked the blackberries which grew lushly and abundantly on either side of the lane. Father did not pare back the hedges often as the lane was not used much, and the brambles grew in profusion. We would take our hooked sticks, basins and baskets, arms and legs well covered to protect against prickles, and set off for a day blackberrying. Blackberry and apple pies were an autumn treat much looked forward to, and apple and blackberry jam another satisfying delight.

David's Plat Lane also provided our source of hazelnuts, along with the Mowstead which was the rick yard. Hazel bushes lined the hedges of both, and picking nuts was another enjoyable annual ritual. The hooked sticks and baskets were needed again, and then we would take the nuts home and lay them out to dry. They would then be packed into the big Huntley & Palmers biscuit tins and stored in the dairy ready for Christmas.

*

The first time I can remember looking forward to food and a meal with real anticipation was a "harvest home" at Wansley. It was the tradition to invite everyone who had worked on the farm during the year to an evening meal, usually after the last of the crops had been gathered in. All the preparations filled me with great excitement, and I ran around getting in everyone's way. The dining room table was a huge oak one with ornate carved legs. It could be made even bigger by cranking a handle which slowly opened it in the middle so more leaves could be inserted. It then took several white damask cloths to cover it. Just to have a meal in the dining room was a real thrill, for the room was only used on special occasions.

At the first harvest home I can recollect, my eyes were almost level with the top of the table; by standing on tiptoe and holding on to the table's edge with my fingers I was just able to look along its length and survey the glorious offerings. I had never seen such plenteous bounty: plates of cold ham and beef, parsley pasty and egg and bacon pasty (we would now call it quiche). There was a brawn which Mother had made in a china mould, and it shone and wobbled on the plate in pink glory. She had also made jellies and blancmanges in china moulds, and they sat there like quivering, glistening castles. There was also rice pudding, blackberry and apple pie and of course lashings of Devonshire cream. There was not much hot food, for this was still the era of the open fire and hot food was difficult. Mother provided boiled potatoes to accompany the savoury dishes and of course various homemade pickles and chutneys. It was a feast fit for a king and this was bang in the middle of the war, so there was no shortage of food on a farm despite rationing.

I expect I was three or four years old at the time and I can remember a few harvest homes, but the tradition petered out due to the war and demanding times. Increasingly work on farms was being done by Land Girls and Displaced Persons, and a celebration of any sort was no longer appropriate or fitting. When harvest suppers were later revived, they became a community effort involving the church and parish and were usually held in the village hall.

*

The pig killing was another busy time. During the war there was a limit on the number of pigs which could be killed for personal use, and permits had to be obtained. In those days before fridges and freezers, although the meat was salted and cured, it was still a large amount of meat for one family to dispose of, and the bounty was shared with friends and neighbours. I know that my parents arranged pig killing with our neighbours, the Waldrons, also with my grandmother who lived at High Bickington. This meant the meat was staggered throughout the year and everyone kept record of how many hocks or sides of bacon etc. were owed to each other.

It was no use Father sending me indoors when Mr Rogers came to kill the pig, the squeals penetrated even those thick walls. I used to cover my ears with my hands but I could still hear the shrill terror. I always felt glad if it was a school day and I was well out of the way.

The dead pig was heaved onto the pig form and carried across to the little courtyard. The only beam which was suitable for hanging the carcass was under the slee, slap bang outside the back door, between the door and the pump trough. While it was hanging there, cold and stiff after the skin had been scraped and the innards removed, it was so easy to open the door forgetting it was there, and walk straight into it. It is amazing how cold, hard and clammy a pig carcass is. Not exactly a pleasant experience in the dark, late at night when dashing out to the pump for a cup of water or making the last trip to the lav across the yard before going to bed.

My mother was the best brawn maker and Mrs Waldron was the best hog's pudding maker, so whenever either family killed their pig, Mother made the brawn and Mary's mum made the hog's puddings. I loved both, and these days it is difficult to find brawn or hog's puddings which taste anything like those of my memories.

The brawn was made from the pig's head. This would be soaked in brine for a few days. Then after soaking and washing, the head would be gently boiled, usually with some peppercorns. When cold, the meat would be cut into small pieces or minced and then put into basins and bowls with the stock. Mother usually pressed them down with a weight and left them several days to set. As well as using pudding bowls and basins Mother also used her china jelly moulds. I think this was the point at which I became confused, and muddled brawn with jelly. I remember being left alone in the kitchen when I was very little; there was some emergency outside with the cows and all hands were needed. There was brawn and cream on the table. I liked brawn and managed to help myself to some, but for some reason I imagined that it was always accompanied by cream. I must have been thinking of jelly, and I will never forget my mother's look of horror and disgust when she came back in and found me tucking in to a plate of brawn piled high with clotted cream. I realised that somehow I had got it wrong, but as far as I can remember it did not taste too bad.

Mrs Waldron always had to wash and scald the intestines before she could make the hog's puddings. They were like big fat sausages, and it was the groats which gave them their unique flavour. They were so delicious fried up with eggs and bacon, and it was heaven if it was the time of the year when field mushrooms were available as well.

All the salting and curing of the bacon and hams took place in the salting house. This was a room just off the dairy. It had a red brick floor, and there were several wooden trestles with salters (big, oval, earthenware crocks with flat bottoms and straight sides) placed on them. Mother bought big blocks of rock salt and small amounts of saltpetre. Every farmer's wife had her own recipes for salting. I think that my mother used mostly salt and saltpetre for the sides of bacon. It was well rubbed in all over, and the bacon stayed in the salter and was regularly turned and rubbed for about three weeks. Along one side of the salting house was a bacon settle. This had a bench seat like an ordinary settle, but all along the back were cupboards where the sides of bacon could be hung until ready and needed.

During the war the hams were done much the same way, but later when it was possible to obtain more sugar, Mother added brown sugar and mustard, and sometimes syrup to the mix. Hams took longer to cure, about four to six weeks, and then they were wrapped tightly in pieces of old sheet or pillowcases and hung from the beam in the kitchen. Always, there were hams hanging all along the kitchen beam, the sheet covers gradually turning yellow from the smoky fire.

When fattening the pig at least twenty score was aimed for, as everyone liked fat bacon and ham with fat on it. (A score is twenty pounds.) Quite unlike these days when the golden grail is as lean as possible. There was no doubt though that the meat from those big fat pigs had a flavour and succulence that cannot be matched by the animals bred today.

The salting house, being cool, was a very good place to keep Mother and Father's supply of tobacco. Although Mother smoked shop-bought cigarettes when she was out, at home she always rolled her own. She felt that it was more economical, but she always made them so large it was necessary to put two papers around each one. During the war, White's Stores brought a fortnight's supply at a time.

We had two or three large earthenware jars which Mother called "steins" (we pronounced it as stains) and these were ideal for storing tobacco or cigarettes. They were stood in the salting house against the bacon settle, and I still associate bacon with tobacco.

*

It might sound as though we were entirely self-sufficient and were in no need of outside provisions, and no doubt in times past that had been true. However, Mother no longer regularly made bread, so the baker's twice-weekly round was welcomed. I think he called on Mondays and Thursdays, the butcher called on Tuesdays and Fridays, and the grocer came once a fortnight on a Wednesday. We were very reliant on these weekly rounds people, for there was a period of about ten years when we had no transport of our own. True, there was the lovely Singer car, Father's pride and joy, which was kept in the "trap house", which gradually became known as the "garage". Aunt Leah and Uncle Jack had bought the Singer sometime in the late 1920s or early '30s. Uncle had never learnt to drive, in fact I doubt whether he was even interested in driving, so it was left to my father, who thoroughly enjoyed the experience. I imagine it was probably Aunty who nudged Uncle into buying the car, for she always liked to be one ahead of the neighbours.

Father always loved motoring and cars, and at the time there was not even a driving test. He just learnt by trial and error as did everyone else. He had come to work on the farm with his uncle because he wanted to work the horses and I know he always loved the horses. However, I think he soon embraced the internal combustion engine with enthusiasm and always found cars interesting. Unfortunately, I can never remember him driving the Singer because during the war it had to be laid up. Petrol was rationed and there was none for social use. Like everyone else he was allocated petrol and TVO (tractor vaporising oil) for farm work, but there was none allowed for personal use.

Uncle Jack, my father and Aunt Leah, with the Singer car.

I know Father loved that car, and every so often for a treat he would take me into the trap house and we would sit in it. It smelt satisfyingly of leather and oil. Mother would sit in the front with Father, whilst I sat in the back. We would pretend the war was over and we could go for a drive to Torrington or High Bickington or maybe to the seaside, which actually was not very far away. Father always patted and touched the car with affection and kept it polished; I know that he was looking forward to the day when he could drive it again.

I am not sure why it was sold, and I cannot remember when it happened, but one day I realised the car was no longer there and I would never have a ride in it. I was told that they would buy another sometime. I think it was sold towards the end of the war and probably for financial reasons. Having had to spend the wartime years without transport, they realised that it was not strictly necessary and it was possible to manage without.

*

All our provisions came from Torrington, and it would have been difficult to manage without them. Our butcher was Mr Arthur Squire, no relation, we thought, but almost certainly hinged on the family tree somewhere. It was a Torrington bakery, Pophams, I believe, and our grocer was Mr Jack White of White's Stores, South Street. The orders were regular and did not vary much. During the war they could only deliver what was available and what our coupons allowed.

In later years when we eventually did buy another car we occasionally visited Torrington in between the deliveries, usually on the Thursday market day, and stocked up on a few extras. There was a long counter along one side of White's store and several chairs for customers. Mother would sit down and say what she wanted, and the goods would be weighed out and put on the counter. The sugar and currants were weighed into sturdy, dark blue paper bags. I was always fascinated by the bacon and ham slicer, although Mother never bought any from the shop. It zipped through the hams so quickly and thinly I could not keep my eyes off it.

A trip to Torrington during the early 1950s usually included two special treats: one for Mother and one for me. Mother's treat was a packet of Passing Cloud cigarettes. She could not obtain them from White's Store so she had to visit a tobacconist in the square. It was a small shop run by an elderly lady who I think was called Miss Blatchford. Passing Cloud cigarettes were unusual as they were not round, but oval shaped, and had a scented smell. I believe they were quite expensive and were Mother's guilty secret treat.

My treat was a visit to Mrs Squire's sweet shop. It seemed to be an Aladdin's cave of sugary delight and was presided over by a lovely gentle lady with a kind smile. Apparently, she had several children, and I thought they must be the luckiest children in the world to have a mother who ran a sweet shop

Confectionery was something that rarely came my way, and until I was eleven years old my life was almost devoid of sweets. I suppose the supply of sweets that Mr White could obtain during the war was limited, and the town folk used their coupons to snap up what was available. Whatever came into his store certainly never reached the rural customers, or maybe he did not sell sweets as there was a sweet shop in the town. Either way, Mother never had the chance to use any of our sweet coupons. Consequently, I can remember almost every occasion when I was offered a sweet and it was usually visitors who came bearing the mouth-watering, ambrosial delights.

My first encounter with chocolate was my last for many, many years. It was an old acquaintance of my mother who came to spend an afternoon at Wansley and she brought some chocolate buttons. I was about four years old and it was the first time that I had ever seen chocolate buttons, or indeed chocolate of any description. Mother let me have the whole bagful, probably because it was such a special treat. It was a little triangular paper bag with a pointy bottom.

It was poultry-feeding time and the three of us made our way down the track, under the fir trees towards the pond and the poultry houses in the Mowstead and Lower Court. I walked along clutching my bag of goodies, systematically feeding myself with the delicious chocolate buttons. By the time we reached the Mowstead I was delving for the final few buttons which were hiding in the point. It was then that I began to feel decidedly queasy, and before you could say "chicken coop" I brought all the buttons back up as I was violently sick. Oh dear, what a waste! From then on chocolate always made me feel ill. It made my mouth dry and immediately brought on a headache, and I was in my forties before I could look a Milk Tray in the eye and contemplate eating it with any gusto.

Having had a childhood free from sweets and very few sugary goods of any kind it would be nice to boast of beautiful, gleaming, healthy teeth. Sadly, there is no justice in this world, and by eleven years old I had a mouth full of decay. Several teeth came out and the rest were stuffed with mercury fillings. The dentist, Mr Copp of Torrington, must have done a good job, for more than six decades later those same teeth are still holding their own and serving me well.

*

Christmas brought Christmas puddings which I found quite exciting. Mother always made her own and I enjoyed it because it was "an event", and everyone on the farm had to have a stir and make a wish.

"You must never tell what you have wished for or it won't come true," I was warned.

During rationing, which went on for many years after the war was over, the Christmas pudding recipes were quite imaginative to make up for lack of fruit and sugar. Mother always had her hoard in Lord Woolton's cupboard, but apple and carrot were also used to bulk things up. A sixpence was hidden in each pudding, and after much stirring and wishing, the mixture was spooned into china basins, covered with greaseproof paper and then tied off with a cotton cloth, usually a piece of old sheet, and boiled for several hours over the fire. Mother always made four puddings: one for Christmas, and the other three for our birthday treats. Mother's birthday was in March and Father's and mine were in April.

Mother did not bother with birthday cakes, we had the puddings instead, but she did make a Christmas cake. We all loved marzipan and she only did marzipan icing. She decorated the cake by making marzipan fruit – apples and oranges, bananas and strawberries – by colouring the icing. She made them look quite realistic, or at least I thought so, and the cake always seemed very festive.

There may have been marzipan bananas on the cake, but I had never actually seen a banana. I thought I knew what bananas tasted like, because Mother sometimes used banana flavouring for her little cakes. The flavouring was quite strong and I rather liked it. One day, when I was probably nine or ten years old, I walked into the kitchen from school and she beckoned mysteriously.

"Follow me, I have a surprise," were her enigmatic words.

I trotted along behind her as she led the way down the passage towards the dairy. She clambered onto the slate slab to reach up to the high shelf above and to my amazement triumphantly produced a bunch of bananas. Well, I was excited, as I had heard much about bananas which were unobtainable during the war and for many years after. She peeled one for me and with due ceremony I took my first bite. Oh, what a disappointment, it was so insipid and not at all as I had imagined, not at all like the banana cakes, which I now know tasted more like pear drops than bananas. I tried to hide my disappointment and pretended to be more impressed than I actually was. I could see that Mother was thrilled with her surprise and wanted me to enjoy it. It was some time though before I learnt to appreciate the subtle flavour of bananas and grew to like them.

Christmas puddings and Christmas cake made an impression on me and linger in my memory, but I cannot recall much about the first course on Christmas Day. I know that during the 1950s and '60s we always had goose for Christmas dinner, but before that I really have no idea, so I was obviously not very interested. I do recollect that my parents and Aunty and Uncle liked to get the dinner over and done with in time for the King's speech. We always ate Christmas dinner in the kitchen, even though it was a special day. It was just easier. Afterwards we retired to the dining room and sat around politely to listen to the wireless, and everyone stood for the National Anthem at the end of the broadcast. The rest of the day was spent in the dining room and tea was served there, which made it special.

The one meal of the year that does stand out in my mind however, was a summer feast known as "Roast Duck and Green Peas". This was a ritual meal every summer and was looked forward to by everyone. Back then vegetables were only eaten in season, and the meal was held when all the requisite vegetables had reached their peak. The peas had to be sweet and tender and accompanied by freshly dug little new potatoes, but the one item which was essential was newly pulled little white turnips. I adored white turnips and so did everyone else. There was only one way to prepare them, and that was to mash them with lashings of Devonshire cream and pepper. What a feast, I can think of nothing to beat it.

I loved white turnips so much that I enjoyed them raw. I have many happy memories of walking out in the fields with Father, and he would pull a little turnip out of the ground, wipe off the earth with a hanky or his thumb, produce his pocket knife and peel off the skin. Then he would cut off the leaves to leave a little short stumpy stem. The little white turnip sitting on top of the stem looked rather like an ice cream in a cone, and I used to pretend I was eating ice cream. To me it certainly tasted equally as good.

A real ice cream was quite a rarity and was confined to trips to the seaside, which did not happen very often. During the 1940s I think that the only visits to the sea were Sunday school outings. I always went on the Roborough Sunday School outing although I did not attend the Sunday school. I was ill so often, and Mother said that walking to school five days a week was more than enough and she did not expect me to go on a Sunday as well. I also usually managed to be included on the High Bickington Sunday School outings if there were any spare places, and I think occasionally the Ebberly Chapel trips. That though would have been the total of outings and opportunities to indulge in ice cream.

My other memory of wartime seaside outings (other than ice cream) was barbed wire. Saunton Sands was one of the popular destinations for Sunday school trips and I suppose the dunes were mined in case of enemy invasion. The general public only had access to certain parts of the beach. The path from the parking area down to the beach was heavily lined with rolls of barbed wire, presumably to make sure no one strayed off the path onto the dunes.

There were other unexpected ice cream treats though, but always in the middle of winter when it was snowy and very cold. When it began to snow and it looked likely that we were in for a cold spell Mother would say,

"I think this will be a good time to make ice cream."

Oh, the joy and happiness her words brought. She made her ice cream with milk, eggs, sugar and vanilla essence. All the ingredients were beaten together, then gently heated in a saucepan. Then came the part I most enjoyed: taking the bowl out into garden and pushing it down into the deep snow. Mother insisted that the bowl of ice cream was first placed into a baking tray of salt. She said that would help it to freeze quicker, and we always had mountains of salt for curing the bacon and hams. We then carefully carried it all out onto the lawn where no animals would be likely to find it and piled and pressed the snow all around. Then of course was the excruciating wait while it froze.

Time moved so slowly, and there would be several excursions out to the garden to stir. As far as I can recollect it was always dark before it was ready and could be called ice cream. It was great fun though: dressed in coats and wellies, holding our flash lights and equipped with bowls and spoons, we ventured out onto the snowy lawn in the dark and, literally shivering with anticipation, began to scoop out the frozen delights. It did not matter if it was not frozen in the middle, we scooped around the edge and then when we came back for seconds, the middle would be frozen as well. Mother never set a limit on how much we could eat. Homemade ice cream happened so infrequently that we indulged ourselves to our heart's content and only stopped when we could eat no more, or it was all gone.

Homemade ice cream, roast duck and green peas, Christmas cake and puddings were all once-a-year treats. Our daily meals were much more mundane and plain. We ate lots of rabbit and I loved rabbit pie or stews. One of the men would usually do the skinning and Mother would draw out the innards. Rabbit pies were particularly delicious as the meat seemed to produce a very tasty jelly, and there was often fried rabbit and onions for supper. Everyone loved hotpots and stew with doughboys, and any kind of meat could be used, but I seem to remember, unsurprisingly, a lot of poultry going into them. Old hens or broilers were boiled up and very tasty they were. My favourite titbit when we had poultry was the gizzard, and Mother always made sure that it was on my plate. Pigeon pie was another staple and a very welcome standby.

Breakfast was a simple meal, eaten at about nine o'clock after the milking was finished, the churns taken out to the end of the lane and the stock attended to. On weekdays it was always toast, the exception being Sundays when Father had egg on toast. We had an expanding toasting fork, and the handle could be pulled out so it was possible to sit well back from the open fire, and still hold the bread near the coals and flames. Glowing coals were best, and of course each side had to be done separately. The person doing the toasting always ended up with rosy cheeks despite sitting as far away from the fire as possible, and it was not unknown for the bread to fall off the toasting fork into the flames. When we had the Rayburn, we opened the fire door, and the toast was done in the same way with a toasting fork. Even when electricity was eventually connected to the farm, my parents did not bother with a toaster and continued to use the Rayburn fire and the toasting fork.

A cup of tea was the drink favoured by adults and I gradually grew to like tea with sugar. The adults sweetened theirs with saccharine but I think Mother always managed to provide a little sugar for me. Not a lot of coffee was consumed; Mother and Father usually had one small cup mid-morning. Camp Coffee, which was a chicory essence, was the only kind available. We all drank a lot of water straight from the pump; it was cold and refreshing, and there was nothing better to quench one's thirst on a hot summer's day. The one drink which was available in abundance was milk, but I just could not drink it neat. It was the smell of the shippens, especially first thing in the mornings. I managed it on cereals, and we all often had milk broth for supper. A slice of bread was cut into small squares and put into a china basin and hot milk was poured on. Very often it was a savoury broth and then the bread was soaked in an Oxo or Marmite gravy, or if lucky some beef jelly and dripping.

We had a large vegetable garden which was always crammed with food, although it could be a little late in the season. It was an unspoken rule that crops in the fields had priority and the vegetable garden was not attended to until everything else was shipshape. Main crop potatoes were grown in the fields, but we always had an early variety of little new potatoes in the garden. There were peas, broad beans, runner beans, carrots, beetroots, leeks and an abundance of parsley, shallots and onions. Some cabbages and cauliflowers were grown in the garden but kale and Brussels sprouts always seemed to do better in the fields. A few weeds flourished in the garden as well. The men did their best but at certain busy times such as harvest, the garden had to take a back seat.

There was a certain routine and Sunday was the only day we always had a dessert for dinner. It never varied and was always junket – Miss Muffet's favourite dessert. Mother was making junket for Sunday dinner before I was born and she made it every Sunday until she moved into Torrington at the age of eighty. It was always sprinkled with nutmeg and served with Devonshire clotted cream and was much enjoyed by everyone.

Sundays were also unique because it was the only day of the week when the adults had an alcoholic drink. Mother and Father always had a glass of cider to accompany their Sunday dinner, and I was allowed one from early teens onwards. The meal at one o'clock was always referred to as "dinner", unlike now when it is usually called "lunch", and it was our main cooked meal of the day. The evening meal was "tea" or "teatime", and consisted of bread and butter, and cakes.

We made our own cider, which was wickedly strong scrumpy cider. We never drank it ourselves though, and our Sunday cider when I was young was Whiteways, which was a sweet pleasant drink commercially produced. Later we bought Sammy Inch's cider, which was made locally at Winkleigh.

I think that cider had been made on our farm for many, many years, probably from time immemorial. An old 1852 map showed that both the two Rushy Plats were originally orchards, so there would have been several acres, and there was a big cider press in a building called the "pound house". This was a two-storey building which adjoined the stable and ran in front of the main house and turned part of the lawns into a sheltered courtyard. There were two rooms downstairs: the one on the left was known as the "teddy house" or "potato house" and was where we stored our winter crop of potatoes. Father also stored the onions in this room. He strung them up in the same way as the Breton Onion Johnnies and then hung them all around the walls. The room on the right was the "pound house". There were two rooms upstairs as well, but they were never used for anything and were quite bare and empty.

It was obvious that the building had once been a dwelling, and Great-Great-Great-Uncle Francis had apparently always called it "Servants' Hall". There was a fireplace in the potato house and behind the door a staircase wound its way up to the next floor, where a door connected the two upper rooms. The pound house was bigger and wider than the potato house, and on the garden side where it jutted out beyond the potato house was an outside lavatory. It was a double lavatory where two people could sit side by side. Mother and I found this very amusing. Perhaps the lavatory had been used for keeping ducks or geese in the more immediate past, for there was a wire netting enclosure in front. It was south facing and the sun streamed in. It was an excellent place to escape and read a book, especially if I felt that I was required for unwanted chores. I could tuck myself away in there and no matter how much they called or searched, no one discovered me.

We made cider most years, and there were many cider apple trees in the two orchards. In the pound house much of the room was taken by the big cider press. I suppose it was a typical cider press, with a large square wooden base with a lip around and a channel for the cider to drip out. There was an upper board, and by turning a handle, the gears and cogs brought the upper board down for squeezing. There was an apple crusher as well. Against the far wall next to the stable was wooden racking where the barrels were stacked. There was one huge barrel – a hogshead, I believe. It held about sixty gallons; the other barrels were smaller.

Collecting the apples for cider making was a completely different occasion than picking for winter storage. Ladders were not used, as the apples were shaken out of the trees and then scooped up with the fallers and put through the apple crusher. They were then put onto the base board of the press on layers of straw. This was called "the cheese". I cannot remember how many layers there were, but the cheese was quite thick. Then the handle was turned and the top board was gradually brought down and the cheese would be subjected to a substantial pressure. It was left like this for some time and the juice was collected and put into a barrel to ferment. I know that when rationing was over, Mother used to put sultanas or raisins in as well, and eventually quite a potent brew was produced. We never drank it ourselves but it was enjoyed by all the men on the farm and was relished at harvest time and threshing days. Father never passed it around until it was time to go home as a parting thank you, as no doubt the work would never have been finished.

*

Threshing days were busy days both indoors and outdoors. A large contingent of men was needed, and all the farms around lent each other men for the big day. Our threshing was done by the Murch family of Umberleigh; for many years it was Leonard Murch, (my "sixpence for a kiss" friend) and then Harry Murch. The big steam engines were gleaming noisy monsters, and while they were in the area they visited all the farms that needed them. Occasionally Mary and I would meet them on the way home from school. It was quite a frightening experience to meet these huge noisy machines because they filled the narrow lanes. I remember an encounter one evening just as we reached Molland Hill. The hill was very steep and I guess the brakes on the threshers were nothing special. The men shouted and waved and hollered at us to get out of the way. We were both terrified and dived through the hedge and ran down through the woods.

Threshing days were always quite fraught indoors as well, as there were usually ten or a dozen men to feed. For the morning drinking Mother sent out teddy cakes with bacon on the top and plenty of tea, the same as she did at harvest time. Everyone came in for one o'clock dinner and somehow we had to squash them all round our kitchen table. Mother always cooked a ham for threshing day, and it was accompanied by boiled potatoes and pickles. "Afters" was often apple pie but I remember her making suety pudding with golden syrup sometimes. After the frenetic morning rush to prepare everything on time, we then collapsed and had a bite to eat ourselves.

I was always needed indoors to help Mother on threshing days, but there was one occasion when I had to go out and help the men. I think I was about sixteen or seventeen, not long after leaving school. They were a man short, and they decided that I would be capable of standing on the rick and pitching to the thresher. I think that I managed quite well and I certainly enjoyed it. It sticks in my mind though, because I lost my wristwatch. It became entangled with a sheaf and went into the thresher. I know I should not have worn it but I didn't think. I did not realise that I had lost it until we stopped for drinking. I was upset because it was special and the only item of value that I had ever possessed. My parents had given it to me for passing the entrance exam to grammar school and I was very attached to it. Nowadays people change watches to suit their clothes but it was a rare possession back then; not many people had one and I had expected to keep it for the rest of my life. Mr Leonard Murch saw that I was upset, and later in the day when we had finished the work he spent some time searching through the straw and douse. He came into the kitchen later with the remains in his hand; it was all in pieces, many mangled pieces. He was a kindly man and it was very good of him to look for it, as searching through all that straw must have been like searching through a haystack for the proverbial needle.

There was one other element to threshing days in later years when Harry Murch came with the machinery. Aunt Leah's sister, Polly, was Harry's mother-in-law, and when she became elderly she went to live with Harry and his wife, Ida, who was her daughter. Threshing days at Wansley were a good opportunity for the two sisters to meet up and have a chatter, and Harry used to bring Polly out for the day. Leah and Polly were always very pleased to see each other to begin with, but as they were both talkative, opinionated and argumentative ladies, by the end of the day they had always fallen out, and poor Mother was even more stressed trying to keep the peace between them.

It is fair to say that we were reasonably self-sufficient and most of our food was grown, produced and made on the farm, and that applied to fodder for the animals as well. The baker, grocer and butcher supplemented our needs, and likewise the cattle feed firms who brought scientifically balanced meal and cattle cake for the cows, poultry and other stock. Almost every rep or delivery driver stopped to have a cup of tea, and several of them arranged their rounds so that their stop coincided with either a lunch or a dinner break. They would gladly seek out the chair nearest the fire, gratefully accept a cup of tea and tuck into their sandwiches and have a chatter. They could then set on their way again rested and warm, for in those days vehicles did not have heaters and it could be very cold when driving for long periods.

Our food was plain, simple and fairly basic, and had probably been much the same for many generations. Recipes were handed down, and daughters learnt cooking skills from their mothers. I knew no one who had foreign holidays or even travelled very far in Britain, so meals such as spaghetti bolognaise, pizza, lasagne, paella were totally unknown. Cheese was either Cheddar or Stilton and no one drank wine. We enjoyed fish, particularly herrings which Mother usually baked in vinegar. I was about thirteen before I came across a curry, and vegetables such as aubergines, courgettes, mangetout and sweet potatoes were a complete mystery. Our food was good honest stuff though. It kept out the cold and provided the fuel for our hard-working days, and, looking back, many of the people I knew lived healthy lives well into a good old age.

Pastimes

We were always busy and there was not a great deal of leisure time. Farming activities always came first, particularly the animals. It went without saying that the welfare of the stock was of the utmost importance, and no matter how tired we were, how late it was, if an animal or animals needed attention, their needs came first.

During the winters, it was not unusual to return home in the early hours of the morning after a dance or hunt ball, change out of my finery into trousers and old clothes, warm some milk, grab the Tilley lantern and battle my way out into wind and rain, up into the shelter in the orchard or one of the sheds to feed the tame lambs. When little lambs are young, like babies they are unable to last for long periods without a feed. Normally I would feed them late, about eleven o'clock, and then make sure they were fed first thing in the morning, but if they missed that late feed then they would have to have sustenance during the night. It was an annoying chore after dancing the night away somewhere and then driving home, often many miles. However, I was always welcomed with such rapture and joy, sometimes almost being knocked over by the greeting when I eventually made it to the shed, that my heart melted and I forgave them all the inconvenience they had caused.

Fortunately, sometimes hobbies and necessities overlapped, and as far as Mother and I were concerned, knitting and sewing fell into this category. A large majority of clothes were homemade, and making a dress or knitting a cardigan was something that we both enjoyed. I had learnt the basics of hand stitching at primary school and had made garments during domestic science lessons at grammar school, but I really learnt how to sew from my mother. She taught me everything: how to alter patterns, how to lay them on the material, the order in which to make up a garment, the tricks to make sure a hem was even or seams did not sag and the importance of a neat seam inside and out. I learnt how to make button holes, where it was important to tack and where it was possible to get away without tacking, and I learnt the importance of pressing and finish.

Mother aspired beyond Butterick and Simplicity patterns. For her nothing would really do except Vogue. They were always more stylish and of course more complicated, and when money became a little more plentiful she subscribed to *Vogue* magazine as well. She made all my school clothes during the 1940s and into the 1950s when life was constricted by clothing coupons and lack of availability of all necessities.

About 1952 or 1953 things began to brighten up, and as I gazed into shop windows I noticed that clothes and materials no longer looked so drab and utility; gratifyingly materials with pretty colours and patterns were emerging. After leaving school at the age of sixteen in 1954 I made almost all my own dresses and skirts and pinafore dresses. Our huge dining room table was most useful as it was easily possible to lay out the material and patterns for cutting on the table, and it saved having to crawl around on the floor to cut out, as many people did.

Mother was very proud of her hand Singer sewing machine. That machine certainly earned its keep, for it not only made our clothes but was used to produce curtains and soft furnishings as well. Sometime in the 1940s Mother had acquired a vast amount of parachute material. There seemed to be acres of it. It was a rather pretty turquoise colour and we used it for linings for skirts and dresses for years. We were still using it in the 1960s, and I believe I used the last of it to line a skirt in the 1970s.

As life began to brighten and lighten up in the 1950s, colourful materials for furnishing as well as dressmaking started to appear in shop windows and magazines. Mother and I looked at the rooms in the farmhouse with a critical eye and we agreed that the place needed a makeover. Very little had been done during the war years and immediately after, except the occasional coat of distemper, and now there were pretty new emulsion paints available, so much easier to use. We eyed the faded blue and white gingham curtains in the kitchen which had been there all my life, and we knew they had to go.

Mother didn't do things by halves and she could not resist bright colours and patterns. I believe she bought the material in Banburys in Barnstaple and she brought it home in triumph. It was a David Whitehead fabric, upmarket and probably quite expensive. It was bright red with a modern black and white motive on it. It was definitely going to transform the kitchen and wow everyone who walked through the door. She had bought enough to not only make curtains but also to cover a small sofa, cover cushions for Aunty and Uncle's fireside chairs and make seat pads for the dining chairs.

By the time she had finished, our kitchen would not have disgraced any glossy magazine and we basked in a glow of favourable comments. There was only one small hiccup that we discovered later. The pattern on the fabric was futuristic and Mother had decided that it was tulips, and hung the curtains accordingly. We then found out, probably from a magazine, that it was supposed to be lampshades and

Mother in the kitchen with Bob, Judy and Ginger, the upside-down David Whitehead curtains in the background, 1960s.

so it was upside down. We decided that it did not matter, as no one knew what it was meant to be anyway.

Mother was delighted when I passed my driving test and was then available to take her places, especially sales (house sales or farm sales). She loved sales and rummaging around in secondhand and junk shops. I sent away for my provisional licence in April 1955 on my seventeenth birthday and I took my test the following September, the week after Barnstaple Fair. I had been driving the car in and out of the lane and around the yard for some time, and of course I had been allowed to lurch around on the tractor in the cornfields and up and down the lane since I was ten. My Uncle John, Mother's brother, took me out for driving lessons, and I always had the opportunity to drive Father to market and other places and get in some extra practice. When I took my test I had done quite a lot of driving. Our car at the time was a Hillman Minx. We had to double de-clutch to change gears and the brakes were capricious, and not to be relied on when reversing.

My uncle was a thorough and exacting teacher, and the first thing he made sure I could do was to hold the car on a hill with the clutch and throttle, as we could not drive any distance without meeting steep hills. Before long I could have held the car on the side of a mountain. About a month before my test I had some lessons to polish up my driving and get in some town practice with Mr Bartlett. He was a retired farmer from Bradworthy. He was interested in, and involved with, the Young Farmers' Clubs and gave driving lessons to members. He had a pilot's licence and had his own light aircraft which he kept at Wrafton. We would spend an afternoon driving around Barnstaple using the routes the examiners took, practising three-point turns and other necessities, then sometimes we would drive over to Wrafton where he obviously had business interests. He often took his pupils up for a spin in his plane and I had been offered a trip, however for some reason or other it did not materialise.

I knew the streets of Barnstaple like the back of my hand before I took my driving test. I was well versed in the Highway Code, I could manage all the hand signals with aplomb (right turn, stick your hand out of the window; left turn, twirl your hand; slowing down, flap your hand up and down), but one thing which could not be included in the test was traffic lights, for there was not a traffic light in North Devon when I took my test in 1955. We had to drive to Exeter to experience such modern innovations.

*

The car may have been central to plans for leisure activities during the later 1950s, but during my primary school years there was no such luxury. Everyone walked or cycled everywhere. Social events were severely limited during the war and its aftermath, nevertheless the year was punctuated by gatherings and get-togethers of one sort or another. I went to the occasional social held in the school room which doubled up as the village hall. There were whist drives, especially poultry ones at Christmas time, and Mother sometimes went to those. As a member of a large family she had grown up playing cards, but she said that she disliked the whist drives for prizes, as everyone was so intense and unforgiving of a mistake.

We regularly visited Uncle Jack and Aunt Leah after they moved to Norhill Cottage and my aunty and uncle and cousins at Newcombes Farm. I think that most of our socialising was done in the evenings after the work was finished, and I have many memories of walking the long distance back to Wansley from Roborough, in the dark under the stars. When night had fallen, we did not attempt the wood or field but walked the long way all around the road and lane.

Mother was very interested in the stars, and had a reasonable knowledge of the constellations, which she enthusiastically pointed out to me. I can remember nights when the sky was like a black jewelled pin cushion full of sparkling diamonds. We would walk along West Road with our heads stuck in the air, wondering and marvelling at the heavens above us. I must have been doing this from a very young age as I can recall Mother pushing the pushchair, and I can remember riding in it as well as walking beside it. I think she probably took the pushchair for a while after I began school just in case it was needed.

Mother's interest and knowledge of the skies came from her maternal grandfather, Thomas Headon. He was a Burrington man and had farmed at Hill Farm. In later life he went to live with his daughter (my grandmother) and family at High Bickington. During his time at Burrington he became very friendly with the rector, an educated man who passed on a great

Grandfather Headon.

deal of knowledge and information. The rector was an invalid, and Grandfather Headon often wheeled him around the parish in his bath chair. The rector was very interested in astronomy and the stars, and that was how Grandfather Headon gained his knowledge.

Mother told me that when she was a very little girl, Grandfather Headon took her out to see Halley's Comet. The comet passed over in May 1910, so Mother would have been just five years old. Apparently, it was a clear night and they had a good view of the comet. She remembered that her grandfather said to her,

"Well, my dear, you are lucky to see Halley's Comet once, because most people do not see it at all, but if you live to be a very old lady you may see it twice."

The comet passed by again in 1986 just after my parents had moved into Torrington. Unfortunately, it was an overcast evening, however we walked up the garden and gazed in the right direction and imagined it, and thought about Grandfather Headon.

*

I can clearly remember summer fêtes at Ebberly House; I think that they held one for the parish most years. It was quite an exciting event in my life. We would walk along the track to Little Wansley and then follow the winding road as far as the little gate by the "hermitage" and the fishponds. There was a stone cross by the gate and I had been told that a hermit had once lived there. We seldom walked in via the main gates. It was a pretty walk in over the wooden bridge, under the trees by the fishponds, but at the same time I also found it slightly spooky. I knew that a little further along in the corner there was a reservoir which always struck me as being deep and dangerous. I had played there with friends and explored from time to time knowing full well that we were trespassing, and I had never felt at ease in the area.

There was a rumour that there was a secret tunnel from Ebberly House to Wansley, and Mother said that my Uncle Ken's father who had worked at Ebberly for a while had found the entrance near the reservoir. He had lit a small lamp or candle and had walked a little way along the passage, but the light had gone out so he knew that the air was poor and had gone back. I think that this may well have been a fanciful story, told to while away the long winter evenings. When we discussed it in later years we decided that if there had been a secret passage it was more likely to have gone to Combe Farm than Wansley, as Combe was nearer, older and an ancient manor mentioned in the Doomsday Book.

The Ebberly fêtes were a pleasant social occasion and well attended by local people. As I neared the end of my primary school years, Mother and Father did not always go and I was allowed to go with friends, usually Mary and Alice or Cousin Rachel. I always remember the weather being sunny. There were all the usual things – stalls, swing boats, tombola, skittles. I seem to remember toffee apples, and of course there were sports and races on the lawn.

After it was over we would stroll home tired and happy – across the fields past the old barn, following the track down over Stone Park, through the trees and along by the meadow, then up under the elms past the old linhay and pond, and so back to the yard and house.

*

Like most children growing up in the 1940s I did not have many toys, certainly nothing like the amount bestowed upon children these days. I had two or three dolls, a large rabbit called Wilfred and some teddy bears; I enjoyed my colouring books and I had a few jigsaws. One of my favourite toys was my swing. Father had made it from a piece of wood and two stout ropes and it hung from a beam under the slee, just outside the back door close by the pump trough. I spent hours there swinging over and back, often singing if I remember rightly, and it was positioned so that I did not actually get in the way of anyone using the pump or the back door.

One Christmas I had the most amazing present which I have never forgotten. It was a huge dolls' house, so big that the base was fitted with castors and it could be pulled along by a rope. Father had made it in the evenings after I had gone to bed. During the daytime it had been hidden in the second pantry underneath an old blanket. It must have taken him ages. The whole of the back opened and there were four rooms – two bedrooms, a living room and a kitchen – and Mother had done the furnishings. I think that it was made from two orange boxes and the furniture was made from scraps of wood and matchboxes. It was all painted and varnished: there were white walls, green window frames fitted with real glass, and a red front door. The rooms were carpeted which was more than could be said for our own rooms, and the *pièce de résistance* was (wait for it) electric light! Somehow Father had wired in a bulb in each room which was connected to a battery hidden underneath the stairs. It was truly a marvel in those years of austerity towards the end of the war, and I played with it and treasured it for many years.

Mother had grown up playing cards but we seldom played at home. Aunt Leah and Uncle Jack were not interested so there were not enough people to play. I enjoyed a game of cards later when I went to boarding school and also became a fan of Monopoly. I whiled away many an hour at home playing Patience and I also had several different board games. Some of my most treasured memories are playing Snakes and Ladders with Father by the light of a candle on dark winter evenings; this was during the periods when I was ill and confined to bed. He always came upstairs for a while after he had finished the work and seen to all the animals. We always seemed to laugh a lot and had such fun.

*

One of my main delights and a way of relaxation was reading. Books were not plentiful during and after the war and I just could not get enough; I devoured all reading material that I could find.

"Mary's got her head stuck in a book again," was a remark Mother often made.

After the war was over and people were struggling back to some semblance of normality, the county library began to send books to primary schools. I would probably have been about eight or nine at the time. What an eagerly awaited treasure trove they were. When the wooden box was delivered, I couldn't wait for Mrs Blackmore to open it and let us delve inside. As well as reading them at school, we could sign for them and (oh joy!) take them home.

What bliss to curl up in a chair with *Little Women* or *What Katy Did*; to relax in the sunshine in the hay tallet above the turnip house, and wander with Alice on all her adventures, or be whisked away by Enid Blyton on yet another escapade with the Secret Seven. Black Beauty tugged at my heart strings, Just William made me chuckle, and I loved Alison Uttley's Little Grey Rabbit stories. I was enchanted by Beatrix Potter's world of animals. It seemed to me that most of them could be living nearby at Wansley, particularly Mrs Tiggywinkle. I felt an instant affinity with Lucie who could easily have been me, and I wondered if there really could be a place somewhere with the magical name of Cat Bells.

Although I felt that there were not enough books to go around I suppose I was luckier than many children. Having been a teacher, my mother had a collection of books from her teaching days – admittedly not a lot of fiction but there was plenty to keep me interested and happy. Thank goodness for Arthur Mee's *Children's Encyclopaedia*; she had all ten volumes and they were a source of delight. I explored the galaxies, the stars and the solar system; I travelled to far-off lands and met mysterious tribes with strange customs; I learnt about modern inventions such as the telephone and telegraph and how they worked; I was transported back in time to the ancient Greeks and Romans; I was introduced to the wonderful artwork of artists and sculptors from the Renaissance to more modern times (modern being early twentieth century) and the books were bursting with wonderful poetry, legends and literature.

Over the years, Mother must have subscribed to a geographic magazine (I think it was called *People of the World*) and she had a substantial pile. I was fascinated and appalled in equal measure by photographs of women with rings around their long-stretched necks and men in war paint with bones piercing their noses. I could see at once there were parts of the world where our scary war shield, which was hanging on the staircase wall, would come in very handy.

Mother also had several poetry anthologies; she loved poetry and passed that love on to me from an early age. I can remember sitting beside her on the top step of the staircase one afternoon while she read me *The Highway Man* by Alfred Noyes. It was well before I began school and I was certainly only four years old, which Mother confirmed many years later when we discussed it.

I connected with the poem immediately, and rivers of fear ran up and down my backbone. I knew all about the wind as a *torrent of darkness among the gusty trees,* for was it not just like that, when the wild Atlantic gales blew in over the hills and fields, swirled around the yard, and battered and buffeted the old farmhouse and buildings. I would snuggle down into my feather mattress and pull the eiderdown over my ears, thankful for the strength and security of the stout, thick stone walls.

Many times had I seen the moon as a *ghostly galleon, tossed upon cloudy seas*; as for the road as a *ribbon of moonlight over the purple moor,* well, I had seen that many times also, mostly from my pushchair as my parents walked back from the village on moonlit nights after visiting relatives. *Over the cobbles he clattered and clashed in the dark inn yard,* just like the cobbled yard outside our back door. So much of the poem was relevant to my life experiences, and although I could not quite understand it all, I was able to capture the flavour and essence of the words. I was even used to guns, for Father had a shotgun and the men regularly shot rabbits, pigeons and rooks, though thankfully not damsels with *dark red love knots in their long black hair.*

When I mentioned to my mother many years later how the poem had affected me and captured my imagination, she said that she realised that I had been moved and terrified by it. She had only read it for her own pleasure really, and had thought that it would have just gone over the top of my head. Afterwards she worried whether it had done me any psychological damage, but she need not have been concerned, for I think that children soon sort out fact and fiction, and what is real and unreal. Just think of all the fairy stories full of wolves and bears and trolls. Nevertheless, I have never forgotten sitting there at the top of the stairs, listening as Mother read. Everything in the house was listening, even the reindeer with the glassy eyes and the Egyptians. For many years after, when I turned the pages of the anthology and came to the page with the poem, I always shivered and all my ridge hairs stood on end.

We all enjoyed reading, and usually passed the long winter nights either reading or listening to the wireless. Mother and Father particularly liked detective stories and westerns; Agatha Christie, Ngaio Marsh, John Buchan, Raymond Chandler and Zane Grey were some of their favourites. During the war I think they suffered from a book famine like mine, but later during the '50s when they once again had transport and could visit Torrington, they were able to borrow books from the town library. Round about then they came across an author who was a farmer called A.G. Street, who wrote about farming life in Wiltshire. His tales set in the rolling chalklands of Wiltshire seemed as though they were from another country, and little did I know that one day in the future those same rolling downs would become very familiar to me.

During the six years in the 1950s when I was working at home on the farm, we always laid the dinner table with a book beside the plate. I know of no one else who did this, and probably most people would consider it to be bad manners. The hour from one o'clock until two o'clock was a little oasis of peace and leisure in the busy day; the men had all gone home for their dinner and usually we did not need the hour to socialise or discuss anything of importance, as we had been working together since crack of dawn, and would be toiling away at farm work until the end of the day. As we enjoyed the only cooked and main meal of the day, each of us was transported to our own fictional world. It was a very welcome period of relaxation and tranquillity, as we each read our book in amicable silence.

Our other source of entertainment and pleasure was the wireless. It provided us with all the essential war news, which I knew was grim and worrying much of the time, but there were also programmes meant to cheer and lighten everyone up. I adored Tommy Handley in *ITMA* (*It's That Man Again*). It was broadcast three times a week – the original broadcast plus two repeats. I listened to all three, sitting with my ear pressed closely to the crackly Bakelite loudspeaker, trying to catch every word. It was all above my head really but I loved the wit and repartee and laughter. I laughed along with it, and my favourite was Mrs Mop ("Can I do you now, sir?"). Any innuendoes were completely lost on me, I just spent the half-hour laughing because it was funny.

Dick Barton, Special Agent was another favourite which everyone enjoyed. I was allowed to stay up and listen while Dick Barton, Snowy and Jock got themselves into impossible situations. Each episode ended with a cliffhanger and then it was bedtime. I made my way upstairs wondering how on earth they were going to extricate themselves this time. There was another good detective series with Paul Temple and his wife, Steve, and Mother and I also enjoyed a detective series on *Children's Hour* about Norman and Henry Bones, the Boy Detectives. My parents also enjoyed Valentine Dyall in *The Man in Black*, but I was not allowed to stay up and listen as it was too late and considered not suitable.

Suzette Tarry the comedienne made us laugh. Gracie Fields, Vera Lynn and John McCormack were household names who charmed and beguiled us with crackly songs through the loudspeaker. Another singing duo that springs to mind were Anna Zeigler and Webster Booth, but my favourite was a group who called themselves Big Bill Campbell and his Rocky Mountaineers. It was American hillbilly folk music and I loved it. I think they broadcast on Sunday afternoons and my favourite song was "The Yellow Rose of Texas", which was sung as a ballad slowly, with heart-rending harmonies, and I sobbed all the way through.

During the 1950s when I was working at home on the farm, the wireless would be the background for our daily tasks in the kitchen.

Workers' Playtime, *Round the Horn*, *Much Binding in the Marsh* helped us forget we were washing clothes, washing and packing eggs, scrubbing the table, preparing dinner, sterilising the milking machine, or oiling the lamps. We did the ironing to *Mrs Dale's Diary* while she worried about Jim, and later in the day we followed the lives of another farming family, *The Archers*, who replaced *Dick Barton*, the only series, of course, to survive into modern times. I also remember a series about a West Country family called the Luscombes who had rich Devonshire accents, and I imagined lived on Dartmoor somewhere, and then there was always Wilfred Pickles ("Put it on the table, Mable!").

Another weekly "must listen to" was Alistair Cooke's *Letter from America*. Aunt Leah in particular never missed it and would often sit in the dining room to listen, away from the hustle and bustle of the busy kitchen. Altogether the wireless provided much enjoyment and escapism, and truly was a blessing, and the actors, fictional characters, music and musicians accompanied our work and blended themselves into our daily lives.

*

Mother was a very good fiddle player. The word fiddle conjures up thoughts of folk or Irish music these days, but she played a lot of classical music as well. It was surprising how many country folk could play a fiddle, especially going back to Victorian times, but locally as far as I can gather, they always used the word "fiddle" and not violin. The great beauty of a fiddle is, it is portable and easy to take to a party or night out. Mother played a lot when I was young, but Aunt Leah frowned upon too much time being wasted on frivolous hobbies and gradually she played less and less.

Mother continued to have lessons even after she was working as a teacher. She taught at Frithlestock School from about 1924 until 1933 and lodged at Pencleave Farm with Mr and Mrs Bond and their young son, Billy. Mrs Bond was an Appledore woman, and on Saturdays she drove the pony and trap to Appledore to visit family and friends and buy fresh fish on the quay. Mother always went with her as far as Bideford, where she had a fiddle lesson at the Bideford School of Art. Mrs Bond and Mother hit it off well, and Mother often talked about those times and the stories and tales about Appledore which Mrs Bond passed on, for Appledore was quite a closed community at the time with its own culture and heritage.

After returning from Bideford, later in the day Mother would then cycle home to High Bickington to spend Saturday night and Sunday with her family. During that period in the 1920s the new road bridge over the Torridge by the station was being constructed, and she said that as she cycled along Rothern Bridge she would watch the progress being made on the new bridge.

My Uncle Gerald, Mother's brother who lived at High Bickington, could also play the fiddle and he formed a dance band. Tom Loosemore played the piano, Charlie Chapland the drums, and Francis Pidler from Filleigh played accordion and viola, and they played in local village halls. All our family could sing, and Mother had a strong contralto voice. Her other sisters and brothers enjoyed singing as well. My aunties Audrey and Dot were both clear sopranos and some of my most treasured memories are of the musical evenings around the piano in the "Lower Room" at Prospect. Lorna played the piano and everyone sang and harmonised; even my Uncle Peter, who was only eight years older than me, was learning to play the fiddle. I think they were mostly self-taught, as my grandparents would not have been able to afford lessons. I have wondered in later years how Mother learnt to play but never thought of asking while I could have had an answer. Probably she had lessons at the Bideford School of Art when she was a teacher because it was the first time that she had been able to afford them. Even the in-laws could sing, and my Uncle Bill Norman, who was married to my mother's sister Audrey, had the most magnificent bass voice. He always rounded off the evenings by singing "Bless This House".

Mother's strong voice was useful at other times, especially to call the men in to dinner when they were working out in the fields. She could easily make herself heard right over to Little Wansley, and even

Frithlestock School, 1920s. My mother, Molly Snell, back row, far right.

Mother playing her fiddle.

if the wind was in the wrong direction the dogs would hear her and start to whine and howl, alerting the men. Her voice at times travelled to neighbouring farms, and my friend Elizabeth who lived at Ebberly Barton said that sometimes their men would hear Mother shouting and they would say,

"Mrs Squire's calling her lot in so must be time for dinner, us'll pack up and go in as well."

It would seem that fiddle playing went back through the generations in the family. Uncle Gerald said that his fiddle was a hand-me-down from his uncle, Jack Gulley, who was a tailor and lived in Burrington. Aunt Leah told Mother the tale about when she first met her maternal grandfather; he would have been my great-great-grandfather. He was called Alexander Chanter and came from Bishops Nympton. For most of his life he had been a shoe and boot maker, also known as a "cordwainer". After his wife died when he was elderly he moved into South Molton, and according to Aunty he was the choirmaster at South Molton church.

Aunt Leah could remember her mother taking her to see her grandfather when she was a very little girl, probably about four years old. She was born in 1878 so it would have been around 1882. The day out obviously made an impression on Aunty, for she remembered it well. No doubt they went in the pony and trap, which would have been very enjoyable, and it would have taken some time to travel from their home in Burrington to South Molton. When they arrived at her grandfather's house, Aunt Leah said that her mother introduced her to her grandfather by saying, "This is my baby" (meaning the youngest of the family). The old gentleman said to Leah, "Well, I'll show you my baby," and he went to a cupboard in the wall, took out his fiddle and played her a tune.

*

Aunty was quite artistic and enjoyed drawing and painting. She had studied art while she was training to be a teacher, and we still have a few of her paintings and sketches. She also had a piano made of rich golden-brown wood with brass handles and brass candlesticks. Polished and gleaming, with photographs and ornaments along the top, it took pride of place in the sitting room at Norhill Cottage. She was unable to play so I think it was more of a status symbol, which she felt was required of someone who was an ex-headteacher and a farmer's wife. She also tried her hand at writing short stories, and I later discovered one of her efforts which she had obviously sent to a magazine. There was a polite note back from the editor thanking her, saying they were unable to use her story at the moment. Strangely it appears that it was alright for Aunty to indulge in her hobbies, although other people, such as my parents, were not encouraged to follow their interests.

*

It was largely due to the war that I had little chance to partake in what would now be called extra-curricular activities – the war, and the fact that we lived in such remote isolation. The war was the Big Black Wolf prowling around the edges of our lives. I was shielded from its realities but I still sensed it was the worrying doom which was hanging over everyone. Life was tough; life was hard; everyone was suffering and we all had to pull together and not complain or moan. We were to be thankful for the basic necessities of life and not to expect any extras. I was told that all the better things in life would happen one day when the war was over.

Living deep in the countryside, none of us children were aware that we were missing anything. It was not until I was catapulted to a grammar school in South Devon at the age of eleven that I realised there were other dimensions to life. I discovered that despite the war, there were children of my age who had had music lessons, had attended ballet classes, had learnt to swim or had riding lessons – all things which I would have been thrilled to be able to do. I was lucky though, I was able to catch up to a certain extent.

I soon knew with certainty that I wanted to be able to play the piano. There was an old piano in the prep room and as I listened to some of the older girls playing pop songs I was filled with envy. It took me about a year to persuade my parents that I really, really wanted to learn. They did their best to put me off, and explained that a lot of practising was involved, and they did not want to waste their money on a whim that would soon peter out. Eventually they gave in and I have never regretted learning. I may have started rather late and not have been a fantastic pianist, but it has certainly given me an enormous amount of pleasure and has been very useful, especially as a teacher.

People sometimes express surprise that I did not learn to ride. In fact, sometimes I am surprised myself, for I lived on a farm and my father loved horses. I can only put it down to the war. There were so many more important things and everyone was so busy, with so much else to think about. There just did not seem to be the time to purchase a pony and set up riding lessons.

I did learn to swim, however. Like everyone at Totnes High School I learnt to swim in the River Dart, or more accurately the Leat, which fed from the Dart to Harris's Bacon Factory. Every night during the summer term, after prep and before high tea, whatever the weather, the matron would walk us down across the playing fields to the Leat, and we would spend a glorious half-hour swimming up and down amongst the weeds and the ducks. There were no public swimming baths in Totnes and this is where our scheduled school swimming lessons took place as well. The teachers were very good and during the summer would give up their time to take us swimming in the dinner hour. We did not mind if it was raining, in fact the water always felt warmer if the weather was wet and rather cold. We taught ourselves to swim, and the older girls would hold us young ones up until we could doggy paddle on our own.

They were good times. The railway line from Buckfastleigh to Totnes ran close by and sometimes a steam train would chug past. The cows would raise their heads and look, a few nervous heifers would kick their heels and run away, we would wave wildly and the driver would wave back and give a toot on the whistle. After our evening swim, as we walked back through the playing fields looking forward to tea, the day would be rounded off very happily if some of the boarders from the King Edward VI Grammar School were in their field for a game of cricket. There would be much giggling and blushing and nudging, especially amongst the older girls for they would know some faces and names.

*

Eventually the war was over, and gradually some luxuries began to filter back into our lives again. Having known nothing except stricken, penny-pinching, rationed, war-torn years, and the austerity of the years following the war, it was all new and exciting to me. I had wept when I realised that I was never going to experience the longed-for ride in the Singer car, but in 1949 Father threw caution to the winds and purchased a little square Austin Seven. We were all thrilled, for we were now independent people of the world and no longer reliant on Mr Rockey's taxi. It was true there was a weekly bus that went from the village to Barnstaple on Fridays, but I was always so ill with travel sickness that the whole journey was purgatory for me, and consequently for my mother. The petrol fumes just reeked through the bus and I could feel waves of sickness almost from the moment I stepped into the vehicle. I felt that I would have preferred to go to school, do arithmetic all day and eat semolina, rather than take a ride on the Barnstaple bus.

Suddenly my parents were free and mobile, for in 1949 I went to boarding school and so was off their hands, and they had transport. Indeed, about that time a spontaneous feeling of freedom, confidence and liberation was seeping into the psyche everywhere – at first tentatively like the first stirrings of a warm spring breeze after a cold winter, but gradually gathering pace and shaking everyone's conceptions. People dared to be optimistic, to look to the future with hope and confidence, and shake off the shackles of the long hard years.

This buoyant reawakening showed itself in many ways as people began to move about and socialise more. In North Devon within a few years there was a sudden craze and upsurge in "Old Tyme" dancing clubs. It appeared that everyone wanted to learn the Lancers, the Valeta and the Military Two Step, and the floorboards of local village halls were well trodden. Weekly dancing clubs sprung up like mushrooms in the local villages as people became more mobile and were eager to socialise. My parents were in the thick of it all. When I came home during school holidays I was whisked off to local villages to dance. I can remember one week going out every night, I think it was about Christmas time. Obviously, that would not have happened during lambing time or in the summer, but there was no doubt that my parents made many friends during that period, and my father especially enjoyed the socialising as much as the dancing. In the years after the war, the Old Tyme dance craze encompassed all age groups, young and old alike.

There was always an MC or instructor to demonstrate and help with the steps. If it was just a class there would be a gramophone or pianist, but if it was a proper dance the music was provided by a band. I remember doing a lot of dancing to Roy and the Blue Stars. My parents often practised the steps at home in the evenings after finishing the day's work, dancing up and down the middle of the kitchen to a wind-up gramophone on the kitchen table.

I suppose the dances were very sedate compared with today. We always had an interval at half-time with refreshments – sandwiches, homemade cakes and a cup of tea. Nothing alcoholic, although if there was a pub nearby the men always disappeared for half an hour, but the ladies would not dream of going. It was still not socially acceptable for women to drink in pubs.

Aunt Leah had never been in a public house as a customer in her life, although she had almost certainly visited pubs as a family member, for three of her brothers had been publicans. Her brother Alec kept the Hare and Hounds in South Molton, as well as being a blacksmith and agricultural engineer. Her eldest brother, Harry, was for many years the proprietor of the Halwill Junction Hotel, and was also a well-known cattle dealer, and another brother, Jack Snell, ran the Portsmouth Arms Hotel alongside some farming activities.

One summer in the mid '60s, when Aunty was nearly ninety years old, my parents had a rare day out. I must have been at home on holiday from my job as a teacher in Bristol and Aunt Leah was living at Wansley with my parents. Uncle had died a few years earlier. We decided to spend the day at Ilfracombe, as none of us had been there for some time. An excursion did not happen very often and it was eagerly looked forward to.

The day did not disappoint: the weather was kind; Aunty, well wrapped, had enjoyed the beach; and the picnic was pronounced a success. We did a little gentle sightseeing, for Aunty liked Ilfracombe and when she was younger used to visit her sister and brother-in-law (Nellie and Philip Balsden) who ran a dairy farm at Bicclescombe Mill. As we drove home we decided to round the day off by calling in at the Foxhunters' Inn, which was on the way back to Barnstaple. (No drink drive laws in those days.) Aunt Leah made no comment about the decision, although we knew that it was most unlikely that she had ever been in a pub. It was busy, but we found a corner for her to sit and ordered her a sherry. She sat as ever, straight-backed, genteelly sipping her sherry and surveying the proceedings in silence. Eventually, she put her glass down and turned to us and said,

"Well, I suppose if the Last Trump was to sound now, all these people would go to Hell."

It amused us and we wondered what she thought would happen to her. Perhaps she considered she had special dispensation, as she had been innocently lured into the den of iniquity.

*

A trip to the cinema was a rare and special treat. I had absolutely no background of films or theatre. Until I was eleven I can only remember going to the cinema once and that was when I was very young, probably three or four. Mother and her sister Audrey took me to Barnstaple to see a George Formby film. Mother and Aunty Audrey were like two schoolgirls let out for the day and laughed and giggled all the way through. I soon became bored and as far as I can recollect, spent most of the time on the floor investigating the fluff, sweet papers and cigarette ends.

The first film that I can remember is *The Red Shoes* with Moira Shearer. We were taken to see this sometime during my first year or two at Totnes. It was considered to be educational, and we were whisked off in coaches to Torquay to have some culture and enlightenment thrust into our unrefined little souls.

It was not until I was in my teens in the early 1950s that a visit to the cinema became a common occurrence, and by that, I mean once or twice during the school holidays. There were two cinemas in Barnstaple and two in Bideford, but we rarely visited those. The highlight of the school holiday was a visit to Torrington cinema, which was tucked away down an alley leading to the churchyard. A trip to Torrington cinema was usually highly entertaining. Almost certainly at some point during the proceedings the projector would break down and there would be stamping of feet, booing and shouting. It all added greatly to the evening's entertainment; then off home to supper, which might be fried rabbit and onions, or soused herrings, and in later years fish and chips were available. What bliss.

At the time, many people did not have cars, and rural bus links did not cater for evening entertainment of any kind in the local towns. Some enterprising gentleman saw an opportunity and bought himself a generator, projector and screen, hired some films and set up a business showing films in local village halls. I think that Roborough village was considered too small to be economically viable, but he came to Dolton and High Bickington. Each village had a set night and we knew which film was coming the next week. It was wonderful. During the winter months in the school holidays, I would walk up to High Bickington church hall with the aunties. Armed with rugs, cushions and hot water bottles, we would settle down to a blissful evening as some Hollywood stardust performed its magic, transporting us far away into other lives and lands. I clutched my hot water bottle in suspense as I shadowed Orson Welles in *The Third Man* and secretly shed tears into my blanket at the close of *Shane*, as Alan Ladd rode off towards the distant mountains.

*

The first time I saw a television working was in a shop window at the top of Totnes High Street. It was in 1952 and I was impressed enough to record it in my diary. Like many other people, the first time I watched anything on the television was the Queen's Coronation on 2 June 1953. It was entirely unexpected, as few of the local villages were electrified. The national grid had reached Beaford before the war, but progress then stopped and was not reinstated in our patch of Devon (Roborough) until the 1960s. However, Aunty Dot had electricity at the Golden Lion. Eddie Owen, who ran the High Bickington bakery, had a generator and could provide power to a few other properties as well, and the pub was one of the lucky ones. Aunty Dot and Uncle Ken adventurously decided to buy a television, and so became one of the first in High Bickington to own a set.

Ownership of a television set was not a problem in Totnes where I went to school, provided you could afford one, of course. I doubt if any of my contemporaries there had much idea about life without electricity, but that was another land; when we children from the rural backwaters went home for holidays, we not only travelled many miles, but we also travelled back in time.

What excitement and build-up there was towards Coronation Day. Truly Britain must be great and blessed, we thought, for literally we were on top of the world, Edmund Hillary and Sherpa Tenzing having just conquered Everest in time for the great event. The day was declared a holiday, and I was up bright and early and waiting in the gateway at Little Wansley, where the farm track met the Ebberly road. Uncle Bill Norman came to pick me up on his motorbike.

There were many of us crammed into Aunty Dot's living room, but as it was not a very big room we all had a reasonable view of the tiny black and white screen. It was amazing, and we were all aware and overawed by the fact that we were watching an event which was taking place 200 miles away, as it actually happened! It didn't matter that it was black and white, or the picture was tiny, or frequently there were blips and zigzags across the screen; "just a hechnical titch" someone would shout and Uncle Ken would twiddle knobs as the picture lurched and rolled. Other than a newsreel at the cinema it was the first time we had seen close-up pictures of royalty, the famous, the great and the good. "*Prince Philip nearly knocked the Queen's crown off when he kissed her,*" I wrote. It was fascinating and we all knew that we were watching history as it happened; we were privileged, and it was something we would never forget.

There was no doubt it was raining in London, for we had all cheered Queen Salote of Tonga as she passed by in the procession – a huge regal figure beaming and waving in her open carriage as it filled with rainwater. It was not quite as bad at High Bickington. "*We all went down to the Church Hall for a free tea,*" I wrote in my diary, but I suspected that perhaps I should have been at Roborough, for that was where my Coronation mug was (or was it a Coronation pencil?) and also where my parents were. Luckily, no one seemed to notice there was one too many, and after tea we did floral dancing around the playground, then went back to the hall for more games. I noted that Cousin John played the piano for Musical Arms, Mrs Tapscott won the prize for the best-decorated house, and my cousin Barbara won the prize for the best-decorated tricycle or pram.

The day finished with a bonfire, fireworks and a sing-song in the field. My parents came from the Roborough celebrations at about eleven o'clock and we finally left at midnight. It was all very simple and unsophisticated, and whether a fifteen-year-old child today would have found it all so thrilling and satisfying is doubtful, but we were all very happy and according to my diary, "*Had a smashing day.*"

*

Well, we certainly knew how to live it up and enjoy ourselves when we had the opportunity, but mostly our leisure-time activities were quietly linked to rural pursuits and the countryside. Father and Uncle enjoyed a spot of hunting, in fact we all did. We only had to hear the hounds or the horn, and a thrill of anticipation rippled up our spines and we were away. Father did not ride, which was a shame, because I am sure he would have loved it. Once again it was Aunt Leah and Uncle Jack who discouraged him from spending much time away from farm work; they thought hunting was a bit of a time waster. Happily, they did not object to following on foot, and when we heard the hounds, we just left everything and ran. We did not lock the doors, although we did shut the kitchen door to prevent the cats from jumping up on the table. We ran across fields and jumped up on hedges, joining our neighbours to get the best view. Our lane on the high ridge provided the best view for miles and we could follow the hunt from Great Wood, under Barlington and towards Beaford. Then we could run down to Whitsleigh Cross, and follow to Kingscott and St Giles. It all made for a few enjoyable hours, and later when I had learnt to drive I used to take Uncle in the car. He was elderly then and appreciated getting out and meeting neighbours.

The high ridge was always our outlook upon the world, and the two fields, Burridges Hill and Cow Field, which ran quite steeply down from the ridge, were south facing and basked in the sun. At drinking time when we were harvesting those fields, we always sat for our refreshments at the top against the lane hedge, and surveyed a sizeable chunk of Devon and Cornwall while we munched our sandwiches and drank our tea. I never tired of the view. We gazed over the top of Ten Oaks Farm into a patchwork of woods and fields – beyond Barlington, beyond the little spire of Beaford church peeping through the trees and onwards eventually into the misty bulk of Dartmoor, a bulwark on the horizon. If we turned our eyes to the west the fields went on seemingly for ever until they were absorbed by the high ground of Bodmin Moor.

Torrington Farmers' Foxhounds meet at Wansley. Frank Heal, huntmaster, on horse. Faggots of wood leaning against the end of the pigs' houses, early 1950s.

Father forecast the weather by looking at Dartmoor, and he preferred it when the moor was hazy on the horizon. That meant settled weather. If the moor was very clear, or as he sometimes put it "If you can see the hedges on Dartmoor it's going to rain," and his predictions were usually right.

It was standing on the ridge of our hilltop kingdom that my parents had witnessed the bombing of Plymouth. Even the vast bulk of the moor had been unable to hide the destruction, and the night sky had lit up as bombs were dropped and flames flared and flashed.

Many years later, we stood on the ridge again and gazed even further out beyond our world into space as Sputnik passed overhead twinkling and winking as it made its way across the night sky. Perhaps during the centuries, the ridge has always been a spot where man has stood and thought about life, or pondered the world, the universe and his place in it. The shadows of the clouds chasing each other fleetingly across the fields and woods were a sombre reminder of the insignificance and brevity of our lives; how true the biblical words:

> *For we are strangers before Thee, and sojourners as were all our fathers.*
> *Our days on earth are as a shadow, and there is none abiding.*

Aunt Leah told me that they celebrated the end of the Boer Wars with a picnic at the top of Burridges Hill. (It must have been in the early days of Uncle's courtship.) She recorded it in the Roborough School logbook:

> *June 3rd, 1902. Holiday to celebrate the Peace with South Africa.*

I can just imagine the ladies in their long elegant Edwardian dresses and wide hats. No doubt they had harvest baskets packed with food, and would have sat back against the hedge to eat and drink and chatter, and of course to admire the view as many others had done before and since.

*

The seasons came and went, and interests and pursuits followed the turning of the year. Another enjoyable pastime, which was also a necessity, was the garden. The vegetables were mostly the men's domain but Mother loved flowers, and the smells and colours of summer which are engrained in my being were intrinsically linked to her flower garden. Marigolds, pansies, granny's bonnets, snapdragons, mignonette, love-in-a-mist, larkspur, love-lies-bleeding, poppies and cornflowers all jostled for space and attention. Rambling roses trailed and festooned the fence, the lilacs sprouted along the hedge, and the great laburnum near the end of the potato house rained down showers of gold, majestically watching over the vegetables and the flowers.

Everything grew for Mother, and that included the grass and the weeds. She did the best she could in the time that she had, but what couldn't be done was left. It did not seem to matter, for the garden was colourful and packed full of flowers. In later years when she had a little more time she extended her activities and planted bulbs and spring flowers around the walnut trees, and daffodil bulbs in the lane hedge. She brought the garden indoors as well, for she seemed to have a gift for flower arranging. Nothing small and pernickety, but big bold statements which she seemed to fling together in no time at all. There was always a large bowl of flowers on the dining room table and in the sitting room. The hall table was adorned with flowers, and there was usually an arrangement in a jug on the staircase landing. It was true she was not too bothered about housework and cleaning and dusting; she felt that life was too short and there were other more important things. However, the flower arrangements caught the eye, lifted the spirit and deflected attention from any shortcomings in the housework department.

*

With one thing and another we were always busy and active. We would work hard all day, then scrub up and go off dancing at night. We milked the cows, fed the fowls, knitted our jumpers, sewed our dresses, scalded the cream, beat the butter, played the fiddle, drenched the sheep, carried the corn and sang round the piano. We all of us walked or cycled for miles in connection with work and our pleasures. There was no television in my life until 1972 when I was thirty-four. Then we bought a little twelve-inch black and white set, although Mother and Father had bought a set in the early '60s when electricity made a long overdue appearance in Roborough. My life seemed to be a television-free zone, for there was no telly available to students during my three years at Bedford Teacher Training College, and my seven years of flat life in Bristol also did not include television. It was not a very high priority and even now I can take it or leave it.

Those childhood and teen years passed quietly and comfortably and mostly enjoyably. I never actually was a teenager, as the term which no doubt came from America was not coined until I was firmly in my twenties. The rules and boundaries of life were stricter, and harder for those who broke them, but generally we worked and played within the strictures. During those years, everyone, whether old or young, still felt relief that the war had come to an end and we had been victorious. We had lived through hard times, but there was no doubt, life was getting better and we felt as though we had earned it.

Church and Parish

The year turned, the seasons came and went, and it was not only the farming calendar which was dependent on the annual cycle, but the daily business of the church and parish was also locked into the sequence. Aunt Leah and Uncle Jack were both involved with parish affairs, especially with the church and the school. Aunty was a school manager from the time that she gave up teaching until the 1950s, and much of that time she was the chair of the managers. Her involvement with the school had an agreeable side-effect for me, as Mrs Blackmore often needed to send notes or documents to Aunty: papers needed signing, queries needed answering and replies were required. Almost no one had a telephone, and primary schools did not have secretaries in those days. Once I reached the Big Room I was the "general factotum" and entrusted to run errands and deliver documents. Oh, what bliss to escape the tedium of the classroom for a while, breathe the fresh air and stroll down through the village on legitimate business.

Uncle Jack was a churchwarden for many, many years. He was the "parson's warden" and probably held the position from before I was born until only a few years before his death in 1960. I believe that he also served as a school manager from time to time as well, so all in all Uncle and Aunty were deeply involved in parish life and there was always much discussion about various matters at home and at Norhill Cottage. My parents stayed on the sidelines as far as church and civic duties were concerned, and they let Aunty and Uncle get on with it.

The rector when I was young was The Reverend Barnard and he was blind. He had been at the parish for many years since about 1913, and he lived at Roborough rectory with his wife and three children. When I knew them towards the end of his time as rector, his two daughters, Phyllis and Dorothy, were running the rectory and helping manage parish affairs. Mr Barnard was a talented and interesting man and read quickly and fluently from a braille bible. His hands moved swiftly across the pages and he also used braille notes for his sermons. I was too young to realise that this was anything out of the ordinary; as far as I was concerned that was what rectors did. I gradually began to gather from adult conversation that he was an unusual and gifted man and was much admired for the way he coped with life.

When they were younger he and his wife rode a tandem. He had an inventive turn of mind and had built a crystal wireless set mostly by himself, and had also been involved in setting up a braille printing press. Aunt Leah and Uncle Jack being quite involved with the church knew them very well, and there was no doubt that they did a lot for the parish. The two Misses Barnard, Phyllis and Dorothy, like so many middle-aged spinsters of the time, were the backbone of the parish and kept the well-oiled wheels turning.

Every summer they held a bazaar in the rectory grounds, and this was another event which I looked forward to. As well as the usual stalls, lucky dip, tombola and other money-spinning amusements, there was always a tableau and an opportunity to dress up. The Miss Barnards had dressing-up boxes which were full of colourful materials, even during the war. They would drape the material around us children and turn us into African women or Indian ladies, and we would enact an Indian street scene or an African village scene, and we were instructed how to tell a story by miming. At this time during the war Britain still felt that it had an Empire, even if its days were coming to an end. We were encouraged to think about the children and people who lived in those far-off lands and to help them if we could.

Every year we were given boxes to collect for the Zenana Missionary Society. I seem to recollect that the boxes were shaped like an elephant. We were told it was to help "the poor little black children in Africa", and we were to put our pennies in. I suppose my parents must have put the money in my box as I did not receive any pocket money; it was superfluous as there was nothing to spend it on anyway. There was a shop and post office in the village run by Mr and Mrs Rockey, and I had been there with Cousin Rachel or Alice when they were running errands for their parents, and possibly they were given a few pence to buy a packet of crisps. I had never personally ever bought anything there and I suspect most children, like me, did not receive any pocket money as it just was not needed.

Alice was the only child I knew who earned some money each week. This was for pumping the organ for the morning and evening services, and I think that she was paid sixpence a week. On a few occasions when I had been in the village on a Sunday, I had attended the service with her and given a hand. It was not a job for wimps, as the large wooden bar had to be lifted and then firmly pushed down evenly and regularly all through the hymns and psalms while the organist was playing. The organ blower had to remain attentive during the service and be ready to prime the organ with air from the bellows, and anticipate this before the playing and singing began, or else the notes came out with a wheezy rasp. Once or twice this happened when I was with Alice, and of course it brought on a fit of the giggles and we could hardly control ourselves. She probably managed much better when she was on her own.

The other annual event which was run by the church and the Miss Barnards was the Christmas party. It was an evening event which was held in the schoolroom and was joyfully anticipated. There was a Christmas tree, which I thought was wonderful; we played games and had tea and then Father Christmas came. It must have taxed the resourcefulness of even the Miss Barnards to provide a present for each child during those stricken and penny-pinching years, but somehow they managed to come up triumphant. I have realised since, they must have spent a great deal of time making, knitting and sewing toys.

I received a teddy bear on two successive years; they were different, but nevertheless there was a similarity between them. The first teddy bear was made of green and brown check tweed, rather like skirt material. He was soft and cuddly and had a pleasant expression on his face. I called him Carlo. The next year Father Christmas presented me with a close relation. He was made of black and grey striped tweed which could have been coat material. He was the same size and shape and had the same expression on his face, and I called him Zebo. I commented to my mother that the two teddy bears in some ways resembled each other and she agreed with me. She thought that maybe Father Christmas had a lot of bears that looked like that, and perhaps they were brothers.

It was during the Christmas period that it really hit home that I was an only child, especially on Christmas Day. It was the only time I felt lonely and a little sorry for myself. We always went to church on Christmas morning, and then we would call in to see my aunt, uncle, cousins and grandfather at Newcombes Farm. The house was always bursting with excitement and expectation, and overflowing with presents and food. Apparently, they hung up pillowcases for Father Christmas; I wasn't sure whether it was true or if they were having me on. For me it was a stocking and I couldn't understand why there were different rules in different houses. My cousins all seemed to be having lots of fun and were rushing about laughing and chattering. It was bedlam compared with Wansley and I loved every minute of it.

They also had a Christmas tree and I was envious. It was always in the sitting room and it had real candles fastened on with little clips. They could only be lit when the adults were in the room as there was a danger of fire, but I thought it was so beautiful.

We never had a tree. I suppose Mother had never had one and it was just not part of our tradition. She said that Aunt Leah and Uncle Jack did not celebrate Christmas at all except by going to church, and she was really surprised and disappointed after she was married and spent her first Christmas at Wansley. They made no effort at home in any way, either by decorations or food. Christmas Day was just like every other day of the week, so presumably that was how it had been for my father, as he had been living with them since the age of fourteen. Mother was one of a large family and there was never much money, but she said that her parents always did what they could to make Christmas special for them.

Mother did her best to change things at Wansley and even if they did not consider a tree essential for Christmas, she always made sure there was lots of greenery, which I think is an even older tradition. On Christmas Eve we would walk down to the woods, and wander around the hedges and gather armfuls of holly and ivy for decorations. Soon all the house was decked out with greenery: the pictures sprouted holly; the fox mask which hung on the wall above the kitchen table looked festive as he peeped out from the ivy with his glass eyes, and surveyed father carving the goose; the buffalo horns over the back door were also bedecked, and all the downstairs rooms were made to look cheerful and welcoming. I always loved this part of Christmas and enjoyed helping with the decorating. We did not have many paper decorations, although we were all allowed to bring our paper chains home from school.

I might not have had a real Christmas tree but I did have a little carved wooden one. It was about six inches high and stood in a little red wooden pot. It was given to me by my kindly Aunty Gwen, who may have seen me gazing at their beautiful tree and realised that I would have loved one. I treasured my little wooden tree and kept it in my bedroom for many years.

The first and only Christmas tree we had at Wansley was for the Christmas of 1967 when I was twenty-nine years old. Brian and I had just got engaged and his family were coming to spend Christmas with us and meet my family. His mother, two sisters, brother-in-law and two nephews aged about two and four were coming, and I felt that we must have a Christmas tree, especially for the little boys. Father was enthusiastic and thought it a great idea, so took little persuading to go down to Burridges Wood to chop one down. Most of Burridges Wood was deciduous but there were two small stands of fir. The tree was duly decorated and helped to make the sitting room look festive and was a focal point for all our presents.

I believe it was that Christmas when the turkey walked in the door, much to Brian's surprise. Mother had ordered it from someone at Beaford and they rang to say they would be bringing it that morning. The vehicle duly arrived and we opened the door expectantly. The man walked into the kitchen leading the turkey by a piece of binder cord which was tied around its neck. Mother also expected it to be dressed ready for the table but there was no doubt it was still very much alive, and suddenly there was some extra unexpected work.

*

At some point during the 1950s, when Mr John Reed was the rector, we were introduced to the idea of a midnight service for Christmas. It was certainly not a tradition in the area and none of us had heard of such a thing. Although it seemed a little strange the first time, we all agreed that it was atmospheric and a spiritual prelude to Christmas Day and the midnight service soon became a Christmas fixture.

We had much colder winters back then, although there were not many white Christmases. It snowed almost every winter during the 1940s and '50s but usually in January and February. I can remember one white Christmas though, when it snowed quite heavily on Christmas Eve. We decided we would walk to Roborough for the midnight communion rather than not go at all and planned to walk via Roborough Mill, so the two Miss Brights could walk with us instead of going on their own, as they were both quite elderly by then. We dressed warmly, wore our wellingtons and took our flashlights.

It seemed on that Christmas Eve as though there was a touch of magic in the air. Although very cold it was a still evening, and the snow was crisp but not too deep. As we walked along the edge of Great Wood the silence was profound and the boughs hung over us heavy with snow. The hedgerows were a soufflé of white, our lights casting blue shadows as we tramped past Owlacombe Mill, and made our way up Scottington Hill and into the village. It seemed to me to be quite exciting to be making our way through the snow to the church in the dark. It would have been about two miles walking that route to the village. I was still in my teens, but the adults seemed exhilarated as well, and the two Miss Brights had glowing cheeks and sparkling eyes, even though they would have been in their seventies. We also felt that it was a little daring to be arriving at church in wellington boots. People dressed quite smartly for church in those days and always wore a hat. I have a feeling that Bessie and Frances Bright took a pair of shoes in a bag, as they would have considered it disrespectful to wear their boots in church. Mother and I just hoped the Good Lord would make allowances for the circumstances and realise the effort we had made.

*

During my growing-up years it was the tradition that Wansley ladies decorated the font. I helped from an early age, and at Christmas time it was festooned with holly and ivy. The festival that I enjoyed helping with most of all though was Easter. For me it was a two-day event, as Good Friday was spent picking daffodils and primroses. During my primary school years Mary Waldron and I spent all day picking flowers. I would walk down through the field and the wood and along the lane to Burridges Cottage where Mary would be waiting for me. We took two large baskets, some wool and scissors, then made our way chattering happily up and down the hills to Roborough Mill, then along the Beaford road to the meadows under Barlington Farm. Here where the brook babbled along the bottom of the meadow was a sea of wild daffodils, bobbing and blowing in the breeze exactly as Wordsworth had described in the Lake District many years before.

We picked steadily all the morning, tying the daffodils into bundles of twelve with the wool. When the baskets were full we carried them back to Mary's house and transferred them into bowls of water. After dinner we would take the baskets and begin again, this time picking primroses, often from the sheltered roadside hedges that led down to the Mill. Sometimes we walked along a track under the trees called "Castles". This was another good sheltered spot for primroses, and the track overlooked our daffodil meadows. Once again, we tied the primroses into little bundles and then carried the full baskets back to Burridges Cottage.

There was only one ingredient left to perfect our decorations and that was moss. There was an abundance of moss at Wansley. One particularly good place was a stone gully in the little copse at the bottom of Rushy Plat. The gulley ran the length of the copse and separated our land from the Pethericks'. It was covered with every type of moss imaginable. Usually I would pick the moss on Saturday morning and stuff it into a sack to take to church.

On Saturday morning, the church would be busy and bustling with an expectant atmosphere. Ladies from around the parish would arrive with their baskets of flowers. The flowers were shared, although the person who had picked them had first choice. Mary and I enjoyed making the font look pretty, and Mother and Aunt Leah supervised us. We hid the jars of flowers amongst the moss and tried to make them look as natural as possible, as though they were growing. By the time we had all finished almost every surface in the church was covered with flowers and moss, and a damp woodland smell filled the air. The sweeping brushes were found to tidy up the mess and then we stood back to admire our efforts, knowing we were ready to celebrate the Easter festival.

*

At the age of eleven I went to boarding school and not long after that the Waldron family moved into Torrington, so our Good Friday ritual of flower picking came to an end. Mother and I still went out picking daffodils and primroses around Wansley, but it didn't bring quite the same thrill and pleasure as when Mary and I set off on unaccompanied excursions during our younger years. However, as one tradition ends another often begins and so it was with our Good Fridays.

It was in the early 1950s and Mother and I had picked a useful amount of daffodils on Good Friday morning. We had returned to the house for dinner and were preparing ourselves for a primrose-picking excursion, when we were sure we heard a loud "Coo-ee". Hurriedly looking out of the courtyard door, to our delight and surprise we saw Aunty Kathleen and Cousin John walking up the track from the pond. As it was Good Friday, High Bickington Post Office was closed and being a very pleasant day they had decided to go for a walk. They had walked around Millbrook and Yelland to Ebberly, then realising that they were not too far from Wansley, they had kept going and walked in along the track from Little Wansley.

We were all pleased and happy, and amongst all the excitement and chatter we rustled up some food, then set off to pick primroses. Afterwards they stayed for tea, my Uncle Arthur coming later in his car to take them home. Well, that set a precedent, for everyone decided that the day had been so enjoyable it was worth repeating. From then on it was a family gathering on Good Friday, and most of the members of the High Bickington family descended upon us. They came to dinner and Mother did a roast, then we all went picking daffodils and primroses and then they stayed to tea. Although we did not realise it at the time, this annual family get-together was to last for about fifty years.

In 1970 my parents sold the farm and moved into the farm cottages at Melland Hill but everyone still looked forward to the get-together, although in 1975 it was moved from Easter to the August holidays. This was because of snow on Good Friday that year. We had spent an enjoyable afternoon walking around the lanes picking flowers, and were sitting around the big dining room table (which my parents had managed to squash into the cottage) tucking into a well-deserved tea. To our surprise, suddenly and unexpectedly it began to snow quite heavily. Before you could say "cutrounds and cream", the room cleared, as everyone raced to their vehicles to make an escape, for Melland Hill was situated in a valley with two very steep hills in either direction. All the family managed to get away before the roads became impassable – well everyone except us, as Brian and I were the last to leave. There was no way out for us, so there was a telephone call to my cousin in the village who rescued us with his tractor.

From then on, the gathering of the clans was moved to August and that meant cricket on the lawn, splashing around in the brook, an inspection of flowers and vegetables in the garden (the men were all keen gardeners and quite competitive) and lounging around in deckchairs. The weather was always kind and the sun shone, and this continued even when all the family moved into Torrington. The photographs show summer dresses, shirtsleeves and tea on the lawn at Underhayes.

*

There were two places of worship in the parish: St Peter's Church in the village, and the Methodist Chapel at Ebberly. Almost everyone owed an allegiance to one or the other and certainly attended the main

A summer gathering at Melland Hill.

Spring gathering at Melland Hill. L–R, back row: Arthur Down, Kathleen Down, Molly Squire, Mary Ann Snell (Granny), Lorna Snell, Keith Snell, Diana Snell. L–R, middle row: Bill Squire, Brian White, Audrey Norman, John Down, Barbara Barrett. L–R, front row: Stephen White, David White, Ian Snell, Andrew Barrett, Dot Gill.

services during the year, even if they did not put in an appearance every Sunday. The two denominations rubbed along quite well, and there was a small amount of drift from one to the other if it suited. This was certainly so in our family, for Grandfather Squire and Uncle Jack were brought up at High Downs at Ebberly and the family had always been C of E. However, High Downs was only a few hundred yards from Ebberly Methodist Chapel and it was nearly a two-mile walk to the village, so naturally they often attended the chapel instead, and several of the family were married and buried there.

When looking through Aunt Leah's papers and belongings after her death in 1981, I came across a little piece of blue paper folded neatly into four. On opening it, I discovered that it was Uncle Jack's baptism certificate. I knew my uncle was a pillar of the church and had been a churchwarden for many years. To my surprise and amusement, I discovered that he had been baptised at Ebberly Chapel.

I always had a sneaky suspicion that the children who attended chapel had more fun than us church-goers. Every year they had an anniversary and it all sounded good fun. They had to learn "pieces" to perform and there usually seemed to be new dresses. They were allowed to practise at school and perform their poems etc. to the rest of us. We had to do boring things such as learn our catechism and were then tested by the rector; it just did not match up.

Looking through the school logbooks it seemed that the chapel had always played some small part in school life, even though it was a Church of England school. During Victorian and Edwardian times there are records of the school closing for visits and treats at the rectory, and teas and treats at the chapel. There was no doubt though that the rector was all-powerful and was entitled to keep an eye on things. Aunt Leah became headmistress on 7 October 1901. That morning the rector, The Reverend Edward May, wrote in the school logbook:

Oct 7th. School reopened this morning by Miss Snell who has been appointed Head Mistress. The Rev. E.H.E May and Mr Bishop were present at 9.15 am for the assembly.

The rector had the authority to visit at any time and check attendance and registers.

On 11 October, Mr May wrote again in the logbook, and he had obviously visited the school five days in a row.

October 11th. Visited the school on the 8th 9th 10th 11th. In spite of the inclement weather the number of children attending was exceptionally good. The plan of room with regard to the arrangement of desks has been altered to the satisfaction of the new mistress.

Examined registers on the 11th and found them to be correct. E.H.F.M.

Aunt Leah often laughed about the letter she received from The Reverend May when she applied for the position of headmistress. We still have the letter and it is essentially a bribe. In it he states that if she will take the Sunday school and keep the children in order in church, he will do his best to get her elected. It was quite plain from the letter that if she did not agree to take the Sunday school, she would not be offered the position of headmistress of the day school.

In the event of getting you elected, would you be willing to help me with the Sunday School? For the past fifty years the Master or Mistress of the school has always gladly taken the Sunday School and kept the children in order in church; and I believe in this little parish this piece of voluntary help has been the means of creating strong feelings of attachment between Scholars and Teacher. Being so near home the thought at once occurs that you might be wanting to go home every week from Saturday to Monday; but on the other hand it is far from my wish to make the Sunday School compulsory or binding on the teacher, and any Sunday you would wish to be away we could make arrangements for; or if you would take the morning Sunday School I could always relieve you for the rest of the day. The Sunday School here is one of the most important parts of our Parish organisation, and is a great means of support to the Day School and that is why I have laid particular stress on the subject.

Will you kindly let me know as soon as possible whether you will fall in with my wishes – if so I will do my best to get you elected here.

I am
Yours faithfully, Edward H.E. May

The Reverend May wrote back to Aunt Leah on 13 August and offered her the job.

After looking over your testimonial the managers were unanimous in electing you as the Head Mistress of Roborough National School at a salary of £70 per annum with lodgings, and at the same time they hoped you would be willing to do what you could to keep together the Sunday School.

Your duties will commence here on Monday October 7th, 1901, and you will be required to sign the necessary agreement.

The one service each year which resonated with the whole community, no matter which place of worship they attended, was Harvest Festival. Almost everyone was connected to farming either directly or indirectly, and we all felt we should give thanks for the bounty of the land. It was certainly the service that Father was most engaged with. Father did not go to church as regularly as Mother. He said that churches made him feel funny. I am not quite sure what he meant but Mother said that it did not matter, because he was more of a Christian than most people who went to church every week, and I could only agree with her.

Father and I loved preparing the fruit and vegetables; only the biggest, the best and the shiniest would do. We went into the potato house and examined the strings of onions hanging around the walls and selected the biggest and glossiest. Likewise, the potatoes, turnips, swedes, carrots, runner beans and any other vegetables which were available. Everything was washed, the apples were gently polished with a soft cloth and our offerings were put into large baskets ready to transport to Roborough. Some years Father would have sheaves of wheat. He grew wheat from time to time when he needed wheat straw for thatching the ricks, and when available he sent one or two. I think that the long, slow deliberation about which vegetables or apples to send to the church was not entirely altruistic. All the farmers eyed each other's contributions with a critical eye, and I have heard remarks such as

"Farmer So and So's onions bain't up to much this yer."

Once again, the ladies of the parish set to work and transformed the church into a cornucopia of delight. By the time we had finished, the windows, ledges, font, pulpit, in fact every surface, was groaning under the weight of the offerings. Michaelmas daisies and chrysanthemums were secreted into every available space, and the smell of fruit, vegetables and flowers permeated the air.

The harvest service was always in the evening. Normally we went to the morning service because it fitted in with the milking and the animals better than the evening one. I liked the evening service; maybe it was something about the music, the calmness of "The Magnificat" and the "Nunc Dimittis", or perhaps it was the cosy glow of the oil lamps which hung down on their chains and bathed us all in a soft light. At harvest time there were wonderful hymns to belt out as well. Who could resist "We Plough the Fields and Scatter" and "Come Ye Thankful People Come"? After the service was over, we all retreated to the schoolroom for refreshments, and the fruit and vegetables were auctioned off.

During the six years in the 1950s when I was working on the farm after I had left school, Mother and I, Uncle Jack and Aunt Leah all went to church most Sunday mornings. Father came sometimes but not regularly. Mr John Reed was the rector then, not only of Roborough but of Beaford as well, for by then the two parishes were amalgamated. The diocese sold off our beautiful rectory and built another one at Beaford. Mr Reed was a country man with Cornish connections, and he had a sincere and simple approach to life. He was well liked and we became good friends. The services were straightforward and plain – the Book of Common Prayer and Hymns Ancient and Modern.

At the time the lessons were read by Mr Guy Watts who resided at Ebberly House. This brought a touch of class to the service, for his beautifully modulated voice lifted the lesson out of the ordinary. It was like listening to Sir Laurence Olivier, and his words fell into the air like golden droplets. I had been going to church all my life, but it was listening to him on Sunday mornings that opened my eyes and ears to the beauty of the King James Bible. In my mind, I can still hear him reading from Psalms, Ecclesiastes, The Song of Solomon or Isaiah, and the poetry and beauty of the words have always remained imprinted on my mind. For me, the bland modern versions just do not compare.

Not everyone went to church on Sunday, but there was no doubt that during those years the Sabbath was entirely different from the rest of the week. No one worked unless it was essential. The milking had to be done and the animals fed and attended to, but other than that, it was considered wrong, or indeed sinful, to do anything other than those things which were strictly necessary. No one worked in the fields or tended to crops on a Sunday. It did not matter if it had rained during the week and Sunday was the first opportunity to gather in the hay or corn; it was taboo to venture out into the fields on a Sunday.

This attitude encompassed life in general, not just work but hobbies and interests. Mother thought that it was permissible to read on a Sunday but not much else was allowed. She would not dream of knitting or sewing on Sunday. When I went to boarding school we were all encouraged to keep ourselves busy and occupied, and Sunday, apart from attending the morning service, was like the rest of the week. We played board games and cards, although during the summer we did not play tennis, rounders or cricket in the field. Hot and sunny Sunday afternoons had to be spent sitting in the garden. No one thought twice about knitting, sewing, crochet or any other creative hobby though. On returning to the farm one holiday, I remember getting the sewing machine out on a Sunday to finish making a skirt and to my amazement Mother burst into tears. I had forgotten her outlook on such matters, and she obviously thought that I was sliding downhill into a dissolute lifestyle.

*

Aunt Leah and Uncle Jack confined their civic duties to the school and the church and did not become involved with parish council or county council affairs. Politics were not discussed a great deal, although round about election time their views would be aired. I can still remember the shock the adults felt, when Mr Atlee became Prime Minister after the war. They were expecting Churchill to be elected.

It was impressed upon me from an early age that being able to vote was a great privilege and was not to be taken lightly. Aunty was born in 1878 so she would have grown up being aware of the suffragette movement, and I suspect that she would have followed its ups and downs keenly. Women were not able to vote until 1918, and then only if they were over thirty and their husbands owned property. Aunt Leah would have qualified on both counts, as by then she was forty and Uncle Jack owned property and land. Votes for all women over twenty-one did not happen until 1928, and this would have encompassed my mother who would then have been twenty-three.

Voting took place in the village schoolroom and when I was young I accompanied the adults. We always went in the evening after finishing the milking and tending to the animals. It was an occasion, and everyone wore their best clothes as though they were going to church and Aunt Leah always wore a hat. Many of the farmers of the parish went at about the same time, afterwards standing around outside the school gravely passing the time of day, discussing the weather, farming or parish matters, all with an underlying air of importance and duty well done.

No one discussed politics, but everyone had a good idea how their neighbours had voted. As a rule of thumb, Church voted Conservative and Chapel voted Liberal. There were only one or two in the parish who were considered to be socialists. As a matter of fact, at the time it did not matter where loyalties lay, for unless you were a Labour supporter there was only one candidate anyway. He was The Rt. Hon. George Lambert, and he stood for parliament as a National Liberal/Conservative and so mopped up all the votes regardless.

It can sometimes be a salutary experience living closely with someone much older and so easy to be unaware of their life experiences. I returned home on holiday from school during the 1950s, and for some reason Uncle Jack and I were discussing history and he asked me what I had been studying at school. I told him that at the time we were revising about Disraeli and Gladstone for exams. It seemed so far back in time to me. Uncle began to laugh and said, "Oh, Gladstone," as though it was someone he knew. I suddenly realised that Gladstone had been a politician during his younger days, much as Atlee and Churchill were politicians in my life. It suddenly made the past seem so much closer.

As one year flowed into the next there was a sense of continuity as each season brought its festivals and customs. Interspersing the orderly humdrum of everyday life were the highlights of the year, eagerly anticipated and hugely enjoyed. During the 1940s most people still found their work in the parish or neighbouring villages, and leisure-time activities were also close to home. This was all to gradually change during the rest of the century, but at the time it all seemed so orderly and reassuring. The pattern had been repeated since before living memory, and it was difficult to visualise that the future might be different.

Roborough church, 1940s.

The Rev. and Mrs Barnard on a Sunday school outing.

(Left) Leah and Molly, 3 June 1968. Leah was almost ninety.
(Right) Wedding day on Wansley staircase.
Scary war shield and Egyptians peeping through.

Bill with guests outside the church, 3 June 1968.

(Left) Leah Snell.
(Right) Teachers at Roborough School in the early 1900s.
L–R: Leah Snell, headmistress. Annie Friend, pupil-teacher. Katie Clarke.

Roborough School, 1907. Aunt Leah sent this photo as a postcard to
Jack and it is dated 19 September 1907. She also says she had a stiff neck and
could only turn her eyes. The other teacher is Katie Clarke. Frances Bright
is third row from back, fourth child from right.

Medical Matters

"The doctor came and we didn't have to pay him."

I heard Mother's words with a slight jolt, as it had not occurred to me that he had to be paid. I knew there were the vet's bills to pay but I was until  then unaware that my parents also had to pay the doctor. I knew that neither the vet nor the doctor was summoned without a very good reason, and until about 1948 it meant a trek to the nearest telephone which belonged to Mr George Squire the builder who lived at Roborough Mill, half a mile away. I believe that was the year when we installed a telephone of our own. I cannot remember exactly but it was round about then, after the long and devastating winter of 1947. That winter which made everyone take a long, hard look at their lives and living conditions, and consider what could be changed to improve things.

There was a buzz of excitement in the air as the adults contemplated having a phone of their own. Father had been told that the GPO would connect him but he had to provide his own poles. This was a substantial number, as it was about a quarter of a mile from the farmhouse to the end of our lane where the telephone lines passed by. Inevitably this meant a trip to Burridges Wood to size up how many suitable poles could be obtained from our stands of fir trees. On thinking about it I have been wondering whether that was one of the reasons the fir trees near the pond were cut down; I really cannot remember now. However, at least a dozen poles were needed and we obtained them from somewhere. I remember the fir poles lying on the grass near the great oak tree – all branches stripped off and the bark removed from the bottom three feet, which was coated with a black tarry substance. We all stood around contemplating the felled firs and imagining agreeable thoughts of telephone conversations in our own home. There was still some way to go before it happened, as Father and the men had to dig the holes and erect the poles, which were to be inspected by the GPO before the wires were attached.

There was no debate about where to put the phone because as we all knew, phones always went in the hall, and naturally there was no choice of design or colour. When the momentous day arrived and we were connected and able to lift the shiny black Bakelite receiver and talk to someone, actually there were very few people to talk to. Not many people had a phone, and calls were mostly confined to business and essential calls. The only member of our family to have a telephone was my Aunty Kathleen who kept High Bickington Post Office. Nevertheless, it gave us a feeling of independence and great relief, not to have to walk half a mile and trouble someone else when we needed to make an essential call.

There was no doubt Wansley was extremely isolated, and for about ten years we had no transport. Consequently, we never visited our doctor's surgery which was at High Bickington; the doctor always came to us. I think it was the isolation and distance from a doctor that prompted my mother to return to the family home at High Bickington for her confinement when I was due, and so I was born at Prospect and not Wansley. Other influences which probably led to her decision were the fact that there was also a nurse at High Bickington and of course her own mother had had eleven children.

Medical Matters

Aunt Leah and Uncle Jack were a childless couple with no experience whatsoever of midwifery or childbirth. Of the two I guess that Uncle Jack would have had the best idea, having assisted numerous cows and sheep over the years. Anyway, I would definitely have made the same decision as my mother.

Childbirth was still a hazardous experience in those days. My grandmother and my great-grandmother had both died in childbirth. There were many other risks along life's path as well, and parish registers record clusters of deaths, mostly children, from infectious diseases almost every winter, even in small country parishes. There was a dark side to life and the logbook at Burrington School, where my grandfather and Aunt Leah were pupils, recorded many instances of childhood diseases such as scarlet fever, measles, whooping cough and even typhoid. The real scourge though was diphtheria, and the school was closed on many occasions by the medical officer. There was one particularly severe outbreak in the winter of 1897/98. Aunt Leah was a teacher at the school at the time. The school was closed at the end of November, reopened in January after six weeks, then closed again on 2 February and not reopened again until 12 April with only thirty-three children present… 114 on the register.

Aunt Leah recalled the tragic deaths of the children in the Woolway family of West Pavington. Five children in the family died: one in February and the other four all died during one week between 7 March and 13 March. They were aged between three and a half and thirteen. Aunty went to the funeral and I still have the funeral card. She said that obviously people were very frightened of diphtheria and were afraid of catching it. As she had been teaching at the school and had attended the funeral, people avoided her and she told us that as she walked along the village street, people crossed over and walked on the other side of the road. I remember that she was quite indignant about it, but I can understand people's concern. I wondered whether the Woolways had any remaining children who escaped the epidemic, so I checked the 1911 census. There is a section on the census with quite intrusive questions about children, i.e. total children born alive, children still living and children who have died. It was all obviously too much to contemplate filling in, so the Woolways had written "No children" across the section. I think they are two of the saddest words I have ever read.

Diphtheria was to be a scourge for many more years and my mother's little sister Betsy died of the disease in January 1922. At the time my mother would have been nearly seventeen and she was training to be a teacher at High Bickington School. The illness and death is recorded in the High Bickington School logbook. Mr Ham, the headmaster, wrote:

January 16th, 1922. Dr Good thinks that Betsy Snell is suffering from diphtheria, and has directed the other children of the family not to attend school. The Pupil Teacher Mary J. Snell is included.

Betsy died on the 19th and Dr Good recommended closing the school from 25 January as there were other suspected cases in the parish. The school was not reopened until Monday 13 February and the Snell family did not return until the following Monday, the 22nd. While the school was closed, Mr Ham recorded that:

The premises are being disinfected, lime washed and thoroughly cleaned.

My mother did not return to school for another month as she was obviously run down, and Dr Good advised four weeks' holiday.

I was surprised that children were not whisked away to an isolation hospital when they were diagnosed with diphtheria as the disease was so infectious, but apparently that did not happen. I was told by one of my aunties that when Betsy was ill, my grandmother hung a sheet in the doorway of the bedroom, and the rest of the children were forbidden to go past the sheet. I am not quite sure why a sheet was used, unless there was less risk of infection than there would be from touching door handles or latches. Granny certainly managed to contain the disease, although she was lucky. Mother told me that there were several others sleeping in the same bedroom until Betsy became ill, and either Aunty Audrey or Aunty Kath, or maybe both, had been sleeping in the same bed.

Mother said they thought that Betsy was over the worst and hoped she would make a full recovery. She remembered that Kathleen had been sent to shout to her (either up the stairs or through the sheet) and ask her if she would like a boiled egg for breakfast. Betsy replied that she would, but by the time Granny took it to her she had died. Dr Good thought that it would have been her heart, as there were quite often cardiac complications with diphtheria. Once again the fear that diphtheria instilled in people became apparent. Mother said that at the funeral she overheard someone remark,

"If I had realised what the child had died of, I wouldn't have come."

Although people were rarely admitted to hospital in those days unless it was for something quite serious, there must have been some kind of public health initiative, as my mother had had her tonsils removed when she was a child. It was the only time she had been in hospital until she was nearly eighty-five years old, and I could tell from the way she spoke about it that it had not been a very pleasant experience. Her admittance to hospital must have been instigated by a routine visit by the school doctor, almost certainly Dr Good. Mr Ham, the headmaster, wrote in the school logbook:

November 20th, 1915. Beatrice Beer and Mollie Snell both have enlarged tonsils, and were taken yesterday to the North Devon Infirmary in order that operations might be performed in the course of the next few days. They will be absent from school the whole of next week.

It did not sound as though either they or their parents had had any choice in the matter, and the two children had been whisked off for their own good.

*

Aunt Leah fell down and broke her thigh when she was ninety-eight years old, and that was the first time that she had ever been admitted to hospital. Due to her great age she had "retired" three times. She and Uncle Jack had retired to Norhill Cottage in about 1942, leaving my parents to run the farm. They then moved back to Wansley to live with us in 1955, as by then they were finding it difficult to cope on their own in the cottage. Finally, in 1970, Aunt Leah retired again with my parents when they sold the farm and moved to Melland Hill.

Uncle Jack had died in 1960. He had cancer, although the word was never mentioned. "He has something in his stomach" was all that was quietly said if anyone asked, the sombre faces and worried looks conveying more than a thousand words. We nursed him at home as people did in those days, and towards the end as he needed round-the-clock care, Mother looked after him at night and I did the days. There was a mountain of bedlinen to wash everyday – still no electricity or washing machines, just our old-fashioned "washer" with the mangle. He was delirious much of the time, with lucid periods in between and a lot of pain, although the doctor did come regularly to provide some pain relief. Mercifully he quietly slipped away on an April evening, four days after his eighty-seventh birthday.

Aunty had always enjoyed a daily walk, and even at ninety-eight, weather permitting, she would walk along the lane leading to Burridges Cottage. Unfortunately, one morning she slipped on the cobbles outside the

"Suffer little children to come unto Me."

The cup was bitter the sting severe,
To part from them we loved so dear,
Our loss is great we'll not complain,
But trust in Christ to meet again.

"Beloved by all."

In Loving Memory
OF
SYDNEY JOHN,
Died Feb. 7th, 1898, aged 8 years,

HENRIETTA,
Died March 7th, 1898, aged 9 years,

THOMAS MANNING,
Died March 8th, 1898, aged 13 years,

GERTRUDE FANNY,
Died March 11th, 1898, aged 3 years 6 months,

WILLIAM MAYNARD,
Died March 13th, 1898, aged 11 years,

THE BELOVED CHILDREN OF
WILLIAM & EMMA WOOLWAY,
West Pavington, Burrington.

Great Aunt Leah when she was ninety-eight.
Not long after she fell and broke her hip.

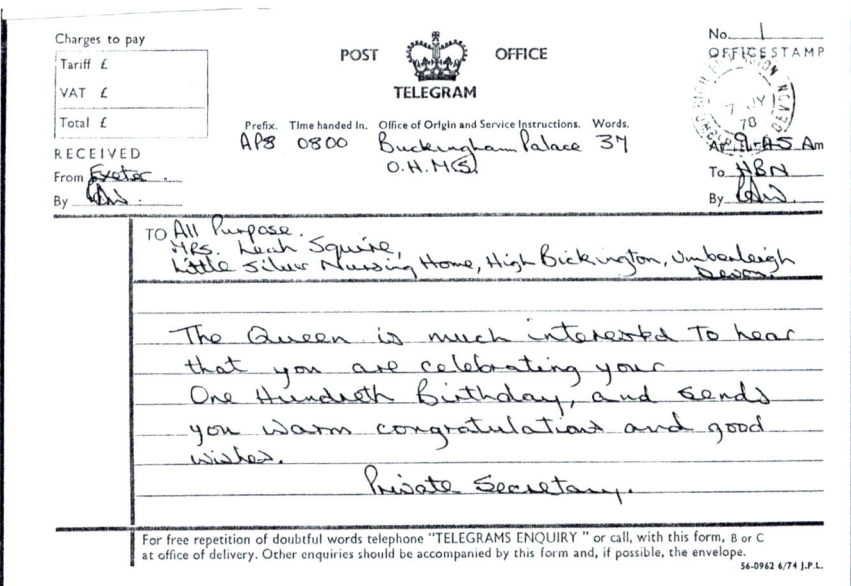

Leah reached her hundredth birthday on 7 July 1978. She was then living at Little Silver Nursing Home, High Bickington. They rang the bells for her at St Mary's Church and the parish council sent a congratulatory telegram. She also received a congratulatory telegram from David Ennals, the Secretary of State for Social Services, as well as the all-important telegram from the Queen. There were many visitors and cards, a birthday cake, strawberries and cream and a glass of sherry for tea.

house, and so she ended up in hospital. She took it all in her stride and the hip was pinned; in fact we decided that she had rather enjoyed her hospital stay, although she would never admit it. She probably liked the attention, for she told us that the nurses stood around and watched her do her hair. As usual she was quite indignant about it.

"Molly, they all stand around and watch me, you would think they had never seen anyone do their hair before!"

She had long silvery white hair which she brushed and then wound into a braid at the back of her head. Apparently the nurses were also amused that she put Oil of Ulay on her face every day. She seemed a little annoyed about that as well, but I say, "Good for her. Keep up appearances and slap on the face cream for as long as you possibly can!"

*

There was no doubt that being ill could be expensive, and tried and tested home remedies were always used first. The doctor was only summoned as a last resort if it was really serious and all else had failed. At home, run-of-the-mill mishaps such as cuts and grazes were always treated with iodine. There was an excruciatingly painful reaction when it was first put on the wound, and Mother said that proved it was working and killing all the germs. The surrounding skin became stained a yellowish brown, and was proudly displayed for the rest of the day. Germoline was a soothing cream used on sores and spots, and Calamine Lotion was always available for rashes and bumps. If our stomachs were giving trouble we took two Carter's Little Liver Pills, and coughs were always treated with Handford's Cough Mixture, which was a unique recipe made up by Mr Pringle, the Torrington chemist. We used dock leaves for nettle stings, and resorted to the washing day Blue Bag for bee and wasp stings. Lemon and honey soothed our sore throats, and we rubbed Vicks on our chests. Goose fat was useful stuff as well. It was also rubbed into chests and used to soothe red, rough, washday hands. If Father pulled a muscle or twisted his knee he always used Elliman's Embrocation, a horse embrocation which he kept in his veterinary cupboard. A spoonful of cod-liver oil was administered each night, and also something which was much more pleasant called Minidex. This was for swollen glands. If we needed a laxative there was always a bottle of syrup of figs in the cupboard. The best medicine of all though was Woodward's Gripe Water for hiccups and indigestion, and I could easily have drunk the whole bottle.

I also remember Mother making something called a bread poultice, which she would use to put on boils. She mashed up some bread with boiling hot water, then laid it on a bandage, usually a piece of sheet, covered it with lint and placed it on the infected area. This helped to draw the discharge out.

The doctor and dentist both regularly visited the school and also the nurse to inspect our hair (Nitty Nora the bug explorer as we irreverently called her). I was thankful that Mother did not expect me to have treatment from the school dentist and she took me to Mr Copp in Torrington. I always felt sorry for the children who had to face up to the dentist at school. I think that Mother disliked the doctor as much as I did. I was always underweight and under height, and I know she felt there was implied criticism of her child-rearing skills. It annoyed her, and she would draw herself up to her full four feet eleven, glare at them and retort, "Well, what do you expect? Just look at me!"

Diphtheria was a disease of the past when I was growing up, and the childhood disease which took its place was polio. We had all of us seen pictures of people in iron lungs and children hobbling with leg callipers and braces. There was no protection from the disease and everyone just kept their fingers crossed. A jab for whooping cough became available when I was young so I avoided that, but I had chickenpox and measles as they swept through the school. We were a small, isolated community, and I did not come in contact with mumps or German measles until doing teaching practices when I was training to be a teacher. I caught mumps from a child in Northampton and German measles from a child in Wellingborough.

*

Mother's remark about not having to pay the doctor must have been made when the first green shoots of the National Health Service were budding, probably about 1948. Within a comparatively short time from the commencement of the NHS, I was admitted to the Royal Devon and Exeter Hospital to have all my problems investigated. I have wondered in later years whether I would actually have gone to hospital if the NHS had not come into being. If the doctor had to be paid, then certainly hospital care must have been costly as well.

The doctor came quite regularly, especially during the winters. I hated being ill and did my best not to let on when I felt the pain and soreness begin. I fought it for as long as possible, sometimes for days, before I knew I had to give in and tell Mother. My problem was cystitis which brought searing pain to the nether regions. I really disliked always being ill in the unmentionables and wished I could have some more glamorous condition, such as a broken arm or leg, or even swoon occasionally with some exciting, undefined ailment.

There were no antibiotics in those days and the doctor's solution was M&B tablets. These were large and round and tasted terrible. Mother crushed them up and fed them to me in teaspoonfuls of blackcurrant jam. Nurse Stear, the High Bickington nurse, called regularly in between the doctor's visits. One winter she advised Mother to be more cautious with the M&B tablets. Apparently I had become listless and dazed and was not responding naturally, and my lips had turned blue. Her opinion was,

"Dr Morrish is too fond of giving out M&B tablets. If I were you, I would stop them for a while."

Mother did as she suggested and within a day or two I had returned to normal. Mother realised that she had probably been poisoning me.

I was admitted to the Royal Devon and Exeter Hospital round about April or May in 1949, when I was just eleven years old. At that time the hospital was situated at Southernhay and was a pleasant red brick building. I think that my hospital stay was the spur that prompted Father and Mother to buy the Austin Seven, so they could come and visit me. Even so, the visits were infrequent. They were so busy and the farm work was so demanding and just could not be left. There were all the animals and poultry to tend to and care for, the milking twice a day, and there was arable work in the fields which was important as well. I quite understood and knew that I could not expect them to visit more than two or three times a week. Once again I was home sick and looked forward to those visits with all my heart.

I was admitted to the hospital several times during that summer, and on only one occasion was I put on a children's ward; all the other times I was on adult wards. It was all quite bewildering and to some extent frightening, as I did not understand any of the procedures or what was happening. I dreaded the catheters and injections but I had to endure it all without my parents. I know that everyone tried to be kind but they had to do whatever was necessary. Strangely, underneath it all, I was glad that I was somewhere where hopefully they could sort out my problems. I had lived with the pain and the illness for so long and it was grinding me down. I knew that I could not go on like it for much longer.

When Mother and Father came to visit, thankfully they brought lots of books. They must have made trips to Torrington Library to keep me in reading material. Enid Blyton helped me to get through those long days and nights, particularly the nights. I was deeply into the "Adventure" stories then: *The Sea of Adventure*, *The Valley of Adventure* and *The Island of Adventure*. I remember reading them all in Exeter Hospital. They were easy-to-read page turners, pleasingly thick, with lots of mystery and excitement which enabled me to forget my own troubles and woes.

After many tests and X-rays a conclusion was reached. I had tuberculosis. I was a rare specimen apparently and the youngest known person to have a tubercular bladder. My parents were told that, previously, the youngest person to have the condition was aged eighteen and had lived in Scotland. My mother explained that my bladder looked like a balloon which had been blown up and then let down again and it was saggy and full of pockets. I suppose it was a death sentence really, although I was unaware of it. I was sent home and prayers were said for me in church.

My parents were given strict instructions on how to care for me. It was the way all patients with tuberculosis were treated in those days, and the recipe was fresh air and rest. Well, growing up on a farm I had lived in the fresh air all my life. However, they were told I must not put foot to ground, and I must be outside all day if possible. Father put an old sofa out on the front lawn underneath the lilacs, by the rambling roses which trailed the fence. The great laburnum stood guard, in golden splendour, and every day Father carried me downstairs to the sofa, then every night he carried me back up to my bedroom again. At night the sofa was covered with a hailer (tarpaulin) to protect it from the dew. I remember that summer of 1949 very well: it was the most beautiful summer with long hot sunny days and very little rain; there were very few days when I had to stay in my bedroom.

My little abode on the lawn, tucked under the fence and the roses, soon became the focal point for the household, and all the jobs which could include me were done in the front garden. I was able to help prepare dinner by shelling the peas and beans, and any other small tasks which could be done while lying on my bed-sofa. Everyone spent as much time as possible with me so that I did not feel isolated, and friends came over at the weekends to play, although of course they were the ones who played and I had to watch. Nevertheless, it was good to see them and I really enjoyed their company. Mary, Alice and Cousin Rachel visited a lot. I missed the companionship of my school friends and of course I was missing a lot of schooling. I had returned to school for the first day of the summer term after the Easter holidays. I was in pain all day and as I trudged back up the road (on my own, as Mary had already left to attend secondary school), I knew that I was going to have to give in and tell Mother I was poorly again. Little did anyone realise, that would be my last day at Roborough School.

From my vantage point on the sofa by the garden fence, I was able to peer between the roses and look up the lane and keep track of everyone as they visited and left the farm. The one person I dreaded seeing was Nurse Stear. She had moved on from her motorbike days and was now the proud possessor of a car. She was an extremely capable woman and a very good and well-respected nurse, but somewhere in her training, the technique of administering injections must have been completely overlooked (perhaps she was away that day). She had one style of approach, and that was to use the syringe much like a pneumatic drill and thrust it into the flesh with great force.

Nurse Stear holding Cousin John at his christening.

I was reminded how lucky I was, as the new wonder drug penicillin was available and I was being treated with it. I cannot remember now whether Nurse came every day or every other day. It felt like every day but it may have been alternate days. I dreaded her visits and my heart sank as I watched her car carefully make its way down the bumpy lane. My buttocks and thighs were black and blue with bruising, and I screwed up my eyes and turned my head away as she surveyed the combat zone, and tried to select a relatively unscathed area.

After about two months of living outdoors, complete bed rest and penicillin injections, I had to return to Exeter to see what progress, if any, had been made. Dr Morrish, to his credit, had always dismissed the hospital's diagnosis. He said that he couldn't see how a child living on a farm in North Devon could possibly have tuberculosis. I suppose my parents thought back to those six Scottish cows who were all reactors, although as Mother said, I didn't like milk and did not drink much. Cereals, and bread and milk broth were the only ways I could be persuaded to imbibe a little. Unfortunately I did not like it neat, and refused to drink it either at home or school.

I was not keen to return to the hospital, and once again I was in an adult ward. The day after my arrival I was given an injection in my upper arm, administered with deftness and little pain. I soon forgot it and there was nothing to see. After a day or two there seemed to be much interest in this injection, and I was asked to point out where it had been. They all seemed extremely excited that there was nothing to see, and a large group of doctors gathered around my bed eagerly discussing the matter. They seemed very pleased and happy and even cracked some jokes with me. I was doing some knitting at the time and one of them picked up the ball of wool and played catch. Apparently, that injection was the equivalent to what was given to the cows, and I definitely had no reaction, so I had never come in contact with tuberculosis.

Well, after the very pleasant shock of finding out that after all I did not have the dreaded disease tuberculosis, they soon decided that my problem was a muscular one which could soon be sorted by a few minor operations. During the preceding year I had had my teeth sorted; they were not in a great state in spite of a childhood with very little sugary food, and several of them had been removed. Each time this had involved a trip to Torrington Hospital and chloroform administered on a cotton wool pad. How I hated the sickly smell and being held down while I counted to ten. I fought it in every way imaginable.

On one occasion Dr Morrish had visited the farm with Mr Copp, the dentist, and administered the chloroform in my little bedroom. Perhaps they thought it would be less frightening for me. It didn't work; he was unable to put me to sleep. Apparently Mother asked him if he could have one more try; I suppose she was hoping to avoid another trip to the hospital. She told me about it afterwards. Dr Morrish refused; he said that I was fighting it, and he had already given me enough to knock out a bull and I would have to be admitted to Torrington Hospital and be sedated first.

Consequently, after all my experiences with the teeth, I was not overjoyed at the prospect of yet more operations, even if they were minor. I loathed the sickly smell of ether. At Exeter it drifted out of the operating theatres, wafted into the wards and permeated the air. One ward in particular, where I spent a few days, must have been quite close to the operating theatre. The sickly odour drifted across and it was impossible to avoid.

After the decision about my treatment was made, it all happened quite quickly and I did not have time to worry about cotton wool pads, chloroform or anything else. I was sedated, whisked off to the theatre where the chloroform was expertly administered and I was allowed home the next day. I was told there would be two more small ops about a month apart. It was all worth it, for the difference even after the first op was amazing. It dawned on me that I had lived with the pain for so long that I had completely forgotten what it was like to be pain free, and I only told Mother when it was nagging me all day and I could not put up with it any longer. After the second op everyone was so delighted with the results, it was pronounced that normal life could be resumed, and I could join the wider world again.

Well, this brought problems, as the wider world no longer included Roborough School. By now it was August and at eleven years old I was ready for secondary education. My year group (all four of us) had sat the selection exam at the beginning of the year, Thursday 13 January to be precise, according to my 1949 diary. It was not called the Eleven Plus in those days. At the time, although the school year ran from 1 September to 31 August as it does now, the ages of the children followed the calendar year, January to December. Consequently, almost everyone was still ten when they took the exam. My birthday was in April and I was the oldest in my school year, and the youngest had a birthday in October.

We had to go to Torrington Secondary School to take the exam, which was quite an exciting experience in itself. We went in Mr Rockey's taxi, and I remember that it broke down near Whitsleigh

Cross on the way back. Fortunately, after some pondering and fiddling under the bonnet he was able to restart it.

Even though Torrington Secondary School was probably at least twelve years old in 1949 when we took the exam, it was still considered to be a showpiece, and was talked about with awe because of the wonderful facilities. Until it was built sometime in the 1930s, everyone stayed at their local primary school until they were fourteen. We all found it quite daunting, and the hall seemed huge compared with our two small classrooms at Roborough. We sat in well-spaced-out rows and endeavoured to do our best with the exam papers.

The results came after Easter, and to everyone's delight and a certain amount of surprise I had passed to go to grammar school. It had been hoped that I would pass, but I had missed so much schooling it was considered doubtful. I think that much of the credit should go to Arthur Mee's *Children's Encyclopaedias*. They were always strewn all over my bed during those long bouts of illness and enriched my life in so many ways. My friend Alice had passed the exam as well, so it was a double delight.

There was one big problem with living at Roborough: it was impossible to attend a grammar school daily, and Roborough was certainly not unique. In a large rural county like Devon, there were many pockets where daily attendance at a grammar school was out of the question. It was considered to be unfair on children who had passed the exam not to be able to take up their place, and so the Devon Education Authority provided free boarding education for children who had passed the exam but were unable to attend a grammar school daily. At the time the county boarding school for girls was Totnes High School for Girls, and the boys likewise, at Totnes King Edward VI Grammar School. They were both day schools with small boarding houses attached, each for about thirty-five boarders.

Well, the question of attending Totnes was superfluous for me, for by the time the results came through I had been diagnosed with a life-threatening illness, and it was considered unlikely that I would take up the offer. When eventually I was given the "all clear" and told that I could get on with my life, it was already August. My parents were worried about me being so far away after being so ill. Sixty miles seemed much further in 1949 than it does now, also it was sixty miles from the north to the south of the county on a circuitous roundabout route. Then, as now, the main routes through Devon flowed from east to west. My parents thought that there might be an alternative solution as there was a scheme whereby it might be possible to attend Barnstaple Grammar School. There were families, approved by the education authority, where pupils could lodge during the week and then go home for the weekend. Mother wrote to the education authority to ask whether that might be possible, as I had been so ill.

After some deliberation their verdict came back. They said that the matron of the boarding house at Totnes had been a nursing sister and in their opinion, as I had been so ill, it would be a much better situation for me to be in a boarding house under her care, than it would to be in Barnstaple living with a family.

Mother had no answer to that, so off to Totnes I went.

Further Afield

If they had put us into a rocket and fired us off to Mars the difference to our lives could not have been more startling. Having been an avid reader of books such as Enid Blyton's *Malory Towers* and *The Naughtiest Girl in the School*, I felt that I had a fairly good idea about boarding schools, especially the bit about midnight feasts. Alice had an older sister, Mary, who had been at the school for several years, so she must have had some knowledge about what to expect, which was probably more realistic than mine. It was a big new adventure though, and, looking back, I think we took it in our stride very well. That is not to say I did not miss my parents and the farm, I did terribly; and in the beginning I suffered desperate bouts of homesickness.

Alice and I always did our own thing and made our own friends, but it was good to have someone else there from Roborough – someone who knew everything without even having to talk about it; a shared secret knowledge of a previous life.

The last ten days or so of my previous life had been spent in a whirlwind of activity. I had suddenly been promoted from an invalid to more or less fit and able, with only one small op to go, and my mother was faced with a mountain of last-minute tasks. Boarding school at Totnes meant a school uniform, which I found exciting as no one wore uniforms in primary schools in those days. There was a long list of requirements which necessitated a whole day shopping in Barnstaple, plus sending for requisite items such as badges, blazers, ties, hats (navy blue beret for winter, white panama for summer), grey shorts, green aertex gym shirts and a green girdle for the standard navy blue gymslip. The list was endless: we each needed a gabardine mac, a warm woollen winter overcoat, school blouses and cardigans, and then there was all the footwear – sturdy school shoes, plimsolls, hockey boots, and the boarders also needed house shoes, which were black and buttoned with a single strap across the instep.

The really daunting task however, was sewing name tapes on all the items. How my mother managed to acquire the name tapes in such a short space of time I do not know. I think she must have lived in hope and ordered them earlier. It was a last-minute job; not many days before term was due to begin, and Mother recruited everyone she could think of. Miss Frances Bright, Mrs Hilda Rockey and several of the aunties arrived bright and early one morning, settled themselves around the big dining room table, which had the mountain of clothes heaped in the middle, and then frantically sewed all day. Everything had to be named, even down to socks and hair ribbons. Of course, as a boarder all our personal and leisure clothes needed naming as well, including vests, liberty bodices, stockings, nightdresses and the inevitable, hated, huge navy blue knickers with pockets in which to keep our hankies.

I spent those last few weeks at Wansley in a happy daze; I think I just wandered around with a smile on my face. It felt wonderful just to be normal and not in constant pain and of course there was the added excitement of boarding school – all the new clothes and eagerly anticipated midnight feasts. It made me feel special to see my name embroidered in red on the name tapes on all my new garments, and there was also a brand new trunk, blue with wooden bars around.

*

The boarding house was a sturdy Victorian or Edwardian building, situated on the Ashburton Road across the playing fields from the school. It was called Hawkmoor, which ironically was the name of the sanatorium up on Dartmoor where my parents had once feared I might end up. Happily, this did not happen and early in September 1949 our doughty little Austin Seven pulled up outside Hawkmoor, Totnes, and I gazed at the house which was going to be my home for most of the next five years. We had arrived quite early, and as I was the first of the new first formers to arrive, I had the choice of beds in the dormitory. It was all just as I thought it was going to be and I looked around in happy wonderment.

Mother, I discovered later, was not quite so impressed. I heard her remark that she thought it was all very spartan. Goodness only knows, we were not used to much luxury and our own homes were furnished very basically, but I heard her say that she had expected there to be some floor covering in the dormitory. It had quite passed me by that the dormitories had bare floorboards, although there was a small mat beside each bed. These days it is fashionable to have bare floorboards but then it was a sign of poverty. We each had a little iron bedstead, much like my own at home, and there was a locker beside each bed, which was the only place where we could keep our own personal possessions. We shared the use of wardrobes and chests of drawers.

There were between thirty and thirty-five boarders while I was at Totnes, and apart from a handful of evacuees from London who had stayed on into the sixth form to complete their education, I think that the rest of us came from similar backgrounds. Most of us were country children from the rural backwaters of Devon, and we were all receiving a free boarding education, presumably at the expense of the taxpayers of Devon. We came from the wilds of Dartmoor: such places as Widecombe in the Moor, Mary Tavey and Bovey Tracey. We came from numerous small hamlets and remote communities such as

Sutcombe, Smeatheharpe and other villages scattered the length and breadth of the county. At the time there was quite a contingent from Lynton and Lynmouth, so obviously they were unable to travel daily to a grammar school, which would presumably have been Barnstaple. There were three of us from Roborough, two or three from Dolton and one or two from Chulmleigh, but no matter where we came from, we felt like a family. There was comradeship amongst us and we looked out for each other in the wider school world, and I always felt happy and comfortable with my life in the boarding house.

There were about 250 pupils at the school including us boarders. The day children came from quite a wide area: some were bussed in from Paignton and Brixham, others arrived by train from Buckfastleigh and of course many lived in Totnes itself and nearby villages.

Within a very short space of time, realisation dawned that I was the owner of a broad Devonshire accent. It had never occurred to me before. Everyone within my circle of family, friends and acquaintances spoke with a ripe country burr and used the same idioms and expressions, and I had never thought of such things. All of a sudden I was confronted with the fact that many of my contemporaries spoke a "bit posh" like they did on the wireless. Alice and I definitely had two of the most authentic Devonian accents in the school but there were quite a few others much the same. It was one of many eye openers, one of a myriad of things to absorb and deal with during that first term.

Hawkmoor would originally have been a private dwelling house, and when it was converted into a small boarding house attached to the school, an extension had been added at the back. The first floor of the extension provided two additional dormitories, and the ground floor area was known as the prep room, but as well as being the room where we did our prep, it was also our dining room and area for leisure-time activities. The ground level sloped from the front to the back of the house, and therefore an additional third floor at the back was possible; a cloakroom had been built into the slope, and there was a covered veranda area where we could play on wet days.

Alice and I soon settled into the routine, and bells became part of our life. The first bell sounded at seven thirty, when we rose sleepily from our beds and stumbled to the washrooms. The seniors had their own bathroom with a door that locked, but we juniors way down the hierarchy had to queue in a line and wait (shivering during the winters) for the use of four wash basins placed in a row – no door, no privacy. "For goodness' sake, hurry up, stop admiring yourself," and other remarks could be heard, especially from the end of the queue where the late risers were standing, huddled against the wall with only a few minutes to spare before the breakfast bell sounded at eight o'clock.

Before going downstairs, we each had to strip the bedcovers back to the end of our bed so that it could air while we ate our breakfast. There was always an inspection while we were eating, and woe betide those who had forgotten or could not be bothered. It was a walk of shame to leave the dining room and bad luck if you missed part of your breakfast. Actually, the breakfasts were rather good, certainly better than anything I had ever had at home. There was cereal followed by something cooked, which was unheard of at Wansley, and we finished off with toast. It set us up until lunchtime and meant we did not feel the need of a mid-morning snack, although most of the day-girls brought one.

When we did make our beds after breakfast there was a regulation way of doing it and the matron, Mac, insisted upon "hospital corners" for the sheets and blankets. We were taught how to do them when we first arrived, and it was expected that we always made our beds in that manner and mostly we did – in fact I continued to do so until duvets became fashionable. Recently I was a visitor at a hospital and watched two nurses change the bedding, and I can report that even nurses no longer always do "hospital corners". After making our beds it was time to ram our prep into our satchels, fling on our coats and berets and scurry off to school in time for the ten to nine bell.

No one messed with Mac, short for Miss McKean. She ruled the boarding house with a rod of iron and not much got past her. She was strict and firm, and we were in trouble if we broke the rules. The worst punishment was being grounded, which meant losing our Saturday morning two hours of precious freedom. Mac was tall with steel grey hair and perceptive brown eyes. We would never have dared call her Mac to her face but she knew full well that was her name. She was fair, understood us better than we realised and looked after us well. We moaned and groaned about our lives under the strict regime, but we respected Mac and, if pushed, we would have to admit that all in all she wasn't a bad sort.

The daily routine in the boarding house was the same all the time I was there and our lives fell into an orderly pattern. After returning from school we changed, put on our house shoes, and were given a cup of tea and a biscuit in the prep room. Then it was time to knuckle down to our prep (homework). Everyone except those in the sixth form had to sit in the room and do their work. There was total silence from four thirty until five thirty, while we wrote essays, learnt poetry and wrestled with algebra, irregular verbs and declensions and other dreary necessities. Mac always supervised us, perhaps doing some paperwork of her own or some knitting. No matter what she was doing though, she kept an eagle eye on us all and could soon spot someone who was reading a novel, or doing something surreptitiously under the guise of schoolwork.

By six o'clock the room had been transformed into a dining room. We laid the tables ourselves and Mac served high tea. The food at the boarding house was nutritious and mostly enjoyable. I had never been used to a cooked evening meal, and two cooked meals a day, plus the fact that I was no longer walking at least three miles to and from school, meant that by the end of the term I was definitely beginning to look more rotund, much to my parents' delight. Our midday meals which were cooked in the main school canteen were reasonable, not wonderful but mostly edible, and compared with the offerings at Roborough Primary School, definitely Cordon Bleu standard.

The war had been over for four years when I went to Totnes, but most essential food items were still on ration. Luckily Hawkmoor had a large garden. We were allowed to use part of it, especially in the summer, but there was also a large vegetable garden which provided fresh fruit and veg in season. There was a greenhouse tucked away amongst the vegetables, and raising seedlings and tender plants was not its only use. Alice was well acquainted with the greenhouse, as Mac made it quite clear that was where she had to go to do her violin practice.

Mac kept some hens, so fresh eggs were available much of the time and she also kept bees. There were two or three hives at the bottom of the vegetable patch. Alice and her sister Mary were used to bees, as their Aunty Elsie who lived next door in Roborough had several hives and both girls gave their aunty a hand. Mac was delighted to have some boarders who had experience of bee keeping; she made good use of them, and frequently dragged them down the garden to help.

Her honey was a good substitute for sugar, and she and the kitchen staff used it in imaginative ways. In season there was a great deal of rhubarb sweetened with honey, and very good it was too. It was not long after I became a boarder that I gave up having sugar in my tea. Sugar was still on ration well into the '50s and only one sugar bowl was permitted during mealtimes. It was such a chore wandering around the dining room trying to find it. If it was empty there was no more available, so I decided to learn to like tea without sugar and save myself the bother.

We children were allowed to keep our sweet coupons. It was all a complete novelty to me, as confectionary of any kind had played no part in my life. There had never been an opportunity to even use our coupons at Roborough, as there were never any sweets on the grocery van that visited the farm once a fortnight.

Suddenly, I was initiated into the delights of Woolworths' sweet counter. What to choose was the first pleasure, and I was definitely into quantity over quality. Then of course it was the nervous pondering of how to ask for it, for I had never been to a shop and bought something for myself, and I was shy and unsure about the procedure. I was eleven years old; I could drive a tractor, I could milk a cow and I could drench a sheep, but I had never been to a shop on my own and purchased anything.

To the delight of us first formers there appeared to be sweet coupons in abundance, for the older boarders seemed to be uninterested in, and surfeited by, sugary treats, and in a world-weary way were willing to sell their coupons to us lowly creatures. Not only that, but we soon heard about the shop in Ticklemore Street, where it was possible to obtain sweets for no coupons at all! Mac had also heard about the shop and lectured us about "dirty backstreet shops" and forbade us to go there. All to no avail, and Saturday mornings would find us making our way furtively along Ticklemore Street to make under-the-counter purchases to add to our swag.

Saturdays were the best day of the week, for they brought precious freedom – at least two hours of wandering around Totnes on our own, doing our own thing. We had to do an hour of prep first though, supervised by Mac and as always in complete silence. Then at last, the moment when we could line up to receive our pocket money, the princely sum of one shilling and sixpence a week. We were expected to buy a stamp for the weekly letter home (tuppence halfpenny) and reserve a penny for the Sunday collection in church, but otherwise it was all our own to fritter on any whim that took our fancy. If we needed to buy soap or toothpaste we could ask for extra funds, but Mac had a memory like an elephant and it was no use asking more than once a term. If she was suspicious, the offending person had to fetch their soap dish or toothpaste tube to prove their need.

My great friend during the time I was at Totnes was another Rachel. In actual fact our homes were not far apart, for Rachel lived at Dolton and like me she was brought up on a farm, Woolridge, which was tucked away under the hills near Halsdon not too far from the River Torridge. Rachel was tall and attractive with black hair and green eyes. She should in fact have been in the year above me and had started at Totnes the previous September. However, like me she had been ill with what was euphemistically called "growing pains", and had been sent back to the farm for six months to rest and recover. She was only four months older than me, as her birthday was in December, and so she was very young for her school year. When she returned to Totnes she was put back a year and we ended up in the same form.

She was one of those lucky people blessed with a first-class brain. It was like blotting paper and absorbed information so easily. It certainly had not been necessary to put her back a school year, for she would have coped perfectly well in her correct school year in spite of missing six months. I always had to work to keep up my grades, but Ray, as she was usually known, seemed to cruise along without doing much work and still obtain A grades. Ah well, life never was fair.

Perhaps it was our shared love of books and reading that brought us together, plus the fact that we were both farmers' daughters. We hit it off from the beginning and remained good friends throughout our school days. Saturday mornings meandering around Totnes town with Ray are some of my happiest memories of those years. It was just wonderful to be free for a couple of hours and do our own thing, for at times, boarding school restrictions did make us feel like prisoners.

We always began with Boots Lending Library at the top of the town. In those days most of the larger Boots stores had libraries. There may have been a small fee to join initially, I cannot remember now, but our membership cards allowed us to use all Boots' libraries, and books could be returned to the Barnstaple branch during the holidays. Naturally Woolworths was another stopping-off point, as we gradually made our way down the steep street, and by the time we had reached The Plains at the bottom we had always acquired some sweets, a pasty and a comic or two. One of us always bought an *Eagle* and usually a *Dandy* or *Beano* as well, for we followed the fortunes of the two Dans: Dan Dare in the *Eagle*, the suave and brave commander of the space ship, and Desperate Dan who dined on cow pies, in the *Dandy*, and of course Dennis the Menace in the *Beano*. Occasionally if we were flush with money such as a birthday present we would splash out on a larger purchase, but it would almost always be a book. We never bought make-up (it was not allowed anyway), or beads and baubles, perfume or other adornments.

Hawkmoor.

(Left) Ray and I walking to Dartington on a school visit as first formers.
(Right) Rachel Pickard (Ray), Alice Rockey, Anne Hopper.

After making our purchases we always headed for "The Island" down by the Dart. It was not quite an island, but almost, and we spent a blissful half-hour eating our pasties and watching the ducks and swans and human activity on the river. I have very fond memories of The Island for it was there that I felt reconnected with the human race again. It was life-affirming to watch people going about their business and enjoying themselves – to know that real life still continued, away from the small narrow world of boarding school.

Sundays, like Saturdays, followed a set routine, and after breakfast, which was later than weekdays, we all had to get ready for church. Before we set off there was an "inspection". We lined up in the hall, and Mac and Miss Barton, her friend who frequently stayed and helped, gave us the once-over. Berets and ties were straightened, shoes scrutinised to make sure they had been polished; we had to show that we had a penny for the collection and a hankie in our pocket, and we were also expected to have a pair of gloves and of course our prayer book. Once we had passed all those hurdles, Mac would wield her clothes brush across the shoulders of our warm winter navy blue coats or blazers, to disperse dandruff and hair, and then we would line up in twos to walk in crocodile to church. The summer uniform was green stripe or check dresses, blazers, panama hats, sandals and white socks.

We usually walked in the north door of the church from the Guildhall side and we sat at the front near the beautiful rood screen. I did admire the intricate carvings on the wonderful stone screen, but all of us would rather have cast our eyes over the King Edward VI Grammar School boys, who were strategically placed at the back, directly behind us, so that it was impossible to see them without turning around. They had walked up the High Street and in the south door. Mac's eagle eyes noted every movement and fidget and there was no chance of any communication.

In later years, after being confirmed, other opportunities had arisen, and I was surprised to read in my 1953 diary that Alice, Rachel and I and a few others often rose bright and early on Sunday mornings and headed to the church for eight o'clock communion. This was in addition to the eleven o'clock service which was compulsory. *Were we really that religious?* I thought to myself. As I read on I realised that the main attraction had been the grammar school boys who were altar servers, and there was the opportunity after the service to stroll down the High Street together on the way back to our respective boarding houses.

The weekends as a boarder were actually very enjoyable, and there was quite a lot of spare time to pursue our own interests. Naturally, we were envious of our friends who were day-girls, for their lives were so much broader socially. They lived with their families and enjoyed normal family life. They met friends and went out at the weekends, they went to the cinema and shows. Many of them lived at Paignton or near the sea, and they enjoyed all the amenities and opportunities of living in a busy tourist area.

Nevertheless, as boarders we did have access to things that would not have been the case if we had been living at home. The school grounds and its resources were ours at the weekend. During the summer term the tennis courts were available, and I would never have had the opportunity to play so much tennis living at Wansley. We played rounders or cricket most evenings after tea, and Mac regularly took us swimming in the Leat. There was the sandpit in the field where we could practise "hop, step and jump" and the high jump was often available as well. I loved playing tennis and rounders, they were my favourites, but I also loved the companionship and camaraderie of it all. One thing about access to all the sports equipment at the weekends, it was just good fun, there was no need to be competitive about anything, we could just use it for our enjoyment.

I was not particularly sporty other than I was good at gymnastics. I loathed hockey and could never see the point of rushing around a field, scantily clad in shorts and blouse in the freezing wintry weather, where there was a very good chance of being whacked on the shins with a wooden stick or a very hard ball. I quite liked netball and was good enough to make the Grenville house team, and occasionally the school B team if they were hard pressed. I enjoyed swimming though, and would have liked to have been better at it. There was not a lot of opportunity, as neither the school nor the town could boast a swimming pool. There was a town swimming club known as the Weir Head Club, and it was situated on the River Dart just above the weir, where the Leat fed off from the main river. The school did not use it at all, and when we needed to obtain certificates for distances, or do lifesaving courses where the measurements had to be accurate, we could use the swimming pool at Foxhole School at Dartington.

Foxhole School seemed to us to be very glamorous and *risqué*. Apparently, (and this was talked about in hushed tones) they went swimming with no clothes on, and what was more, they did not have to attend lessons if they did not feel like it. The school was considered to be trendy and modern, and apparently many showbiz parents, as well as some of the great and the good, sent their children there. It seemed astonishing that people paid good money to let their offspring swim in the nude and bunk off lessons if they felt like it. We felt a little envious, and I knew with certainty that if I did not have to, I would never go to another maths lesson as long as I lived.

Boarding school life may have been rather like living in a prison but at least there was plenty of companionship. The prep room was our living room, and during the winter evenings and weekends the focal point of our lives. There was one coal-fired stove, which basically was a modern cream enamel and glass version of the old black tortoise stoves at Roborough School. We sat around the tables companionably in groups, various activities in different parts of the room. Board games and cards were quite popular, and squeals of excitement, or groans of disappointment provided a backdrop to the more muted tones of those who were knitting, sewing or maybe drawing, and chatting about school life, friends, plans for the holidays, boys, pop songs, films or whatever. There was a loud speaker on the wall connected to a wireless somewhere on the premises. It was tuned in to the *Light Programme* and brought us the latest offerings on the musical scene. Guy Mitchell was very popular then, and we sang along to "She Wears Red Feathers and a Huly-Huly Skirt" and "My

Truly, Truly Fair". Donald Peers and Ronnie Ronald also sang to us through the loud speaker. How tame it all seems now compared to rock and roll, Elvis and the Beatles, who were about ten years in the future. Those who needed a quiet space were usually gathered around a table at one end of the room, where it was reasonably peaceful to read, write the weekly letter home, or complete some prep.

Stamp collecting was a popular hobby, and some of my pocket money was spent on stamps. Naturally there was a good deal of swapping. None of us could afford anything of value so they were run-of-the-mill stamps, but I learnt a great deal of geography without realising it – particularly about the British colonies and the French colonies. There were so many far-flung corners of the world where the King's head was on the stamps, and before I left Totnes the Queen's head appeared instead. How strange it seemed initially to sing "God Save the Queen".

Letters and parcels from home were highlights of our lives, especially "tuck parcels". Everyone in the dormitory eagerly looked forward to their arrival, for there was a great deal of sharing. There were usually far too many goodies in a parcel for one person to scoff on their own, and homemade cakes and other offerings could soon go stale. The arrival of the tuck parcel sometimes meant a midnight feast. We all felt that it was obligatory to have one from time to time. The worst part was keeping awake until midnight and we took it in turns, each keeping awake for half an hour – it was not easy.

When we were all finally awake we had to keep very quiet, for Mac's bedroom was on the same floor – just up the corridor. We usually had a fit of the giggles and it really was important not to make a noise, as there was the possibility of being grounded. I seem to remember that most midnight feasts were rather cold affairs. There was no heating at all in the dormitories, in fact central heating was almost unheard of for anyone. We sat around the tuck box shivering with the cold while we sampled the delights within. Intense cold in the bedrooms was a feature of boarding school life, just as it was at Wansley. The new extension built onto the back of Hawkmoor, where we first and second formers slept, seemed to be exceptionally cold, and one year I remember the toothpaste became so hard I could not squeeze it out of the tube.

Bedtime was at seven o'clock and lights out at seven thirty. Mac came around and said, "Goodnight," and switched off the light. No talking after lights out was the rule, so we had to whisper to each other and listen for Mac's footsteps. Most of us had torches and there was a lot of reading under the bedcovers. We also enjoyed storytelling and took it in turns to spin a yarn. There was no doubt that Ray was a brilliant storyteller; her imagination ran riot and sometimes she serialised her tale and it continued for several nights.

The greatest fun of all after lights-out, was playing sardines. It was more fun if two or three dormitories agreed to join in, and of course it really was spiced with danger, as discovery definitely courted punishment. One person hid and then the rest of us had to find her. It all had to take place in silence and we tiptoed around in the dark, searching the dormitories, trying not to giggle and stumble over things. When we discovered the hiding place, we had to creep in beside the person and also hide. Eventually almost everyone was squashed together behind a curtain, or under a bed, or in the lavatory, or wherever, desperately trying not to laugh or give away the hiding place.

One night something happened which definitely was not funny. Alice was a sleepwalker. Her sleepwalking activities began not long after we started at Totnes, and at first we found it alarming and a little frightening, for she walked around like a zombie with staring wide-open eyes. Mac talked to us about it and told us that we must not try to wake Alice or frighten her. We had to gently turn her round and guide her back to bed. This worked well; Alice continued to sleepwalk, and it was normal routine to help her back to her bed.

This continued intermittently for a year or two. One night, probably when we were about thirteen years old and in the third form, Alice woke up herself and discovered that she was not in bed, in fact she was not even in the boarding house. She was lying in a patch of bluebells under her dormitory window. It was in the early hours of the morning and she had evidently been sleepwalking, and had fallen out of the window. She was fortunate that she was not hurt; I think she just had some bruises and a black eye. She had fallen the height of two and a half storeys. The front of Hawkmoor was two storeys high and her dorm was halfway along the house. It was also lucky that she was fast asleep so her body was loose and relaxed, and she had fallen onto a patch of grass and bluebells. It would not have been so good if she had fallen out of one of the back windows, which were three storeys up with a concrete path underneath.

"What did you do when you woke up and found you were in the bluebells?" we gasped as she related her adventure.

"Well, the only thing I could do," said Alice in her matter-of-fact way (I suppose you are bound to be pragmatic if your mother lays out the village dead), "I stood up and found out that I was still alright, so I walked around to the front door and rang the bell."

We gazed at her in wonder, as we tried to imagine Mac's face when she answered the door in the middle of the night and discovered Alice on the doorstep. Apparently she was given VIP treatment – wrapped up warmly in blankets, given hot milk and a medical once-over – and the next day the window was fixed so that it could only be opened a little way.

*

I always enjoyed the daily walk from the farm to the village when I attended Roborough School, and likewise the journeys from Wansley to Totnes. They were little mini adventures of their own, and it is a truism that the travelling is often more interesting than the arrival. There were two ways of reaching Totnes: one was to drive in our little Austin Seven, and the other way was by rail. We always went by car at the beginning and end of term, as there was my big blue trunk to take. Alice has recently reminded me that it was strapped onto a carrier at the back of the car. Half-term journeys though were on the train, but either way I always looked forward to the trip and thoroughly enjoyed myself.

It would be true to say that our journey in the Austin Seven could be more accurately described as an "expedition". About 120 miles there and back, on 1950s Devon roads in an Austin Seven, was quite an undertaking, and not something that happened without some forethought and planning. Sustenance on the journey was important, and sandwiches and a thermos of tea were always packed. Heaters in cars were unheard of then, so Mother and I made sure we were well wrapped up in rugs during the cold winter months. When it was very cold, especially in December and January, we both had hot water bottles to cuddle. Not the soft rubbery ones which are available now but stone jars with a screw top, well wrapped in an old sock. They lasted the journey well though. Father, who was driving, just had to suffer the cold. However, when it was raining he, at least, had a windscreen wiper. There was just the one with one speed only, and it did its best to clear the rain so that the driver could see ahead. If it was raining heavily, Mother and I would be unable to see anything as the rain cascaded down over the windows. The car was not completely waterproof and I can certainly remember on one occasion, sitting in the back holding an umbrella to keep the drops from dripping down my neck and back. None of us thought any of this was the least bit unusual or bizarre, quite the opposite. We realised we were lucky to have a car and to be able to travel from A to B independently, and there were many who would be envious.

When Father turned the starting handle and Amy sprang into life (the registration number was AMV 541, hence the name) we all breathed a sigh of relief, for there was no certainty or predictability with cars in those days. Then we set off gently and steadily out of our long, bumpy and potholed lane, carefully braking down the steep Ten Oaks Hill, and then chugging up the equally steep Molland Hill and so to Roborough village. From then on we slowly and steadily progressed from the familiar, where we could name the fields and the owners, to the countryside which we knew but was not so familiar, until eventually we reached the wider world and anonymity.

We usually left home at about eight o'clock and it was probably about eight or nine o'clock before my parents returned in the evening. As farmers they enjoyed themselves surveying the fields and countryside as we drove past. They commented upon and compared the crops, and as the years passed they remembered what had been planted in fields during previous years. They always passed comment about the beautiful South Devon countryside and how early the crops were. They reckoned about two weeks earlier than in our more rugged and exposed countryside in North Devon.

We chugged through Winkleigh Aerodrome which was quite straightforward, although apparently during the war the route through was like a maze, which was difficult to negotiate without help. We steadily made our way through Crediton, then on to Exeter, past St David's station and then on to the notorious Telegraph Hill (the old one, not the present-day route) and another stiff challenge for Amy. After that it was Newton Abbot where we sometimes stopped for lunch. Occasionally Father varied the route and went via Chudleigh and Chudleigh Knighton. If we did not stop to eat at Newton Abbot, then it was straight on to Totnes and lunch at a café on The Plains.

Mother and Father may have been admiring the crops and the countryside, and we had certainly been driving through fresh and healthy country air, but inside the car it was anything but healthy. Mother smoked most of the time – Craven A and Senior Service were her favourites – and Father managed to drive and stoke up his pipe from time to time. I think that Exmoor Hunt was his preference then. The air was always thick and fudgy with cigarette and tobacco smoke, but we thought nothing of it. It was not considered to be bad or an issue of any kind, and we always drove everywhere in a swirl and fug of smoke and tobacco fumes.

*

If I ever need to make an effigy of someone to sit on top of a bonfire I shall choose Dr Beeching – he who in my estimation ruined the railways. I had grown to love travelling by train, and during the years from when I began school at Totnes in 1949, until I earned enough to buy my first car in 1964, the railways played quite a large part in my life and of course it was mostly steam. My love affair with trains began with my first half-term journeys to and from school. Totnes was on the main Great Western line, (brown and cream carriages) and Portsmouth Arms was on the main Southern line, (green carriages) so that meant changing at Exeter. There was quite a large contingent of boarders as far as Exeter, and a good number travelling on to North Devon, for there were the Lynton and Lynmouth group as well as us Roborough and Dolton children, and one or two from Chulmleigh during my early years at the school.

There was something about trains which captured my imagination. Those big powerful monsters, billowing steam and of course soot, slowly and majestically approaching the platform; the tingle of excitement and the clang and clatter as they drew near. Their arrival was fascinating and there was an element of mystery about them, for they came from exotic places and could transport us away to unfamiliar territory. I enjoyed it all: buying the ticket, the butterflies in my stomach as the train appeared in the distance, heaving suitcases in and finding a seat, preferably a corner seat to gaze out of the window into sidings and office blocks, then people's back gardens (a brief glimpse into other lives), and eventually the green fields and countryside of Devon.

The beauty of trains was the freedom to move about, to be able to walk up and down the corridors, and survey other carriages. Sometimes we stood in the corridor for a large part of the journey from Totnes to Exeter, or sat on our suitcases. The windows opened by tugging on a large leather strap, and we often travelled with our heads stuck out and hair blowing in the wind. This was dangerous and forbidden, as it was all too easy to be hit by an object or another train. It was soothing to sit back and be lulled hypnotically by the rhythm of the wheels: clackety-clack, clackety-clack, hol-i-day time, hol-i-day time, home we go, home we go, clackety-clack, clackety-clack, back to school, back to school clackety-clack, clackety-clack, soon be there, soon be there, clackety-clack, clackety-clack…

It would be difficult to find a more beautiful or interesting train journey than the one from Totnes to Portsmouth Arms. The rounded hills and lush valleys of the South Hams were beautiful, but the highlight of the journey was the section through Dawlish and Dawlish Warren. There was the glorious experience of the sea lapping along so close to the track at Dawlish, and then of course the tunnels near Dawlish Warren were eagerly anticipated. It was wise to close the windows or else the steam rushed in and engulfed the carriage. There never seemed to be lights in the carriages in those days, and we would suddenly be plunged into darkness, and then just as suddenly back into daylight again. We knew the tunnels so well that we could count how long they would last.

After that we kept watch for deer in the great Deer Park belonging to Powderham Castle and then on to Exeter where we had to change. The Great Western trains bringing us to Exeter were on their way to Paddington, and the Southern trains taking us from Exeter to Portsmouth Arms came from Waterloo. After changing at

Exeter, we settled back to slowly chug our way through the meadows and woodlands and many small country stations, until eventually we arrived at Portsmouth Arms.

I enjoyed the rail journeys because they gave me a sense of freedom. It was not just that we could move about on the train, but for a few hours we were unrestricted and nobody knew exactly where we were. Thank goodness there were no mobile phones or easy ways to keep a check on us in those days, for they would soon have discovered that we were not actually on the train at all but enjoying ourselves in Exeter. This escape to the delights of the city always happened on the way back to school, and we would arrive at Totnes on a much later train than our parents fondly imagined. We put our cases in the left luggage office and away we would go.

Alice and her sister Mary had some relatives who lived in the St Thomas area of Exeter and I can remember visiting them on several occasions. We made a short rail journey there using our same tickets; I cannot remember any problems. The thing that sticks in my mind is that they had a pianola, which is a mechanical piano. It was the first one I had ever seen and it fascinated me. It worked by inserting a roll of perforated paper, then when someone pedalled like mad to work the bellows, the pianola played the music. It struck me as a very easy way to churn out a tune without bothering with piano lessons at all.

There was only one occasion on our covert trips around Exeter that we slipped up, and Mac became suspicious. It was a genuine mistake, for after one of our secret excursions we caught the express which went straight to Plymouth and Penzance instead of the stopping train. We realised what had happened as we roared through Newton Abbot at a cracking pace. There was nothing for it but to sit tight as we raced through Totnes station and onwards towards Plymouth. We had to find a phone box and call Mac and tell her what had happened, and then we caught the next train back to Totnes, which meant an hour's wait. We arrived back at Hawkmoor very late to an icy reception, and were grounded. No trips to town the following Saturday.

I feel that I was lucky to have had so much opportunity to ride the trains during those years, for the end of the golden years of railways and steam trains was approaching, although no one realised it. My last three years of glorious travel from 1960 until 1963, when I was at Bedford Teacher Training College, was really the swan song of the railways before Beeching took his hatchet and performed carnage. It was a through line from Ilfracombe to Waterloo in those days, so I jumped on the train at Portsmouth Arms or Eggesford, and stayed in my seat until I reached the great metropolis. Then it was a short journey by bus or underground to St Pancras and another different but interesting journey, much more metropolitan, onwards to Bedford. There was one area where the line passed through clay pits and brickworks in south Bedfordshire, where it seemed as though we were passing through a lunar landscape.

I could not escape trains and railways even when I arrived in Bedford, as the hostel where I lived during my three years in the town was situated close to the station, and the main railway line to the Midlands ran along on the other side of the garden wall. The expresses roared through with whistles and hoots, trains ground to a halt with clangs and reverberations, goods trains pounded through, carriages were shunted into sidings, it was a cacophony of noise all day and all night. Just to make sure there were no silent interludes, there was a busy road on the other side of the hostel with plenty of traffic to add to the din. I had just spent six years living on a farm in remotest Devon. I had been swathed and cosseted in silence; there had been nothing noisier than a tractor and my ears were adjusted to the noise levels of a lowing cow, the cackle of a hen, a barking dog and the dawn chorus from the oak and beech trees. After about two weeks in Bedford I thought my head was going to burst; I was not sure that I could stand it any longer and I was ready to bang my head against a wall and go home. Suddenly, one day I realised that I was not hearing the noise anymore. Thankfully my ears and brain had adjusted to accept the noise level and were able to relegate it to the background.

I was fond of Waterloo station; I suppose because it was the link to home. It was in October 1962, travelling back to Devon at half term, that I stood on the platform at Waterloo and wondered whether I would ever get there again. Kennedy and Khrushchev were eyeballing each other across the waters around Cuba, and the whole world was waiting with bated breath. We had three minutes apparently if the nuclear buttons were pressed, and I just prayed that I would get back to Wansley in time to die there. If it was all going to end, that was the only place I wanted to be.

It was strange how the train from Waterloo to Portsmouth Arms seemed to change character as the journey progressed. It began its journey full of importance, straining at the leash to transport its passengers from a metropolitan station in one of the great cities of the world, to their destination. There were certainly several destinations, for that one train was bound for Ilfracombe, Torrington and Plymouth via Okehampton, not to mention all the other places on the way. Large wooden name boards were attached to the carriages and it was just a case of getting into the correct one. Travellers to Eggesford or Portsmouth Arms were always told to sit in the carriages marked Ilfracombe. The reason for this was because country stations have short platforms, and the trains were much longer. Ilfracombe carriages were the ones which always drew up alongside the platforms once the train reached our little stations north west of Exeter. Not that it worried me very much, as I had jumped out of carriages which were not at the platform more times than I can remember. It is surprising how high a train is when it is not stood at a platform.

By the time the train had reached our little stations along the Taw valley, it had changed from a busy, self-important beast hurrying along and bearing passengers, luggage and mail to the distant corners of the country, into an Adlestrop train which sauntered from stop to stop. It hissed and sighed, let off steam, lingering at each small station. I am not quite sure where the change took place, but it was possibly round about Crewkerne, after sprinting down through Basingstoke, Andover and Salisbury, that the train had a change of heart, and decided to shake off its metropolitan image and take life at a more leisurely pace. Certainly, the other side of Exeter it didn't even pretend to be in a hurry.

There was always a lot of jolting and jerking at St David's station, for this was where the carriages destined for Okehampton, Tavistock and Plymouth were uncoupled. Another engine took them on to Yeoford where they then made their way across Dartmoor. I am sorry that I never made that journey because it is impossible now. Aunty Lorna did part of it though, when she regularly travelled from Portsmouth Arms to Okehampton during the period when she was a "general dogsbody" (her description, although the job was advertised as "matron's assistant") at an Okehampton old people's home.

Eggesford was the station I used mainly on my trips to Bedford because the express trains always stopped there. Apparently, this was because Lord Portsmouth, who resided at Eggesford House during the nineteenth century, gave permission for the railway line to run through his land on the provision that all trains stopped there (how wonderful to be able to make such demands) and this ruling lasted over one hundred years into the 1960s. However, the station that I remember with nostalgia will always be Portsmouth Arms, named after the pub just up the road which was kept by Aunt Leah's brother, my Great-Uncle Jack, for many years. Travelling on the trains was such fun, and there are one or two incidents that happened at Portsmouth Arms which stick in my mind.

Firstly, the only time I can recollect a communication cord being pulled was at Portsmouth Arms. It certainly was not something that was done for fun, as there was a stiff fine, and this daring act was perpetrated by my staid, decorous Aunty Lorna. We had spent a day shopping in Exeter. Shopping trips to Exeter during the 1950s were very much a part of my life, and Mother and the aunties went two or three times a year and we always went on the train.

On this occasion it was just Lorna and me; I suppose I was about seventeen or eighteen at the time. We had had a good day and came back elated and laden with bags. It was a winter shopping expedition, and by the time we returned to Portsmouth Arms it was gone six o'clock and dark. There was no electricity at the station, and the station master was using a Tilley lantern as we all did on dark evenings. Lorna and I had got into the last carriage, and consequently when we reached the station we were not on the platform; only the first two carriages were at the platform and we were way down the line in the dark.

"Don't worry," I said to Lorna, "I will jump down first, you pass me the bags and then you jump down."

I glanced along the line to the platform in the distance and saw the station master holding his Tilley lantern aloft, lighting the way for the few passengers getting off the train. All went well. I jumped down, Lorna passed me the bags, of which there were a good number, but before she had time to jump, I saw the station master blow his whistle, wave his flag and the train began to move. Of course, he had no idea there were some passengers disembarking down the line in the dark.

I shouted, picked up the bags and began to run beside the track and moving train towards the platform, waving and hollering at the top of my voice – all to no avail as he could not hear me over the noise of the engine. As he stood watching the train depart, I could tell when he realised there was a problem – as Lorna glided past him, silhouetted in the open doorway. I saw the Tilley lantern jerk up and down as he also began haring along the platform, shouting and waving as the train picked up speed.

Thank goodness Lorna had the presence of mind to pull the communication cord, although by the time the train stopped, it was a long way off the other side of the platform. Eventually, when I managed to catch up with them, there were three men – the station master, the guard and the train driver – all helping her to climb down backwards. I doubt whether she had ever had so many men making a fuss over her in her life. The whole episode was a little adventure and a real giggle, and we laughed and chuckled over it for many years.

It was at Portsmouth Arms, returning home from school for a half-term break, that we once had problems with a ticket. Someone had lost their ticket – I cannot remember who it was now – but as we approached the station we pondered what to do. Between us we hatched a plan. There were about seven of us getting off, so we decided that as we lined up to have the tickets clipped, the first person in the line would slip back and hand her ticket to the person who had lost theirs, who would be waiting the last in the line.

It was a young porter clipping the tickets, and as the last person in the line handed over her ticket I saw a look of puzzlement cross his face, as of course the ticket had already been clipped. I thought,

Oh my goodness we've been rumbled.

Luckily, he must have decided against querying a gaggle of rather bolshie teenage schoolgirls and metaphorically shrugged his shoulders and ignored the discrepancy.

My one lasting and dearest memory of Portsmouth Arms station must have occurred near the end of my train travel days – in fact, near the end of all train travel in what I think of as the "Golden Years" before Beeching. I think it was during my first year of teaching in Bristol when I travelled home, back to Wansley for a holiday. My father had already said that he would probably be twenty minutes or half an hour late picking me up and I said not to worry, I would be quite happy waiting. I sat down on a seat in the sun and passed the time of day with the worker on duty. I have no idea whether he was the station master, porter, signalman or what his title was – jack of all trades, I suspect. When he realised I had to wait, he invited me up to the signal box for a cup of tea. Well, I was really curious as I had never been in a signal box and definitely never had a cup of tea in one.

I followed him along the track, up the steps and inside. There were a couple of chairs so I was able to sit down while he boiled the kettle. It was obviously his den, equipped with a book or two and a newspaper, but what enchanted me most of all were the pots of geraniums basking in the sunshine on the window ledges; I could not believe my eyes. Of course, it was the signal box and the levers were all there as they should be against one wall; in fact, he pulled one while I was there, as though to prove that it actually was a signal box.

I passed a serendipity half-hour amongst the geraniums and signals, chattering, drinking tea and I believe a biscuit or two was munched as well. There was a good view out of the window and I was able to spot Father when he arrived, and so I bade my host farewell and thanked him for his hospitality. It is true to say though, I have never forgotten tea in the signal box.

Totnes brought a new, different life, and many more people entered my world. Until then, like Alice, Mrs Blackmoor had been my only teacher at Roborough School. Suddenly there was a profusion of teachers for the many different subjects. As it was a girls' school all the teaching staff were female, although the PT mistress with her short back and sides haircut, and robust muscular frame, cut a manly figure as she strode around in shorts, summer and winter. Almost the entire staff were unmarried; another legacy of the Great War, which cast its long shadow down over the century in so many different ways.

We all knew that the domestic science teacher had lost her fiancé during the Second World War, and that was why she had a short fuse and soon lost her cool. She was a beautiful woman, a Grace

The station at Portsmouth Arms, 1930s. The Gill family
– Kenneth Gill (Uncle Ken) is seated left.

Kelly lookalike, and she seemed like a tragic heroine to us, and we forgave her when she lost her temper. The majority of the staff were elderly. I know everyone over forty seems about one hundred years old to a schoolchild, but those teachers, mostly in their fifties and several whom I feel sure were in their sixties, were the stalwarts, like the Miss Barnards at Roborough Rectory, who kept the country running efficiently during the war. Doubtless they had all had their disappointments and tragedies, and potential sweethearts, fiancés, lovers and husbands had been lost in the First World War. They all seemed so old, that it never occurred to us that they too may have loved and lost.

*

There are usually one or two teachers who influence our lives and if we are lucky, send us down paths that otherwise would have remained unexplored, or they tickle an interest in a certain subject. That was how it was for me, and it was definitely Miss Mace who gave me a lifelong interest in history, a fascination for digging around in the past to find out how people lived and what they thought and did.

It was her enthusiasm which was so infectious. She would certainly have been in her fifties, and more likely in her sixties, but she was one of those people who is forever young at heart, and was able to communicate ideas and information in a relevant way, and even inspire us young first formers with a zest for discovering more about the Romans and their way of life. During my first few weeks at the school, history lessons meant tramping Roman roads and looking at Roman remains, of which there appeared to be an abundance around Totnes. I had never been aware of any Roman influence around Roborough, although we had apparently had our Iron Age folk living in the woods at Ten Oaks. Perhaps the Romans, like my parents, had noted that the climate in the South Hams was more equable, and decided to stay in the south of the county.

It was no wonder history lessons captured my interest, for they involved wandering around outdoors in the fresh air, which I had been doing all my life and was beginning to miss in the secluded life of boarding school. We followed Miss Mace as she strode up a muddy track which evidently had been made by the Romans, somewhere in the hills above Totnes High Street. She had short white hair, a round face with rosy cheeks and twinkly blue eyes which lit up with enthusiasm as she regaled us with how life would have been for the Roman soldiers of the time. Over the years I was at Totnes it did not matter which period of history we were studying, her lessons were never dry or dull. She always managed to brighten the subject up, and filled us in on the gossip of the day, or the more gruesome, bizarre or curious titbits of information which brought it all to life and roused our interest.

She had a splendid opportunity to really bring history to life one summer (I think it was 1954) after the young Princess Elizabeth had become Queen. It was the dawning of a new Elizabethan age, and Miss Mace was the organiser of a floodlit pageant in the grounds of Totnes Castle, to celebrate our glorious history. It was the first big public celebration that I had ever been involved with, in fact there had been few jollifications of any kind post war, as austerity and rationing had continued for many years. However, now there was a change in the air. We had all pulled together through difficult and perilous times, and a young and beautiful new queen had acceded to the throne. The country had turned a corner and it was definitely time for joyous celebrations and a knees-up.

I was involved with rehearsals for the pageant because I was in the school choir. I had not joined the choir because I was any great shakes at singing, or even because I was particularly interested in singing, quite the opposite in fact. My ulterior motive for joining the warbling was to escape cold and windy dinner playtimes, twice a week in the winter. Anything was better than mooching around the playground, bored stiff and freezing to death. Ray had already joined, and I was rather worried that I might not be accepted, as there was a test. I could remember my run-in with Uncle John and the nursery rhymes and my abysmal failure with "We Three Kings". I was not at all confident that I would make the grade.

It was my lucky day and I must have strung together a few notes which were acceptable, for I was told I would be a soprano. I might not have joined for the right reasons, but it was not long before I discovered that singing with others was very enjoyable and I never regretted my decision. Through the choir I became involved with a lot of music making at the school and as we were lucky enough to be close to Dartington Hall, our musical lives were greatly enriched. Dartington was within walking distance, and we were able to regularly attend recitals and concerts, and listen to accomplished musicians. Better still, music students from Dartington often joined our school orchestra, and one term we collaborated with them in a production of *Dido and Aeneas*, their music students taking the principal roles.

So, it was as a member of the choir that I was able to partake in the town pageant. It was about Merrie England, and celebrated our history from Queen Elizabeth I to Queen Elizabeth II, and Miss Mace wrote and produced it, with help from many others but she was the driving force. It was done on a big scale, with people on horseback, smoke and canon fire, all set against the backdrop of the floodlit castle. The choirs of all the schools amalgamated and the evening rehearsals were very enjoyable. For the first time I felt as though I was part of the town, and I really appreciated being allowed to stroll up to the castle grounds with Ray after tea, and join everyone else for a rehearsal. The boarding house was a little world of its own and segregated from the town, and although we lived in Totnes, that was the only time I felt part of it.

One weekend Julie White and I went to stay with Miss Hobbs and Mrs Thomas, two elderly teachers who lived in Paignton. There was a problem with the Hawkmoor boiler; it was an emergency and we were foisted upon whoever would have us. Miss Hobbs was science, and Mrs Thomas, a widow, was geography – both quite elderly but a genial couple and they made us very welcome. It was about two

weekends into the autumn term, the weather was balmy and the two teachers thought it would be a good idea to have a dip in the sea. We did not have bathing costumes, but the teachers foraged through their belongings and found some old costumes. I drew the short straw and ended up with Mrs Thomas's swimsuit. Mrs T was a big lady, not tall but definitely large. Her kindly face was well creased, there were several chins, and her hand-knitted jumpers and tweed skirts hid voluminous amounts of flesh. Luckily I was not at all fashion conscious. Like most children who had lived through the war, none of us had had the opportunity to be fussy about our clothes. Clothing was something that covered you up and kept you warm. I did not mind if the costume was big and baggy, provided it covered the essentials and protected my modesty.

We spent a very enjoyable afternoon – I think it was at Babbacombe and there were very few people there. It sticks in my mind because our frolicking on the beach and in the sea was presided over by the most beautiful sailing galleon, which was moored just out in the bay – white sails billowing, silhouetted against the blue sky. It was like something out of a story book, which indeed it was, for we learnt that it was the galleon that had been used in the film *Treasure Island*, and it was now sailing back to wherever it had come from. The film with Robert Newton and Bobby Driscoll was made in 1950, so I would have been twelve years old at the time. It was several years before I actually saw the film, but it gave me a thrill to think I had unexpectedly seen the ship in the flesh, so to speak.

There was not much opportunity to visit the cinema, but I was kept up-to-date with the world of film and screen by a friend, Wendy, who lived in Paignton. It was good to have a friend who was a day-girl, and it was a friendship which provided a wider perspective of life for me. I think that Wendy probably felt sorry for my restricted lifestyle, and she certainly would not have wanted to change places. Wendy and her mum were keen cinema-goers and she lent me copies of *Picture Goer* and *Photo Play*, and kept me informed about films she saw at the weekends. On one or two weekends I was able to stay with her.

It was not often anyone came to take us out, and if family or friends visited and took us out for the day, it was usually to Paignton Zoo. I was not ungrateful, but after five years I felt that I knew Paignton Zoo like the back of my hand. Zoos were different places then and I felt sorry for the animals. Living in a boarding school was rather like being a prisoner, so I could sympathise with the animals – but I knew they had a worse deal than we had, and a worse deal than the animals back home on our farm.

There were one or two teachers who gave up their time and took us out for walks at the weekend, and those walks were very welcome. It was so good to get out in the fresh air. The teacher who spent most time at the boarding house was Miss Shepherd, who taught French. She took charge for one evening most weeks to give Mac time off and she also took us for long walks at weekends. We often walked along the river to Dartington Hall, then to Dartington itself, around Shinners Bridge and back along the Ashburton Road to Totnes. As I drive along that road now I can scarcely believe how we used to regularly walk it, with little regard for the few cars that drove past.

It was during a French lesson one morning in February 1952 when there was a discrete knock on the classroom door. A member of the canteen staff (where they had a wireless) entered and had a whispered conversation with Miss Shepherd, who to our surprise then burst into tears. That was how we found out that the King had died and we now had a new Queen: Elizabeth II. We all had to assemble in the school hall, and the headmistress, Miss Briggs, conveyed the news in a dignified fashion and we sang "God Save the Queen" for the first time. The next day we gathered on The Plains at the bottom of the High Street, while the Mayor made the announcement in an official proclamation.

Miss Shepherd's tears were not the only ones that day, for the King had been well liked and respected. I know my parents thought highly of him, for he had been put on the spot by the abdication of his brother, and had faced the task bravely and with dignity. He and his wife, Queen Elizabeth, were also much loved, because they had refused to leave London during the war and had braved the bombing along with everyone else.

Unfortunately, I did not like Miss Shepherd, despite the fact she gave up her time to take us out. She was one of those teachers who keep control with sarcasm, and she referred to me as "Dear Little Egg Face". She probably did not treat me differently to anyone else but consequently I did not like French lessons. It was a shame, because I have since realised that I would have enjoyed languages and it could have been a strong subject. I gave it up as soon as it was possible when we were making choices for O Levels.

I must give her credit though, for she did bother with us. One May, Sunday morning, Alice, Ray, Ann (another Dolton girl) and I met her when we were walking back from communion and our early morning tryst with the grammar school boy altar servers. I recorded it all in my 1953 diary, so I was just fifteen. When we told her that we would be spending all the afternoon sitting in the garden at Hawkmoor, she said,

"Well, that sounds awfully tame, you need a fairy godmother to whisk you away."

To our surprise and delight she telephoned Mac and arranged for her and Miss Fisher, who taught science, to take the four of us out for the afternoon. We caught the bus to Longcombe and then walked to Stoke Gabriel and strolled along by the water. It was a beautiful spot and a beautiful day. We found a café and sat outside in the sunshine, and were treated to toasted tea cakes and fancies before making our way back. We were going to walk back but missed the way and ended up at Tweenaway, and as it was getting late we then caught a bus back to Totnes. Altogether it was an unexpectedly delightful afternoon which I still remember with pleasure.

*

My greatest friend while I was at Totnes was Ray and we saw quite a lot of each other during the holidays as well, as she lived nearby at Dolton. Her parents, Frank and Jean Pickard, were easy-going and welcoming, and I loved going to stay at Woolridge with Ray and her two younger sisters. Mrs Pickard had spent some time living in India with a family as a nanny for their children, and it was through Ray that I was introduced to the delights of Kipling. I fell in love with his poetry and books, and they have brought me pleasure ever since. I have always felt that I would like to visit India, but once again it was one of those dreams that has not materialised.

It was late one summer evening after helping Mr and Mrs Pickard get in the hay, that Mrs P said that she would make us a curry for supper. It sounded terribly exotic and I had certainly never tasted a curry before, neither had my parents. It was something way outside our sphere of culinary skills. Mr Pickard finished the milking while Ray's mum set to in the kitchen and rustled up the curry. I tried it tentatively while they watched my face. There was no problem, I knew after the first few mouthfuls that curry would be on my list of favourite foods, up there with rabbit pie and hog's puddings.

Time spent at Woolridge always passed pleasantly. They had a wind-up gramophone and a collection of crackly records. There was

Frank and Jean Pickard, Woolridge, Dolton, April 1975.
Photograph by James Ravilious for the Beaford Archive © Beaford Arts,
digitally scanned from a Beaford Archive negative.

Noel Coward singing "Mad Dogs and Englishmen", and we spent a lot of time singing along with "The Foggy, Foggy Dew" and "I Know Where I'm Going", and there was a hilarious song about a pig called Susannah.

Ray and I helped out a bit on the farm, and usually walked the cows to the meadows after milking and fetched them again in the evening. They ambled happily along the narrow lanes around the farm. Sometimes in the summer we would go skinny-dipping in the Torridge down below Halsdon, and after would lie in the grass to dry off. Mr Pickard allowed Ray to use his double-barrelled shotgun when she was about fourteen, and then we roamed the fields looking for rabbits to shoot, not very successfully I might add.

Woolridge was situated in a dip in a sheltered position. There was a delightful orchard full of old moss-covered trees, and many afternoons were spent curled up in a tree with a book, munching an apple, the sunlight dappling through the leaves of the wooded valley. Sometimes though, we went visiting, for Ray had friends in Dolton with a tennis court, so there was the opportunity for a game of tennis.

We spent a lot of time reading; it didn't matter what it was, we read everything from Henry Williamson to Biggles. It was not just Williamson's books about wildlife that interested us, but we became involved in the series about the Maddison family, although Williamson's love of the countryside and nature is always evident. We enjoyed any swashbuckling-type stories with debonair heroes: Leslie Charteris's Saint stories, *The Scarlet Pimpernel* by Baroness Orczy, *The Three Musketeers*, *The Prisoner of Zenda* and *Beau Gest*. We also enjoyed Daphne du Maurier and Georgette Heyer's regency novels, and then of course there was the saga of the Whiteoak family who lived at Jalna in Canada. I spent many, many nights at Totnes reading *Gone with the Wind* with a torch under the blankets. We discovered another author called Mary Webb who wrote dark stories about country folk, mostly set in Shropshire. Her characters were monosyllabic, brooding, in-turned farmers with biblical names such as Gideon or Seth. When, many years later, we heard about the tragedy of the farming family at Winkleigh, who killed themselves rather than move from the farm, I instantly thought of Mary Webb. It could have come straight from one of her stories.

*

I spent time staying with friends most summer holidays, but strangely one summer, August 1952 to be precise, Mother seemed reluctant for me to go. For quite some time I had been friendly with one of the Lynton and Lynmouth boarders – there were several there from the twin villages – and Ann and I got on rather well. It seemed like a good idea to visit each other's home during the summer holidays, as I had never been to Lynton or Lynmouth and Ann had never stayed on a farm. For some reason Mother was not very keen on the idea; she seemed reluctant to say yes, which was unusual. She would not give a straightforward answer, but just said that she felt uneasy about the plan and would rather that I did not go. Quite simply, she just had a bad feeling about it, or a premonition as she admitted afterwards.

There was no logical reason to say no, so of course she had to say yes, and agree to our summer holiday plans. It was only for a few days, after all. I was going to stay with Ann from Monday to Thursday, and Ann would come back to the farm and return home the following Monday. Mother actually rather liked the twin villages, and when she was younger, had on several occasions stayed with cousins who lived on a farm, Croscombe Barton, which was at Martinhoe not too far from Lynton and Lynmouth. During those days the railway went from Barnstaple to Lynton, and Mother and her sisters had loved the train journey. She said that at one point the gradient was so steep and the train chugged so slowly, that it would be possible to jump off the train and run down over the fields to Croscombe, rather than continue to Lynton. I am not sure that they ever did anything so daring.

By 1952 when I made my journey to Lynton, the railway was long gone. I couldn't blame Dr Beeching for that. Mother and Father took me in the car to Barnstaple and then I caught the bus. Mother still seemed anxious and exhorted me to take care, and look after myself.

There was no doubt, Lynton and Lynmouth were everything that Ann had cracked them up to be. The weather was good at the beginning of the week and we spent our time exploring. Ann had friends and knew people everywhere. We walked to some riding stables where she helped out during the holidays. It was just off Countisbury Hill, and we visited friends who lived at Watersmeet. The Valley of Rocks charmed me the first time I saw it, and we spent many happy hours scrambling up over the rocks and cliffs on equal terms with the goats.

We spent one really hair-raising afternoon side stepping adders on Hollerday Hill. It was one of the scariest and most foolish things I have ever done. It was a hot humid day and Ann suggested a shortcut across a rocky plat near the top of Hollerday. It was full of gorse and bracken, and lying basking in the sun in all directions were adders, sunbathing on their hot stones, or on the patches of hot earth amongst the bracken and grass. Ann darted between the stones like a demented goat and I had to follow.

"It's alright, don't worry," she shouted back. "Just be careful where you put your feet."

I made my way across the minefield considerably slower than she had, and felt great relief when we reached a tarmac path the other side.

Whew, I thought to myself. *That must have been what Mother was worried about*, for I had received a letter from home that morning (a letter on a four-day holiday!), begging me to be careful crossing the road, and not get knocked down by a bus, and to be very careful and not go swimming in the sea unless it was a designated area that was safe. I had never known Mother like this.

On Tuesday evening, Ann's parents had treated us to a show at the Pavilion. Their home was at the top in Lynton and the Pavilion was down at the bottom in Lynmouth. We enjoyed the show so much that they allowed us to go again on Wednesday night. As we went into the Pavilion we each bought a programme, and during the interval there was a draw for the programme with the lucky number. On Wednesday night Ann had the winning programme and to our delight the prize was two free tickets to attend another show. Having seen it twice we did not wish to see the same show again, but it changed on Friday night, and we agreed it was a shame that we were supposed to go back to Wansley on Thursday. There seemed to be no reason why we could not go to my home on Saturday morning rather than Thursday afternoon, and I said I would ring my parents the next morning and suggest it.

Well, if I had said we were contemplating swimming the Bristol Channel, or walking a tightrope across the Lyn Gorge, Mother could not have been more horrified.

"Absolutely not," she said. "I did not want you to go in the first place, and you are to come home this afternoon as we have arranged, and you are to bring Ann with you."

I clearly remember how she emphasised bringing Ann with me. She was adamant and there was nothing more to be said.

Well, of course we all know what happened on that Friday night, 15 August 1952. Thank goodness for Mother's premonition of disaster, or I probably would not be sitting here now. It rained all that Friday at Roborough, and my parents said they would take us to a dance at High Bickington Church Hall in the evening. We still felt a little disgruntled that we had been made to return to Roborough instead of watching another show at the Lynmouth Pavilion, but Ann still had the tickets and was going to use them the next week, possibly with her sister or her mother.

By now Father had upgraded the Austin Seven and had bought the Hillman Minx, and as always we drove to High Bickington along the small lanes through Ebberly and around Yelland and Mill Brook.

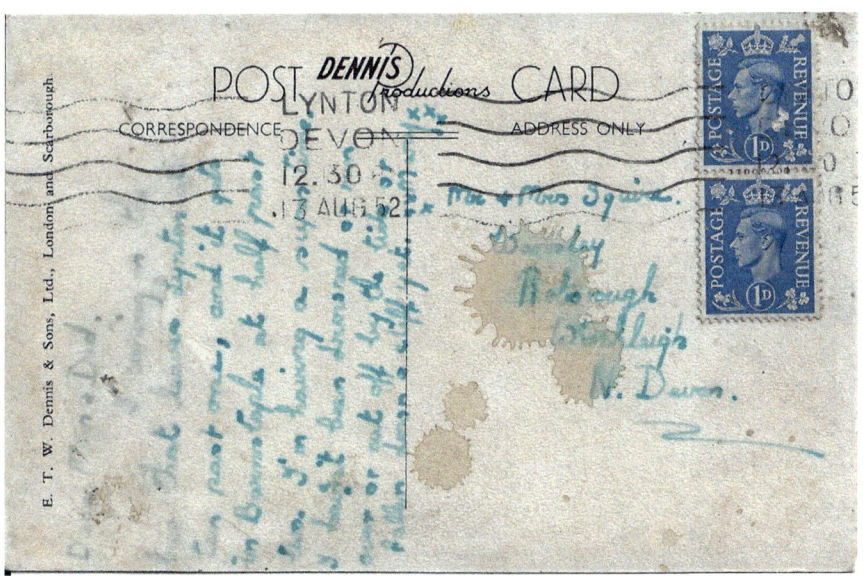

I sent a postcard of Mars Hill to my parents to confirm the bus times for our return journey. This is the back of it, and it was posted at 12.30 on Wednesday 13 August. This was before going to the show on Wednesday night, winning the tickets and trying to change our plans. I had obviously received my mother's letter, full of dire warnings and forebodings, and in a typical teenage retort, had replied: "I haven't been drowned, or run over, or cut off by the tide, or fallen down a cliff yet."

Of course no one – not even my mother – thought of a flood!

While we were at the dance, news began to drift in of local brooks and rivers bursting their banks and flooded roads. We were told that we would have to return to Roborough another way, as the road at Mill Brook was flooded, so we returned home on the high ground towards Dolton Beacon and into Roborough that way.

The next morning Mother brought us a very late breakfast in bed and the news that was on the wireless: that night there had been a disastrous flood at Lynmouth, much of the village had been washed away and many lives had been lost. All during the day the scale of the calamity gradually unfolded, although I think that Ann and I did not really comprehend the enormity of the disaster. On Sunday afternoon there was a phone call from Ann's mum. She said they were all safe and were looking forward to her return the next day, Monday, as the family all wanted to be together. They were obviously traumatised by the events, and everyone in the two villages would have known someone who had been swept away. On Monday morning we drove Ann to Barnstaple. I think my parents had to get a special pass for her to travel on the bus to Lynton, as only rescue workers or people with aid and residents were allowed – definitely no sightseers.

It was difficult to take in what had happened, to grasp the fact that the roads and bridges that we had walked along a few days before, houses and hotels we had passed by, the old Rhenish Tower and many other landmarks had vanished forever. It would never be the same again.

And what happened at the Pavilion?

According to Eric R. Delderfield's account in his book *The Lynmouth Flood Disaster*[*]:

> *The lights failed at the Pavilion where the concert party were performing and the show closed down. The audience, reaching the street, were astounded to find the roads covered with water to a considerable depth.*

---

* *The Lynmouth Flood Disaster*. Eric R. Delderfield. Published by E.R.D. Publications Ltd, Exmouth.

Many people avoided Lynmouth Street and ascended Mars Hill, but some who made the decision to walk along Lynmouth Street were washed away. The Rising Sun Hotel on Mars Hill was open house for the night, and twenty-five of the audience who had been watching the show at the Pavilion spent the night there in safety.

What would Ann and I have done if we had been there? I have often thought about it. Would we have done the sensible thing and walked up Mars Hill and spent the night in the Rising Sun, or would we have braved Lynmouth Street? Knowing us, because we were curious and it was more daring and exciting, I suspect we may well have made the decision to walk along Lynmouth Street. Thank goodness we were not there, but what a close-run thing it was.

Thankfully, all our other Lynton and Lynmouth friends who were boarders at Totnes were safe and their families also. There was a lot to talk about it when everyone returned to school in September, and I think there were quite a few deeds of bravery which did not

(Left) Mars Hill; the Rising Sun is on the right.
(Right) A very treacherous-looking Lynmouth Hill.

View from Mars Hill, looking towards the sea and the old, original Rhenish Tower. These photographs predate my visit to Lynmouth. They were taken by cousins who lived nearby at Martinhoe. I would think they were taken in the 1920s or '30s. The Shopland family lived at Croscombe Barton. There were eight children and like so many in our family, they were either farmers or teachers. None of them married and eventually the family died out.

reach the papers or make the news. It was a big tragedy for two small communities, and Eric Delderfield recorded the bare bones of the disaster in the area. Thirty-four people were killed or missing; ninety-three houses and buildings destroyed or subsequently demolished; twenty-eight bridges (in the area) destroyed or badly damaged; nineteen boats lost; and 132 vehicles were destroyed.

*

There is no doubt that life is fragile and fortunes flip in the twinkling of an eye. Who could have guessed what was going to happen that night? We are all of us at the mercy of the flotsam and jetsam of random events and their far-reaching consequences; an advertisement in a newspaper, the train we catch or the carriage we sit in, an invitation to a party, or the number on a programme, can unknowingly change our lives and send us down paths that we would never have envisaged.

It was a hurried conversation in a bedroom when someone was unwell, depressed and weary that led to the sale of a family farm – that, plus some suppressed feelings of guilt. A way of life ended before anyone really had the time to think through the consequences, and reconsider the decision.

I am pleased that my parents had a carefree retirement at Melland Hill, with no farm work to worry about, although there was Aunt Leah to look after for several years. They could indulge their love of gardening, and when Aunty moved to a home after breaking her thigh, they joined three Old Tyme dancing clubs and were free to dance away as many nights as they liked, and made many friends.

Although not much was said, I know they did regret selling the farm, especially when three grandsons arrived within less than five years. I had never wanted it to be sold, but felt that I should not interfere, after all, they were the people who had devoted their lives to it. They had been generous to me when I indicated that I would like to leave and follow another career. It must have been difficult for them and not at all what they had hoped would happen. With the self-centredness of youth I did not realise that this was not the plan, but there were no recriminations or accusations; they gave me their blessing and always seemed interested in my exploits and adventures. They were proud of my achievements and pleased that I was enjoying myself.

There is no doubt though, that a place can worm its way into your soul. Although I left Wansley it never really left me, and it must have been the same for my father. The pastures, woodlands, hedges, flowers and wildlife from the first snowdrops and smallest star of bright green moss, to the huge elm trees with their safe gnarled limbs; from the newly hatched little chicks to the frolicking lambs and the sheep who died in a snowdrift – all distilled themselves into my being. It was not just the harvests, sunshine and the good times, but the toil, anxieties, rain, mud and mess, the biting winds and winter snows – they had all somehow twisted, twirled and twined themselves around my heart. It was also the knowledge that forebears had toiled on the same land with the same hopes, dreams, worries and frustrations, passing the baton on from generation to generation.

It was sad and I think we all grieved in our own way when it was over. Certainly Father and I did, although he did not talk about it much. I am not so sure about Mother; her time at Wansley was coloured by Aunt Leah and the relationship was always tense and uneasy. I know that I was lucky though. I was blessed with a wonderful childhood, and grew up cherished and loved in an ancient Barton with layers of history and atmosphere. The present custodians are doing a good job, and the old house has been sympathetically modernised. It now looks much more stylish, chic and neat than it did in our day.

Father and Mother were able to stay on in the farmhouse for nearly a year after it was sold while the cottages were being modernised. It was not a happy year though. Without the animals it seemed like a ghost farm, and was strangely eerie. The new owner (not the present one) was busy knocking down ancient hedgerows to create bigger fields, and enlarging gateways for the modern machinery. My father could not wait to get away.

He never went back, which was probably a wise decision, and he lived on his memories for the rest of his life. Happy memories are priceless, and I think we were all lucky to have lived and worked in this hidden corner of Devon. The farm enfolded us within its hills, valleys, fields and woodland, and our family was blessed to have been its guardian and custodian for about a hundred years.

Mary and Brian White, 1968.

A History of the Owners of Wansley Barton

Pre-1066	The land was held by Wulfeva, a local Saxon chief.
1303	Owned by Thomas de Wanteslegh.
1332	Owned by Walter de Wonteslegh, who had to pay a tax of two shillings to Henry III.
1346	De Waltero Vuyng owned what was then called Wantyslegh.
1428	Robertus Wynard was the owner of the then-called Wantislegh.
1515 to 1758	The Wolocombe family lived at Wansley. In St Peter's Church, Roborough, on the north wall is a plaque dated 1652, dedicated to Sara, wife of John Wolocombe. She had ten children, of which three died.
17th Century	The major part of the house as it stands today was built. A dog-legged staircase was incorporated.

There are rumours of a tunnel between Wansley and Ebberly House.

1758 to 1837   The Davey family lived at Wansley.

Early 1800s   The then-called Greater Wansley was enlarged.

1837 to 1870   Thomas and Anne Copp lived at Greater Wansley. They farmed 140 acres, had five children under six years old, and employed two house servants, one carter and two farm servants.

1870 to 1970   The Squire family lived at Wansley Barton.

1970 to 1983   John Arkwright of Ebberly House owned Wansley as part of his estate.

1983 to 1996   Roy and Anne Fielder owned Wansley and lived there with their three daughters.

1996 to present Roy and Sophia (née Fielder) May and their two children live at Wansley Barton.

This history was researched by Roy and Sophia May.

Acknowledgements

I would like to say thank you to everyone who has taken an interest and encouraged me to write this memoir. Thank you to all those who have spent time hunting for photographs, especially Carol Petherick, Margaret Bolt and Ann Harris.

I am also grateful to the Beaford Archive for allowing me to use two of the wonderful James Ravilious photographs. Many thanks to Kathryn Burrell for her interest and help.

Many thanks to Cressida Whitton from the Devon Historic Environment Team who somehow managed to conjure up a 1946 RAF photograph from the depths of County Hall. I was unaware that such photographs existed. Thanks to her also for sharing her knowledge and expertise, and pointing out that the rounded corners of many of the fields indicate medieval origins.

Roy and Sophia May (the present owners of Wansley) must have spent many hours researching the history of the farm. Their hard work has produced a timeline going back to Saxon times which is fascinating, and I am very grateful to them for allowing me to include it.

I would also like to thank John Down for writing the field names on the Wansley map in his beautiful architect's handwriting.

How lucky I was to bump into Sue outside Co-op! I suddenly remembered her artistic skills and when I suggested an illustration or two, I was overwhelmed with her enthusiasm. I really did not have to do much arm twisting. Thank you so much, Sue. Your delightful watercolour illustrations – for the cover, and on the inside pages – have greatly enhanced my story and the book as a whole. I know you have enjoyed the project, but nevertheless I really appreciate all the time and effort you have put into it.

Of course, none of this would have been possible without the guiding hand of the team at Troubador Publishing, and I am very grateful for their help, advice and patience. It must be obvious that I have zero knowledge of anything to do with publishing, and they have guided me through all the ups and downs of self-publishing with patience and good humour. Thank you very much to everyone.

Last, but not least I would like to say thank you to my family, who have put up with a great deal and not grumbled too much when I have been huddled over the computer instead of getting the tea. Thank you all for your patience. I just hope that it has been worth it.

Sue Tudge, watercolour illustrator

Sue was born and grew up in the Forest of Dean before training as an early years teacher in Cheltenham. After qualifying, she moved to Devon to start a teaching career in the Torrington area. She enjoys gardening, watercolour painting and walking her dog around the lanes and countryside.

For exclusive discounts on Matador titles,
sign up to our occasional newsletter at
troubador.co.uk/bookshop